The Rhetoric of Modernist Fiction

The Rhetoric of Modernist Fiction

FROM A NEW POINT OF VIEW

Morton P. Levitt

University Press of New England

HANOVER AND LONDON

Published by University Press of New England,

One Court Street, Lebanon, NH 03766

www.upne.com

© 2006 by Morton P. Levitt

Printed in the United States of America

5 4 3 2 1

All rights reserved. No part of this book may be reproduced in any form or by any electronic or mechanical means, including storage and retrieval systems, without permission in writing from the publisher, except by a reviewer, who may quote brief passages in a review. Members of educational institutions and organizations wishing to photocopy any of the work for classroom use, or authors and publishers who would like to obtain permission for any of the material in the work, should contact Permissions, University Press of New England, One Court Street, Lebanon, NH 03766

Library of Congress Cataloging-in-Publication Data
Levitt, Morton.
The rhetoric of modernist fiction from a new point of view / Morton P. Levitt
    p. cm.
Includes bibliographical references and index.
ISBN–13: 978–1–58465–122–2 (cloth : alk. paper)
ISBN–10: 1–58465–122–9 (cloth : alk. paper)
ISBN–13: 978–1–58465–500–8 (pbk. : alk. paper)
ISBN–10: 1–58465–500–3 (pbk. : alk. paper)
1. Fiction—20th century—History and criticism.   2. Fiction—19th century—History and criticism.   3. Fiction—Technique.   I. Title.
PN3503.L3785 2006
809.3—dc22   2005025778

In memory of Ivo Vidan,
fine scholar, dear friend

And for Annette

Day-by-day talk streams forth;
night-by-night expresses knowledge.

NINETEENTH PSALM

Contents

Contents

Preface

While the idea for this book is recent, its subject has been with me from the start of my career, even before I knew for certain that I would have such a career. The idea was proposed some five years ago by Philip Pochoda, then Editorial Director for the University Press of New England, who suggested that I write "a genuine sequel to Wayne Booth, on the order of *The Rhetoric of Modernist Fiction. . . .*" He was responding to another manuscript which I had sent to the Press and about which he had nice things to say, but which he declined to publish as "a collection of somewhat disparate essays [on some dozen different Modernist novelists]." But he saw in the prevailing themes of those essays a concern for point of view and concluded that it was time for a coherent updating of one of the most influential of all the many studies of narrative technique in fiction, Wayne Booth's monumental *The Rhetoric of Fiction,* first published in 1961.

I had then to admit that I was among the many to be influenced by Booth, whose book came out as I was in the midst of my first faculty position and before I had completed my own graduate studies (both at Penn State). My dissertation, completed in 1965, which I had titled *From a New Point of View: Studies in the Contemporary Novel* (I had not yet learned the term "Modernist" as it applied to literature, or even the term "New Criticism"), used Booth as a starting point and concentrated on largely little-known contemporary novelists from a variety of cultures. (A few of them—Robbe-Grillet, Butor, Simon—make a reappearance here.) I also had to admit to the perceptive Pochoda that my interest in point of view had persisted throughout my career as a critic and teacher, that I had long regarded it as the central, even determining, characteristic of Modernist fiction, and that I had refined my positions considerably since that early effort. It was indeed time to bring it all together in one, comprehensive study. I have never so enjoyed a writing project. (I might add that the manuscript which I had originally submitted has recently been published by the Edwin Mellen Press as *The Modernist Masters: Studies in the Novel.*)

I need also to repeat here a story that I have often told to my students over the years, about my own discovery of the prominence of point of view in the understanding of narrative art. I was beginning my graduate studies in English at Columbia (after an abortive effort to study law there), when I saw the Alain Resnais film, *Last Year at Marienbad*, with its scenario by the then-unknown Alain Robbe-Grillet. Like many of its early viewers, I was bewildered by the film's depiction of reality and its vision of life, but I knew enough as I exited the theatre (in the basement of Carnegie Hall), not to ask, as one refined, elderly woman asked her companion, "But, my dear, what was it about?" Whatever questions had been raised by the film, the matter of the plot was surely not the correct one, I understood—that is, not one that would lead to an answer worth having. The film's reality lay somewhere else.

That somewhere else began to reveal itself three weeks afterward when I saw another film, Federico Fellini's *La Dolce Vita*. With its quite traditional literary approach (its development of imagery and metaphor, its use of irony and, especially, its presentation of point of view), Fellini's film pointed the way for me to question the clearly untraditional, but still literary devices of the Resnais/Robbe-Grillet movie. And so I began my critical study of point of view (which I knew hitherto only from assignments in an undergraduate creative writing course, and so rather simplistically: "first-person protagonist," "third-person eyewitness," and the like). The studies in this book go far beyond, I would like to think, those early discoveries, but I would also like to believe that they retain the same practical, common sense approach and the same abhorrence of specialized jargon.

Studies in point of view, especially of Modernist novels, are immensely subtle and sophisticated and, therefore, require an accessible vocabulary and an absolute lack of mystery. There is no reason that any moderately bright freshman cannot begin to master such studies. I have seen the proof of this over and over again in my teaching career.

Central to this book, as to virtually all of my work as a critic over the years, are certain inter-connected and strongly held beliefs: that the novel as a form reaches the peak of its development during the Modernist era; that the Modernist Masters were not writing for some self-proclaimed elite but for the same general audience that their predecessors had written for; that they expected through their work to help to create that audience, that body of ideal Modernist readers, for they believed firmly that the rewards for their attentive readers would be greater by far than the demands which they had made on them; and that the single most significant of these demands, the key to understanding both individual Modernist novels and literary Modernism as a whole, lay in their myriad, revelatory uses of point of view. That is why I find Wayne Booth's *The Rhetoric of Fiction*—in its strengths and its weaknesses—so vital a text and why I believe that developing and expanding its method will help to resolve many of the problems that have arisen in recent years regarding the Modernist novel. In order to keep faith with this belief, I have avoided detailed discussion of some subjects that might otherwise inevitably adhere to and detract from it, among them the relationship between Modernism and post-Modernism in the novel, as well as the relative worth of the approach labeled Narratology by some literary theorists. I trust that my own readers will have the patience and good will to judge this book on what it does in this regard and not for what it carefully avoids.

If this has been a career-long interest for me, it inevitably means that my debts are numerous and deep, in a sense, to more than forty years' worth of colleagues and students. If I cannot name each one (and at least one of those students does appear here), I can recall them gratefully and fondly. But I do need to single out a few for particular thanks: to Frank Warlow, who first taught me about point of view in 1958 at Dickinson College; to Mitchell Morse, who oversaw my dissertation and ever since has provided a model of good teaching, good writing and good values; to my friends and colleagues at Temple University, in the international James Joyce community, and at the *Journal of Modern Literature,* who read and commented upon various parts of this book and gave me much good advice—among them, Dick Beckman, Ellen Carol Jones, Ellen Rose, Jean-Michel Rabaté, Stanley Sultan, and, especially, Dan O'Hara: if I have not always been wise enough to follow their advice, they can hardly be blamed for that. I also owe a great deal to Diane McManus, both for her assistance and for her advice as a critic of Virginia Woolf; to colleagues at some of the foreign institutions at which I've been privileged to work and who helped provide the atmosphere of literary excitement that made this book possible—Ivo Vidan and Sonja Bašić at Zagreb University, Croatia; Manuel Villar Raso at the University of Granada, Spain; Miguel Tamen and Antonio Feijó at the University of Lisbon, Portugal; and Michael Pretina at the Camargo Foundation in Cassis, France. My thanks also to Murray Beja and David Hayman, those superb scholars of Modernism, for their wise and useful suggestions. I am also indebted to Philip Pochoda for his initial insight and for the nudge which led directly to my writing this book, as well as John Landrigan for his wise and helpful advice. Above all, as anyone who knows us will realize, my best and most trusted reader and most stimulating source remains Annette Shandler Levitt.

The Rhetoric of Modernist Fiction

CHAPTER 1

The Art of Point of View

Confronted by the blank face and tortured psyche of a pathological killer—or so, at least, he seems—a man clearly capable of violent deeds although absolutely incapable of expressing them, the critic, himself rooted deeply in the Western humanist and moral tradition, calls out in exasperation, "is this really what we go to literature for?" (384).[1] This is Wayne Booth speaking, in *The Rhetoric of Fiction,* when faced with Alain Robbe-Grillet's early novel, *Le Voyeur* [*The Voyeur*] (1955; English translation, 1958). It is a powerfully symbolic moment as well, for critics and novelists alike, in the modern history of narrative and in the history of what we have since learned to call Modernist and post-Modernist fiction. When I first encountered Booth's words, shortly after the publication of *The Rhetoric of Fiction* in 1961 and my own discovery of Robbe-Grillet's fictions (in novels and in films), I recognized their surprising limitation; it seemed to me then, as it seems to me still, that where Booth understood better than anyone else of his time the mechanics of the Modernist revolution in narrative which had led to such works as *The Voyeur,* he could nevertheless be strangely unresponsive to their broader possibilities, moral and critical implications included.

The Voyeur is an account, from within—from the point of view of a certifiable psychopath—of the rapes and murders of a series of young girls, crimes which he may have committed, or which he may have seen someone else commit, or which he would have liked to commit, but which he cannot even be certain have actually occurred. And since his is the sole point of view in the novel, the reader, too, cannot be sure whether these acts have in fact taken place, or who their victims may have been, or who their perpetrator is. Indeed, we suspect that the ferry boat on which the protagonist is traveling at the novel's end may be taking him to and not away from the island on which the crimes may have occurred—so that they may be prospective rather than retrospective, present as yet in his mind but nowhere else. The amorality of all this, for Booth, is appalling. "The book," he says of *The Voyeur,*

1

is a brilliant culmination of more than a hundred years of experimentation with inside views and the sympathetic identification they can yield. It does, indeed, lead us to experience intensely the sensations and emotions of a homicidal maniac. But is this really what we go to literature for? Quite aside from the question of how such a book might affect readers who already have homicidal tendencies, is there no limit to what we will praise, provided it is done with skill? (384)

Booth's unease is palpable, and the reader who has admired and learned from his magisterial readings of texts and his ability to make connections among them—the reader of Booth cannot be less than sympathetic. But he has taught us too well for us to be satisfied with sympathy. For I could sense when I first read these words that Booth's moral background had made it impossible for him to apply fully his own theory. There remains, as I see it still, many years afterward, no better explanation than *The Rhetoric of Fiction* of the long history of narrative in the novel up to the twentieth century. But the explorer himself faltered so badly on the shores of Modernist and post-Modernist narratives that it seemed necessary even some forty years ago (when I first approached the subject in my dissertation) to provide the readings and logical connections that Booth had made possible but that he could not himself undertake.

In our putative age of "narratology" and narrative theory, in which Booth and his work have typically been ignored or dismissed or condescended to as naive or simplistic or unscientific but surely out of date, it seems more necessary than ever to return to and re-introduce Booth and to take him through to the narrative frontiers which he pointed us toward but could never himself reach. Undertaking this journey will enable us to avoid the worst excesses of the "narratological" approach, a pervasive a-literary quality in particular.

It was Henry James who both gave us the term "point of view" and provided the first theoretical words on the subject. James is also the principal fulcrum, as novelist, in the development of point of view: eighteenth- and nineteenth-century narrative techniques reach their culmination in his fictions, and twentieth-century techniques are based directly on their foundation. Yet James himself was also a sort of narrative Moses, precluded by circumstance and character from effecting the transition from the old points of view—and from the worldviews which they realized—to the new. Much the same may be said, of course, of Wayne Booth, whose readings of point of view up to and including James—through the Victorians and their Edwardian cousins, that is—may well be definitive. But Booth is obviously discomfited by the development of point of view after James. His sad failure with the well-and-ironically named *The Voyeur* is merely the most evident of his hesitations.

What makes this situation symbolic, moreover, is a series of circumstances that Booth never quite manages to master. He never understood, for example, that Robbe-Grillet himself was both a novelist and a theoretician who, half a century after James, used his own novels to advance his theories about the nature of fiction and of the world and of their inter-connection. More specifically, Robbe-Grillet—whom I have elsewhere called the first post-Modernist novelist (to the extent that such a phenomenon actually exists)[2]—uses Modernist technique (in point of view especially) as a means of assaulting Modernist ideas of the nature of the world and of the place of humans within it. Despite their evident incompatibility, then, Booth and Robbe-Grillet share, along with James, certain implicit understandings about the inter-connections of technique and theme in the novel, more particularly, of the absolute and irretrievable linkage of point of view and worldview. This same understanding is at the heart of the Modernist achievement.

The Voyeur is but one of a substantial body of novels in which Robbe-Grillet attempts to demonstrate his theories that humanism is central to the Modernist experience in the novel (despite the claim of some of the Modernists themselves that their work was outside the old humanist tradition) and that in the post-Holocaust, post-Hiroshima world (although he does not name these events, they clearly occasion for him the death of the old and the justification for the new), the romance of humanism has been replaced by the realities of *chosisme,* "thingism." As he says in *For a New Novel,*

> Is there not . . . a certain fraudulence in this word *human* which is always being thrown in our faces? If it is not a word quite devoid of meaning, what meaning does it really have?
>
> It seems . . . [that there are] those who use it all the time, those who make it the sole criterion of all praise as of all reproach . . . ; if I say, "The world is man," I shall always gain absolution; while if I say, "Things are things, and man is only man," I am immediately charged with a crime against humanity. (51–52)[3]

"[T]he humanist outlook," Robbe-Grillet adds, as if it were a pejorative, "is pre-eminently a pledge of solidarity" (53).

The obvious paradox, however, is that it is only through humans that Robbe-Grillet (indeed, any novelist) can demonstrate the irrelevance of humans in this presumably post-Modernist world (assuming, that is, that the human-centered world against which he reacts is Modernist). For the principal means by which the novelist Robbe-Grillet manifests the ideas of the theorist is point of view. More meticulously even than the far greater Modernists of an earlier generation (he would be among the last to deny this), he limits his novels' perspectives to the fields of vision—in both senses of that term—of his protagonists. We enter their consciousnesses and are privy to all that they perceive through their senses, as well as all that they think. There is not a word, not an image, that we can attribute even hypothetically to an omniscient author or an imagined "narrator." This is the situation that so disturbs Wayne Booth. As the psychopathic watch salesman Mathias in *The Voyeur* reveals his desires, his confusion, his psychoses, his compulsive observation of details and his failure to comprehend their significance, he both illustrates Robbe-Grillet's theories and, at the same time, refutes them.[4]

The real contradiction here, however, is not between the theory and practice of Alain Robbe-Grillet but, rather, between his novels and the readings of Wayne Booth. For these fictions are not merely the "brilliant culmination of more than a hundred years of experimentation with inside views and the sympathetic identification they can yield" (384). They are also proof that the theoretical views of Booth on point of view, applied in close readings and without preconception or prejudice, do work and that, even in this age—perhaps particularly in this age—they remain highly relevant.

✳

My aim in this book is to complete, in a sense, *The Rhetoric of Fiction:* to apply the method and language of Henry James and Wayne Booth to those Modernist and post-Modernist novels which so discomfited Booth and, in the process, to offer a new (yet old) way of reading individual texts, an enriched understanding of Modernism itself as a force in the development of the novel and a jargon-free idiom to describe both novels and movements.[5] For with Booth's unease in the face of certain texts and with a certain Narratological (post-Modernist) bias against the Modernists, it may well be that the storytelling strategies of the Modernist novel—the richest age, I am convinced, in the history of the novel—have never before been approached systematically from within by a method devised for and friendly to its aims and its accomplishments.

Underlying the readings and principles that I provide here are several pivotal assumptions: that neither the art in question nor the critic of that art may be detached from history or tradition if we expect our views to be heard beyond the present moment; that the critic may not invent a vocabulary that is at once private and arbitrary if we desire to communicate with readers beyond our immediate circle; that whether we identify ourselves as New Critics or Post-Structuralists or by some other term, the primacy of the text is not negotiable: it takes precedence over theory and secondary sources alike.[6] Scholars, critics and theorists alike, as I understand my profession, are in the service of the work of art which they would elucidate. They may be as heroic as they would like—or as their admirers might judge them—but they must acknowledge that they remain secondary, in every instance, to the work of art.

✳

No technical term could be more matter of fact, more commonsensical than James' "point of view" when it is used to describe the infinitely complex narrative possibilities of the Modernist novel. And no term is more useful in describing this

The Rhetoric of Modernist Fiction

practice. The paradox here is that "point of view" works precisely because of its generality, its lack not just of specificity but of any pretense to a scientific approach. Because it cannot name, we are led to describe. If such a practice leads frequently to critical ambiguity rather than to certainty, that is not at all inappropriate to the Modernist novel, with its persistent ambiguous worldview. For if anything at all is certain in the novels of Joyce, Proust, Kafka, Mann, Woolf, Faulkner, et al., it is that nothing is certain; the world made possible by those eminent Victorians Darwin, Marx, Freud, Frazer and Einstein, in the aftermath of the First World War, which destroyed a continent's and a century's expectations, and of the Treaty of Versailles, which virtually guaranteed a Second World War, is inevitably a world of ambiguity. This is as true of personal as of national relations. And if, as I believe, many of the novels which we term post-Modernist are, in source, in practice, and in result, effectively Modernist—this same close reading of point of view will work as well for the fiction of that presumably new sensibility and era.

The much more technical terminology that has of late come into favor in some narratological quarters turns out to be, in action, of far less value, as I view it: Because it seeks to name, and thereby to identify, various narrative tropes, it would appear to offer a far greater certainty than "point of view" possibly can. The problem rests with the naming process itself, however, for no one has yet devised—nor, as I see it, is anyone likely to devise—a system of specialized terms that can work generally, for more than an individual novel or two.

✳

It is not the terminology of narratology itself to which I object, but rather the promise inherent in such naming. Narrative, as I read it, is not a mystery to be resolved by nomenclature. Such a practice can too easily substitute for insight; the terms too often take over and assume the place of analysis. This is not the way that I have learned and that I teach my students to read. Neither science nor magic is a viable means to mastering Modernist (or even post-Modernist) narratives.

Another sub-rule, if you will: We must never mistake the name of a literary event (or of any event, for that matter) for its meaning, its seeming form for its function; we must look as closely as possible at its actual practice. "Point of view," in practice, is an effective critical lens because it is here, more than in any other aspect of the novel, that the differences between appearance and naming, on the one hand, and actual function, on the other, may indeed be profound.

Re-reading *The Rhetoric of Fiction*—or reading it for the first time—in the context of contemporary discussions of narrative, we recognize how masterfully Wayne Booth completed his task, as he understood it. Our task today is not just to apply Booth's lessons—but to extend them to the one significant area inaccessible to Booth: the Modernist novel. That this is the novel's great age makes this a not insignificant task in its own right.

CHAPTER 2

Booth, Joyce and Modernist Points of View

*B*ooth's approach in *The Rhetoric of Fiction* is at once moral and rhetorical. Mine is also moral, I like to think, although, coming from a different generation and background, mine is a rather different morality from Booth's; but I am not at all sympathetic to the simply rhetorical, especially when it is detached from and/or takes precedence over the work of art.[1] Where Booth tends to organize his study around types and rules—he is likely to be skeptical about some earlier rules and is not much concerned with establishing new ones (or new nomenclature) in their place, but the organization of his book is based largely on the classification of types—my own strongest desire in following him is to avoid, as consistently as I am able, both rules and types. My approach is more pragmatic: My interest is not in individual texts as illustrations of the various narrative possibilities open to writers of fiction, but in what the texts themselves tell us about Modernist practice in point of view. Whatever generalizations I might reach—and the one or two rules for reading that I might offer—are derived directly from those texts. Close reading, not rhetoric, is both my training and my delight.

Booth's most admirable qualities in *The Rhetoric of Fiction,* at least as I read that pivotal book, are the breadth of his reading and the openness and generosity of his sensibility. But, inevitably, he remains a man of his background and generation, and as I read his readings, they display one definite limit: He reads the texts of Modernist novels with a certain uneasiness, a wariness, a willingness to accept the generalizations of others about them, even, at times—however hard he tries—a lack of sympathy. He thus fails to notice, I believe, the many ways in which these texts support his general theses, as well as the ways in which his methods may elucidate these texts.

Coming from a generation later than his and closer in sympathy with the Modernists, I feel freer to read these same texts through eyes which have also read Booth. In much the same way that writers of short stories after *Dubliners* have access to possibilities that Joyce himself did not yet possess (this does not mean, of course, that they can improve on Joyce, but they can at least build on his methods and expand his vision), I feel that I now have the opportunity to build on Booth and to appreciate more fully the narrative goals and possibilities of what I am convinced is the great age of the novel. For Booth, implicitly, the novel reaches its peak in the late eighteenth and nineteenth centuries; for me, without question, its peak is the age of Joyce, Proust, Kafka, Mann, Woolf, Faulkner, Hemingway, Beckett, Kazantzakis and many others. To understand the centrality of point of view in their great accomplishment is thus an imperative for all those concerned with the history of the novel.

Some Rules for Reading Modernist Novels

Let me begin with my two rules for reading, both rather obvious, I think, yet rarely followed by contemporary critics or theoreticians of narrative. The first is consistent with Booth's reading, the second very much at odds with it. Can there be a credo more obvious than:

RULE 1: A good contemporary reader of novels will read with both eyes—one focused from the perspective of our time, the other from the time of the author: WE MUST NOT JUDGE A NOVEL WITH THE STANDARDS OF OUR TIME ALONE.

For example, to criticize Trollope for being omniscient is ludicrous; to criticize Murdoch or Drabble for being omniscient is necessary. Booth works hard to follow this rule and only occasionally—if significantly—fails to do so. Less obvious, and more important, is:

RULE 2: Just as we suspend disbelief when we enter the theatre, agreeing that what we see is life and not artifice, so we must do so when opening a novel; we know that someone has written these words, but UNLESS A NOVELIST CALLS ATTENTION THROUGH NARRATIVE TECHNIQUE TO HIS/HER PRESENCE, WE ARE OBLIGED TO FORGET THAT PRESENCE AND TO RESPOND INSTEAD AS IF THESE WERE NOT WORDS ON THE PAGE BUT REPRESENTATIONS OF REALITY.

If we constantly talk about the author of these words, we will be forever begging the question and, in effect, labeling all authors omniscient. This rule is particularly imperative when we know that some novelists—as with the Modernists generally—are vitally concerned with eliminating their presence as authors within their texts. (I have elsewhere called this Levitt's Law, building on Hugh Kenner's Uncle Charles Principle.) Here Booth consistently falters, and here, more even than with his abiding morality, is the root of his problems with the Modernist novel.

Some Fallacies of Intention

Students sometimes ask—especially when faced with a surprising interpretation of a text—how we know that this was what the author intended. My own usual answer to this question is that we needn't worry about the author's intentions, that what matters is what he or she has accomplished. (I might add that writers have not been unknown to lie about their work, and that, more innocently, they are not always their own best readers.) Such a response accords to the critic a certain dignity—as well as responsibility—as interpreter of the text. It is also a means of avoiding past excesses of interpretation, which may have relied exclusively on authorial comments and thus missed out on other possibilities within the text. This last is the root of the so-called intentional fallacy, which some contemporary critics think of as the central tenet of the New Criticism. To practicing New Critics, however, the intentional fallacy is more of a guide to teaching than an injunction for reading: more useful for directing uncertain students to the text than as the way to read that text. Thus, for example, we may well need to understand something of a novelist's general intentions about point of view before judging fully his or her work. This is even more imperative when we are dealing not with a single novelist but with a generation of them, and when we can divine in their work a shared, perhaps even a defining purpose.

Modernist Characteristics

The Modernist novelists as a group are linked in various ways, both in technique and in worldview. Chronology, I believe, is not a determinant, at least not in the sense that all those writing novels in, say, the 1920s or 1930s are inevitably Modernists. To my mind, D. H. Lawrence, almost an exact contemporary of both Joyce and Woolf, is not a Modernist novelist at all, for he shares with them neither broad vision nor the particulars of writing novels as a means of expressing that vision. Various theories have been offered of the characteristics of the Modernist novel, one of the best known being that of Maurice Beebe: myth, irony, tight imagistic and metaphoric structure, and self-reflexive usage are the qualities that he cites. While Beebe does not specify innovative narrative technique, this underlies each of his other categories.[2] Every teacher of Modernist novels will offer a different emphasis, of course, and thus may see irony perhaps, or mythopoesis, or a response to the Romantics, or to the modern world (either positive or negative, ironic or moral, or ironic and moral) as central.

For me, at the heart of the Modernist novel lies point of view, every novelist's first decision in writing a novel and the clearest determinant of a worldview as expressed in fiction. Wayne Booth and I are at this point in reasonably close agreement. Where we disagree is in the implications of such a belief. For me, it is evident that the Modernist Masters shared a vision of a world at once threatened and sustaining, of a humanity at once fragile and resilient, and that they manifested that vision—in their very different ways—primarily through innovative points of view whose major purpose was to eliminate the authorial presence within the novel and to substitute for it the presence of the reader.

Booth is far less comfortable with the Modernists than with their predecessors. While he does not assume, as some critics have, that they have deserted the tradition which he so obviously loves, he often does seem uncomfortable with their responses to that tradition, with the ways in which, as I view it, the Modernists have extended that tradition. And so he never appreciates the central role which they have created for the reader; and so he never notices the inherent humanism—the morality—of their creation. It may take another generation's greater distance to recognize it, but the Modernist novel as I read it is being most traditional when it is most innovative, for formal adaptation to changing times is the very essence of the history of the novel.

The Role and Responsibility of the Modernist Reader

Implicit always in Booth's criticism of the Modernists—even when he expresses his admiration for, say, Joyce as their leader—is a conservative, one might almost say reactionary, sense of the role of the reader. It is no accident that *The Rhetoric of Fiction* concludes with a consideration of "The Morality of Impersonal Narration," in which he carefully looks out for the reader as if we cannot look out (or within) for ourselves.

Booth begins his final chapter with a consideration of Louis-Ferdinand Céline, the French Fascist novelist often acclaimed for his style. He is cautious about judging Céline, although it is clear that he approves neither of his politics nor of his point of view: "It is all, of course, completely 'objective,'" Booth writes about point of view in *Journey to the End of the Night* (1932); "Céline is never undeniably there, even in the long-winded commentary" (380). But Booth is hesitant to draw explicit negative conclusions from this. Personally, I have no trouble judging Céline: I believe that the quality of his prose has been over-rated, that his handling of point of view is often clumsy (Booth, too, notices the "heavy-handed symbolism" [382] of the novel but wonders whether it should be attributed to the novelist or to his reliable spokesman within the text), that his politics and morality are despicable. Readers—even the most determined New Critical readers—are entitled to make moral judgments: critical neutrality does not demand that we neglect our values; it means merely that we must not pre-judge an author's worldview or deny him or her the narrative means to communicate that view.[3] Where Booth and the Modernists are concerned, this means that we must not confuse ambiguity with amorality. From Céline, Booth moves directly to Robbe-Grillet and the question, "is this what we go to literature for?"

Booth, of course, appreciates ambiguity, and he cites Ian Watt's suggestion in *The Rise of the Novel* that "the novel is essentially an ambiguous form." Still, Booth concludes, "This does not mean, however, that novels should or must be ambiguous" (386–87). Who could disagree?—except when the reality which the novel attempts to depict is itself ambiguous, when one lives in inherently ambiguous times. Written a decade after the atomic bomb attacks on Hiroshima and Nagasaki, Robbe-Grillet's *The Voyeur* realistically depicts a universe that can never again maintain the certainty of earlier times, a universe whose very core is ambiguity. We may not like reading about such a world, or the idea of living within it—indeed, we may find further grounds for rejecting Robbe-Grillet's worldview (his sometimes sadomasochistic depictions of women, for instance) in subsequent fictions of his—but we must not confuse the messenger with the message, the world in which we live while immersed in the novel with the world in which we would prefer to live our lives. Yes, as uncomfortable as they may make us, the early novels of Robbe-Grillet are precisely (if not only) what we go to literature for: They are not fun to read, but they do show us life as it may be in our age; most importantly, they leave it to us to decide how we will respond to that life.

The reader in the Modernist novel has become a major actor in the elaboration of the novel's events and meaning: This lesson from the Modernists is one that Robbe-Grillet has learned well, although to rather different ends from theirs. Robbe-Grillet may be said to use Modernist technique—in point of view principally, but also in metaphor and irony—as a means of denying the Modernist vision; it is in this sense that he may be considered the first post-Modernist. While Booth does not speak of the Modernists as a group—indeed, the term had not yet been applied to literature at the time that he wrote *The Rhetoric of Fiction*[4]—it is clear that he cannot distinguish between them and Robbe-Grillet and that, implicitly at least, his condemnation of the latter extends also to the former. The humanism inherent in Modernist fiction, a humanism that few critics could see in the 1960s and 1970s but that derives in very large part from the responsibilities entrusted to the reader, is turned against them by Robbe-Grillet through that same point of view.

The Modernists used point of view in an incredibly imaginative variety of ways, all of them designed to incite our involvement within the text, in the working out of its meanings—in minor matters and major ones, in plot and character development, as well as in theme and worldview. They not only avoid telling us what we are to believe, as their Victorian predecessors had done with their passive readers; they induce the modern reader to become virtual co-creator of the text. Joyce and his Modernist contemporaries were not writing for some rare, elitist reader; their intention was to turn us all into new, more self-aware, more responsible readers. It is still common to say of the Modernists that they represented a break in the novel's long tradition as a popular form, among the most accessible of literary forms (so that, for the first time, popular novels and good novels were entities separate and distinct). To the extent that this is true, it is

The Rhetoric of Modernist Fiction

because we have not always as readers been willing to meet the demands made on us by the Modernists. Those willing to do the work, however, have in virtually every case been rewarded for the effort. Once thought the most demanding of novels, *Ulysses* delights increasingly large and diverse groups of readers, from all sorts of occupations and nations, even over the Internet. (There are also international Internet reading groups of *Finnegans Wake*.) Their task is certainly more demanding than that of, say, readers of Tom Clancy stories, but they are unlikely to forget what they have read a few moments after putting down the book.

I do not know whether Wayne Booth also at times reads escapist fiction. I do know how superb a reader he can be of texts such as Sterne's *Tristram Shandy* or Austen's *Emma*. But he has not learned to trust readers of Modernist novels to find their own way and defend their moral base for themselves. And so he precisely misses the key Modernist point when he writes, "From this standpoint there is a moral dimension in the author's choice of impersonal, noncommittal techniques" (388). There is, of course; but where Booth sees amorality because we may be misled by such techniques, I see a new, more intense morality because we are in the process given the tools to judge for ourselves. Implicit in such a reading—in our very ability to make such judgments—is an awareness of the irony which pervades so much of twentieth-century life and which promises to do so as well for the twenty-first century. I am not one of those for whom irony is the most characteristic quality of Modernist literature. But there is no denying that many of the most characteristic techniques of Modernist point of view culminate in irony. Put a bit differently, I would contend that irony for the Modernist novelists is frequently a function of point of view, that it is inherently potential in the distance which may be developed between the reader and the characters (especially those who may serve as unreliable points of view), between the reader and the author, even between the author and his creations. Also, of course—ironically—it may develop when there is too little distance, when we are induced to identify too intimately with a character unworthy of our trust and affection. The novelists and the times have trained us well to judge for ourselves.

Yet it is only by building on Booth's principles that the Modernist reader can refine those tools and appreciate fully the narrative revolution that has defined the novel as a form in the twentieth century. "The author makes his readers" (397), Booth concludes *The Rhetoric of Fiction*: the necessary beginning for *The Rhetoric of Modernist Fiction*.

Booth, Henry James and James Joyce: Distance/Ambiguity/Amorality

Booth does appreciate, however, what he calls—building on Henry James—the "pleasure of collaboration." He understands well what James means when he speaks of "'making his reader,'" for "'When he makes him well, that is makes him interested, then the reader does quite half the labor.' James is not thinking here simply of giving the reader a sense of his own cleverness. He is making his readers by forcing them onto a level of alertness that will allow for his most subtle effects" (302).[5] It is almost as if Joyce and his fellows had read James, had even read Booth on James, so central is this concept to their art, so fine a statement is this of their effort in managing point of view. Yet Booth cannot quite bring himself to recognize this presence in their work. I can only assume that his inability to do so relates in some way to what he sees as their crossing of a moral line. James is the last novelist with whom Booth seems truly comfortable.

Yet even with James, Booth feels a twinge of discomfort. Interestingly, this occurs not with one of the more demanding, more ambiguous late novels of James (of them, he speaks only of *The Ambassadors*), but with the technically more straightforward *The Turn of the Screw*. And his problem is essentially the uncertainty of the plot—the presence, that is, of the ghost—an uncertainty which derives from the potential unreliability of the governess as point of view. Booth answers the question for himself by determining that the ghost is real and that "the governess sees what she says she sees" (314). My reading of *The Rhetoric of Fiction* tells me, however, that this is the wrong question to ask. What matters is not what facts may be true, but what the governess believes to be true: If she is telling the truth as she sees it, she is not inevitably unreliable. Booth's question and answer presuppose that it is possible still to identify an objective reality in modern life. But if the history of our century teaches us anything, it is that certainty is no longer attainable (unless, of course, we all become true believers and ignore those facts that we find disconcerting). Booth's misunderstanding, harmless as it may be for James, foreshadows his more meaningful problem with Robbe-Grillet and all that that implies.

James, says Booth, is not to be blamed for the often conflicting interpretations which critics have formed for *The Turn of the Screw*. "Yet if we exonerate James, must we not blame the critics?" (366) he asks. Again, I would say, this is the wrong (rhetorical) question, formed as it is from a (pre)conception of the world more suited to the nineteenth than to the twentieth century.

> The first readers of *The Turn* never questioned the governess' integrity. . . . [W]e now look for distance everywhere. . . .
>
> Their first readers were more likely to commit the fault of overlooking distance when it was plain before them. . . . But many of us now . . . can't accept a straight and simple statement when we read one. . . .
>
> In short, we have looked for so long at foggy landscapes reflected in misty mirrors that we have come to *like* fog. (366–67, 372)

But can this be bad if the world is, indeed, one of fog and mist? Booth is too fine a critic to suggest that an author—say, a Modernist novelist—actually creates the world which he or she depicts. The artist may make it possible for the viewer to perceive a reality never before seen and in this sense to play a role in creation, but it is events far more powerful than novels (the Battle of the Somme, the Treaty of Versailles, Guernica and Auschwitz, Hiroshima, Nagasaki, the war in Vietnam, the assassinations of great men, the events of 11 September 2001) which create reality. The novelist's job, as always, is to respond to that world, the critic's to measure and judge that response. Where I would blame the critic is in sometimes failing to recognize such facts.

The well-attuned Modernist reader understands fully his or her new role and responsibility. Readers of *Finnegans Wake,* for example—and if we need a single work to stand for a demanding and rewarding Modernism, none seems more suitable than this—are likely to act in concert with others in a reading group; to become researchers, even experts, in the many areas which this encyclopedic text demands our knowledge (among them military and literary history, world geography, foreign languages, Irish culture, the formation of mythopoesis, the formation of the mind); to recognize that we can never be quite finished with this book, never exhaust its potential meanings or our desire to explore them; to delight in the possibilities, with all their uncertainties, of co-creating a world with the novelist. The fact that so many skilled readers of the *Wake* are not academics, not even native speakers of English, attests, I believe, to the rewards which Joyce offers his reader. James' implied contract with his reader is revised and updated by Joyce and the Joycean reader.

The confidence with which I offer this sense of the stature of Joyce within modern culture—a stature that appears to increase even as academics distance themselves from Modernism at large—would not have been conceivable forty years ago, when Booth had just published *The Rhetoric of Fiction.* In the same semester that I first read this book—and also first read *Ulysses* with some understanding—I was assured by a professor that Joyce was a fraud. Booth knew better even then, although his discomfort with Joyce is evident throughout. There is much in Joyce's handling of point of view that he applauds, but much potential as well that he cannot yet see.

Booth's Joyce is demonstrably a "giant" (325), and *The Rhetoric of Fiction* devotes more space to him than to Fielding or Dickens, and as much as to Sterne or Austen, Booth's obvious favorites; only James merits more space, and much of that is reserved for James the theorist of fiction, rather than the novelist. Yet Joyce seems here more an obligation than a labor of love. The fact that Booth chooses to discuss *A Portrait of the Artist as a Young Man* for its management of point of view, instead of the more ambitious *Ulysses* or *Finnegans Wake*—or even the more accessible (and obvious choice) *Dubliners*—suggests, I think, both that obligation and that discomfort. Yet Booth seems uneasy even with *A Portrait.*

To begin, he confuses Stephen Dedalus's theory of art with his creator's (50). For all his awareness of the significance of the distance between creator and character in modern fiction, Booth may have problems with its implications. Thus, "[w]hen compared with Dickens, for instance, James Joyce may seem expliticly amoral. Joyce's overt interests are entirely in matters of truth and beauty" (132). We can recognize today, however, that these are Stephen's interests and that Joyce's distance from Stephen, his presumably autobiographical creation (his "distance from his own hero" [335]), may be intended in part to point up that amorality (or at least that immaturity): to make not just an ironic point, that is, but a moral one. Had Booth had more faith in—or distance from—his own core beliefs, he might have made this connection himself. Not that he is unaware of Joyce's accomplishment: "It is obvious—at least once we have read Joyce—that there is no limit to the number of deciphering pleasures that can be packed into a book" (301). Any participant in a *Wake* reading group will affirm this as fact. Of course, "deciphering" is not Booth's ideal pursuit in reading a novel, and, forty years afterwards, we can affirm that there is much more than such pleasures in both *Ulysses* and *Finnegans Wake*. We know with certainty today for *Ulysses,* and with increasing confidence for the *Wake,* that it is simply not true that they "cannot be read; they can only be studied" (325). Forty years ago, however, that seemed a not unreasonable conclusion.[6]

There is much in Booth's reading of Joyce—in general approach, in specific details—that I find myself in agreement with; forty years ago, I likely would have found even less to disagree with. When Booth declares, for instance, that "no work, not even the shortest lyric [as with Stephen's at the end of *A Portrait*], can be written in complete moral, intellectual and aesthetic neutrality" (329–30), I want to applaud. But I also must note that limited points of view, devoid of any source of commentary, are not inevitably morally neutral; they are likely, in practice—in the hands of the Modernist Masters at least—to be quite aggressively moral (albeit of a morality rather different from Dickens'). "Commentary" is not the only, or the best, or, for a modern reader, even a viable source of moral standards. "Purged of the author's explicit judgment" (333), *A Portrait* does not deny us a sense of the novelist's values, those alike which appear to coincide with Stephen's (about the Catholic Church in Ireland, for example) and those which seem directly to counter them (aspects of Stephen's Romanticism, of his attitudes toward art, even of his vaunted indifference to politics: when Stephen proclaims to his classmates, "I'm not interested in politics, I'm only interested in style," Joyce, I believe, is using the stylistic flaw—the misplaced modifier—to undercut the proud declaration).

Booth goes on to agree that we can neither understand nor appreciate all of Joyce's "refinements" in *A Portrait;* "[f]or some of us, the air of detachment and objectivity may still be worth the price, but we must never pretend that a price was not paid" (336). This exaggerates the novel's difficulty and understates its accessibility (even *Finnegans Wake*'s "refinements" become increasingly clear as we continue to read it). We must also ask to what extent this putative price is a moral one and whether this is not at the heart of Wayne Booth's problems with Modernist point of view. Forty years of reading Joyce and of applying what I have learned from *The Rhetoric of Fiction*—and in each of these pleasures I have frequently focused on point of view—have convinced me that a far greater price is paid when we fail to take the author at his own (figurative) word (the word, as it were, of his work) and thus impose on his work a no longer meaningful standard of values.[7] For we may miss in the process not only the work's virtues (ambiguity intended) but also the extent to which it does fulfill our needs, does adhere to the tradition which we would defend. There is barely a hint of the surviving omniscient author in *A Portrait of the Artist as a Young Man,* none at all—as I read them—in *Ulysses* or *Finnegans Wake.* But none of them is "author-less" (326). We must be careful not to deny the author's moral presence when he is crafting us to serve as his agent and not to insist on it when it is destructive to do so (the "implied author": the very term begs the question).

The Fallacy of the "Implied Author"

"Implied author" is one of the few more or less technical terms that Booth creates, but only to fill what he perceives as a gap in terminology. As opposed to "the omniscient author speaking in his own voice" (171), Booth notes, we need a term to describe the process by means of which a novelist may disguise his continuing presence within his narrative. "It is a curious fact that we have no terms either for this created 'second self' or for our relationship with him"— "persona," "mask," and "narrator" (73), even "diguised narrators" (152) are patently inadequate. And so he settles for "implied author" (73), "the author's 'second self'" (151).

> [I]n this distinction between author and implied author we find an attempt at a middle position between the technical irrelevance of talk about the author's objectivity and the harmful error of pretending that an author can allow direct intrusions of his own immediate problems and desires. (75)

Acknowledging the inappropriateness of outright, Victorian omniscience in the modern novel, Booth nonetheless refuses to countenance an absolute absence of authorial presence. His compromise, the implied author, is asking, I believe, for linguistic and critical trouble: There can be little functional difference, in the end, between an implied author and an explicit one. The latter, like Thackeray, may flaunt his power and personality; the former, for Booth, will continue to exert control where it matters: in avoiding the amorality of ambiguity. To dramatize this central point, Booth chooses the same quotation from Joyce's *Portrait* that I used as epigraph for my dissertation, which endeavored to apply Booth's principles to precisely the opposite purpose (although I'm not sure that I understood at that time just how different our visions of Modernism were). "Even the novel in which no narrator is dramatized," Booth writes, "creates an implicit picture of an author who stands behind the scenes, whether as stage manager, as puppeteer [Thackeray's constructions], or as an indifferent God [Joyce's], silently paring his fingernails" (151). If this is true, then all efforts at eliminating the modern reader's dependence on the author are doomed before they begin, defined out of existence, for all novels by this definition are inherently omniscient; at its most extreme point, such logic would essentially eliminate the Modernist novel. This cannot have been Booth's intention, and it obviously makes no sense. And so we must be willing to suspend disbelief in the author's presence within his novel. This problem becomes paramount in that greatest of all Modernist novels—perhaps the greatest of all novels—Joyce's *Ulysses*.

CHAPTER 3

A Brief History of Point of View in the Brief History of the Novel

Chaucer's Persona

The history of point of view is older by far than the history of the novel. While the term "point of view" is itself only a century or so old, the practice goes back to the origins of oral storytelling. The first decision that any storyteller must make—whether in speech or in writing, whether he or she does so consciously or without thought—is the prism through which the story's events will be revealed to the reader. This is also often the most important decision that the storyteller must make. The choice was limited and easy for the oral bard: He (or perhaps she, if we are to believe Samuel Butler and John Barth) would speak in his own voice, directly to his immediate listeners. But sometimes that choice would be a bit more complex—enriched, one might say—as when Homer empowers Odysseus to tell his own story to his listeners in Phaiakia. As Eumaeus the swineherd tells Penelope of the beggar whom he has entertained, "There was no end to what he made me hear / of his hard roving; and I listened, eyes / upon him, as a man drinks in a tale / a minstrel sings—a minstrel taught by heaven / to touch the hearts of men."[1] We can learn much about narrative in the age of Homer by listening to or reading Homer.

In the age of the novel, point of view has become synonymous with the novel as a form: One can imagine a novel or short story without irony or imagery or metaphor, but fiction without point of view is inconceivable; still, point of view is not limited to fiction. Wherever storytelling—"narrative" (in the larger sense of the term)—is involved, in whatever literary form (in one of the modes of poetry or even in the drama), point of view will be relevant. It is at the heart, for example, of each of the long poems of Chaucer, among the very first writers to develop a *persona* rich with possibilities of irony, of potential unreliability, even

17

of metafiction. For his most famous *persona* is named Chaucer, and he is the bore who speaks only in prose and is the only one of the Canterbury pilgrims to tell two tales—the first is so dull that his listeners interrupt and insist on a different story. That one is no better and is similarly never completed.

Chaucer the pilgrim—fat, middle-aged, unlucky in love and rather foolish, more interested in life lived through books than in living himself—has brothers in the *The House of Fame, The Book of the Duchess* and *The Legend of Good Women,* even in the character of Pandarus in *Troilus and Criseyde.* Never ill-willed or consciously deceptive—even the pander Pandarus means well by Troilus and his sad lover, Criseyde—Chaucer's persona is nonetheless at least potentially unreliable as a storyteller, for his perspective is always limited, and he is always such a bore. One can imagine, however, that Chaucer's own listeners/readers, knowing well the character of the man and the successes of his public career, found yet another level of ironic pleasure in hearing him read his own (unfaithful) account of himself in his fictions. No writer of fiction has ever improved on his practice.

Eighteenth-Century Beginnings: Fielding and Richardson

Everyone agrees that at the heart of English fiction, from the beginnings to the present day, lies realism, but no two critics seem able to agree on just what it is that realism consists of. In his seminal study, *The Rise of the Novel,* Ian Watt identifies two distinct strands, as characterized by the novels of Samuel Richardson and Henry Fielding, respectively. Although Watt says little directly about point of view, it is evident both from his discussion and from these novels that the issue of realism—its very definitions—and the issue of point of view do not simply overlap but are essentially the same. That is, realism as a literary conception may not exist separately from the point of view chosen to depict it. This remains as true in the twenty-first as in the eighteenth century.

Watt points out that Fielding called *Tom Jones* "'A History,' and habitually described his role as that of historian or biographer whose function was to give a faithful representation of the life of his time."[2] At describing public life, that of society at large, Fielding is brilliantly successful. But he is far less successful with private life. "The fact that Fielding's characters do not have a convincing inner life means that their possibilities of psychological development are very limited."[3] Does Fielding choose his particular mode of point of view in *Tom Jones* because he is not interested in the inner lives of his characters, or is it his choice of point of view that determines the failure of those inner lives? Does the narrative chicken inevitably follow or precede the egg? In the novel, the two are simultaneous, at once the form and the function, each serving as both cause and effect. I would argue that this is the key fact in the consideration of the novel form in any period.

Fielding opts in all of his novels, but especially in *Tom Jones* (1749), for what can be characterized only as omniscience, in one of its more extreme forms. Perhaps the best known facet of *Tom Jones* —for those who have gone beyond Tony Richardson's wonderful popular film—is the personal essay with which Fielding opens each of the novel's eighteen chapters. Like the character Prologue in a Shakespearean history play, he both sets the stage and comments on the world for which the stage has been set. He speaks here in his own voice ("As we determined when we first sat down to write this history" (77) and directly to "My reader" (44) and "my friend" (448).[4] He interprets, foretells, talks around the action in these prologues, even comments on the nature of prologues (Book XVI, 738–39), gives advice to other novelists (Book XII, "Showing What Is to be Deemed Plagiarism in a Modern Author, and What Is to be Considered as Lawful Prize," 537) and critics alike (Book X, "Containing Instructions Very Necessary to be Perused by Modern Critics," 446). We need not today take seriously his theory of the novel as a Comic Epic in Prose, but it is clear that he needed his contemporaries to do so; and so he talks much about that. Among those who can be said to have followed Fielding's advice and model, Thackeray and George Eliot did so productively. Among twentieth-century novelists who have done so—those whom I label the New Victorians—his misapplied example has proven disastrous.

✳

The only consciousness into which *Tom Jones* takes us is that of Henry Fielding. For Richardson, in *Clarissa* (1748), the author's consciousness is just about the only one that is not explored. Because the novel's form is epistolary—and the form may be said to have chosen its author, since its predecessor, *Pamela* (1740), began as an exercise book in letter writing for a newly literate servant class—it provides us, by definition, with subjective accounts of the characters and events which populate this two thousand-page text. "With Richardson," writes Watt, "we slip, invisible, into the domestic privacy of his characters . . . we get inside their minds as well as inside their houses."[5] The epistolary novel obviously cannot serve as a model for very many subsequent novelists. Occasional letters do serve in various Modernist novels as a kind of subsidiary point of view—in Proust, in Simon, in Faulkner, in Joyce, among others—but few writers after Richardson have been interested in working in the form, and few readers would likely be interested in reading the result. (The fact that a novel includes a letter, or even a series of letters functioning as a point of view, does not inevitably make of it an epistolary novel.) But virtually all of the Modernist novelists have followed Richardson in exploring the workings of the mind.

The Fielding-Richardson dichotomy appears in other forms in the history of the novel and novel criticism. Perhaps the best known is Hawthorne's division between what he calls the "novel," broadly social in its coverage, concerned primarily with external realism and likely to be either omniscient or objective in its point of view; and the so-called "romance," more private than social, concerned primarily with internal realism (although, three generations before Freud, Hawthorne is not yet confident enough to call this "realism"), and likely to devise essentially subjective points of view. The Modernist Masters may be said to have combined the two modes: *Ulysses* and *Finnegans Wake,* for example, brilliantly evoke both inner and outer realities, thus resolving, one would think, the original conflict. However, those English critics and novelists who assaulted Modernism in the decades after World War II, appalled by the perceived "immorality" and "experimentation" of the Modernists, were never able to acknowledge this union. F. R. Leavis could never quite see how perfectly Joyce fits into and continues his beloved Great Tradition.

Nineteenth-Century English Forms: Dickens, Thackeray, Trollope, Brontë

When crowds of his readers gathered in front of the home of Charles Dickens in London, in the winter of 1841, they were demonstrating two central, determining facets of the Victorian novel: the intimate relationship between reader and novelist and the reader's recognition that in the world of fiction, the novelist was God. Dickens was at that time in the midst of writing *The Old Curiosity Shop* (1841), one of his most popular, as well as his most sentimental novel, and it looked dangerously to his readers as if he were about to kill off Little Nell, his (to a modern reader) sickeningly saccharine young heroine (as well as the prototype of the comic strip and musical comedy character, Little Orphan Annie). Dickens' readers knew well—following his usual pattern—that he had not yet written the serialized novel's next installment, and they were hoping by their demonstration to affect its outcome. In that same cause, a bill reportedly was introduced into Parliament imploring Mr. Dickens to save Little Nell. When the ship bearing the novel's next installment reached New York Harbor, it is said, thousands waited anxiously at the pier for news of her fate. Fortunately, Dickens had the good taste to kill off the little bastard. But that is beside the point, for what the incident really illustrates is a relationship between author and audience that would be inconceivable in any modern context. That relationship is at the heart of the dominant Victorian narrative strategy, equally the cause of omniscience and its effect.

The prevailing image of Victorian narrative is, for me, that of the middle-class household on the Sabbath, after church and mid-day dinner, sitting in the parlor and listening to the father of the family reading the current installment of a novel in, say, *Household Words,* the popular journal edited by Dickens himself, or from the latest three-decker novel by him or by one of his contemporaries. The Victorian novelist is, in effect, that *paterfamilias,* his audience the members of his family listening passively to his reading. He is both omniscient and omnipotent, knowing all, telling all, controlling all, and never reluctant to acknowledge his control: "for novelists have the privilege of knowing every-thing," declares Thackeray in *Vanity Fair* (1848, 37).[6]

In his note to the reader at the beginning of that novel, Thackeray names himself "the manager of the Performance" and speaks of his characters as "his Puppets." He announces throughout his narrative strategies, interprets the actions and intent of his puppets, tells us "the truth" whenever there is even the vaguest possibility of doubt, moves effortlessly backward and forward in time as his story requires, serves as the bridge between characters and reader and speaks directly to that reader in his own voice ("My beloved reader," 228); he even becomes a character in his own fiction: "If, a few pages back, the present writer claimed the privilege of peeping into Miss Amelia Sedley's bedroom, and understanding with the omniscience of the novelist all the gentle pains and pas-sions which were tossing upon that innocent pillow, why should he not declare himself to be Rebecca's confidante too, master of her secrets, and seal-keeper of that young woman's conscience?" (177–78). No author could be more God-like.

Dickens, Thackeray's contemporary and principal rival, masterfully strings together the multiple threads of his complex plots and then, after the conclu-sion has been neatly rounded off, composes an additional chapter in which he can tell us of what happens "afterwards"—two or five or ten years after-wards—to each of his characters. For he understands that his readers want to know all, that they feel as close to his characters as to him, and they know well that he knows all that there is to know about these people, and they are con-fident in and sustained by his control. For they understand that their world is eminently knowable, that even if they themselves have not yet mastered all that there is to know in their universe, such mastery remains for the Victorians, at the least, a possibility, if not a certainty.

And then there is Trollope, who criticizes both Dickens and Thackeray for not being omniscient enough. (He may not name them, but they are clearly his targets.) As he proclaims in *Barchester Towers* (1857):

> But let the gentle-hearted reader be under no apprehension whatsoever. It is not destined that Eleanor shall marry Mr. Slope or Bertie Stanhope. And here, perhaps, it may be allowed to the novelist to explain his views on a very important point in the art of telling tales. He ventures to reprobate that system which goes so far to violate all proper confidence between the author and his readers, by maintain-ing nearly to the end of the third volume a mystery as to the fate of their favourite personage. Nay, more, and worse than this, is too frequently done. Have not often the profoundest efforts of genius been used to baffle the aspirations of the reader, to raise false hopes and false fears, and to give rise to expectations which are never to be realised? Are not promises all but made of delightful horrors, in lieu of which the writer produces nothing but commonplace realities in his final chapter? And is there not a species of deceit in this to which the honesty of the present age should lend no countenance? . . .

> Our doctrine is, that the author and the reader should move along together in full confidence with each other.[7]

The novelist as nursemaid, we may characterize this theory of Trollope's, which represents the furthest expression of Victorian omniscience and all that it implies about the nature of fiction and about the world.

Not all Victorian fiction, of course, is quite so Victorian. There are occasions even in Dickens when certainty is carefully avoided—the opening scenes of *The Mystery of Edwin Drood* (unfinished, 1870), for instance, in which we see, as if in a mist, for a few moments, through the eyes of an opium addict—but the Victorian reader clearly understood that such moments would be brief and certainty soon restored. And even so, Trollope felt the need to protect the reader: and, in protecting him, to shield his family, especially that lowest common denominator, the young daughter: it was her (imagined) sensibility which the Victorians set up as their guide for what may be said or must be said, for defining their world. How perversely apt it is, then, that the one significant sustained deviation from narrow Victorian narrative is written by an unmarried young woman for an audience of young women: Emily Brontë's *Wuthering Heights* (1847), whose dual point of view and potential ambiguity (mixed with a reassuring degree of omniscience) seem to have had no influence on narrative technique.

We must be careful not simply to dismiss Victorian narrative, however, for it is perfectly suited to the Victorian worldview. (Victorian narratives written in the midst of Modernism, of course, are a different matter entirely.) We must also recognize that not all narrative before or just after the Victorians was quite so profoundly omniscient (I use the term to denote both the method and its implications). Nor were all fictions written outside Great Britain during this era so inevitably omniscient. Victorian omniscience is a carefully developed and painstakingly nurtured technique whose purpose was to reflect (and, in the process of reflecting, perhaps to help to create) the Victorian era. Still, I am sometimes surprised to come across a fiction by a nominal Victorian which is not consistently Victorian (in the sense that I have defined it), which might almost be considered a forerunner of Modernist technique. While omniscience, with all that it evokes, is the prevailing characteristic of Victorian English narrative, it is not the sole narrative means available either in England in particular or in the second half of the nineteenth century in general. This distinction will prove central in the mid-twentieth century, as English critics come to assail all deviations from what they consider the norm; it is a distinction that F. R. Leavis and C. P. Snow, among others, never do master.

Nineteenth-Century American Forms: Hawthorne

Their publication corresponding closely to the opening and closing dates of Victoria's long reign, stories by the American Nathaniel Hawthorne and the Russian

Anton Chekhov offer possibilities of narrative that the English essentially denied during that period. I think, for example, of such early stories by Hawthorne as "My Kinsman, Major Molineux" (1832) and "Young Goodman Brown" (1835) and such late stories by Chekhov as "The Darling" or "The Lady with the Dog" (both 1899), which may seem fundamentally omniscient but which deviate from certainty and even from control when the situations and characters demand it.[8] Hawthorne typically falls back on the tics of omniscient control ("In truth they were such," 117; "In truth, all through the haunted forest there could be nothing more frightful than the figure of Goodman Brown," 116) and cannot resist letting us know that the adventure which he records is very likely a dream: "'Well, Robin, are you dreaming?'" (33).

> Had Goodman Brown fallen asleep in the forest and only dreamed a wild dream of a witch-meeting?
> Be it so if you will; but, alas! it was a dream of evil omen for young Goodman Brown. (121)

Yet he endeavors, as best he can, with the limited technical tools available to him, to create a sense of uncertainty. For the psychological reality which he depicts—and which is the subject of his famous preface to *The House of the Seven Gables*[9]—demands an almost Modernist ambiguity: T. S. Eliot and William Empson aside, the Modernists were not the first (after the Metaphysical poets) to discover ambiguity. "'May not a man have several voices, Robin, as well as two complexions?'" asks Robin Molineux' mysterious stranger (29). How interesting that this near-contemporary of Dickens—in truth, Hawthorne was the elder by eight years—should seem so un-Dickensian in such vital ways.

Straddling the Centuries: Henry James, Novelist and Theoretician

The very essence of [the novelist's] affair has been the imputing of knowledge.[10]

These verily are the refinements and ecstasies of method. . . . [11]

Anything, in short, I now reflect, must always have seemed to me better—better for the process and the effect of representation, my irrepressible ideal—than the mere muffled majesty of irresponsible "authorship."[12]

The Golden Bowl (1904) is the first great novel of the twentieth century, one which almost symbolically straddles the centuries; for it is also, in a sense, the last great novel of the nineteenth century. Following James, it is no longer possible to write in the old forms and to succeed in reflecting the new realities. A writer both of and ahead of his time, James understands early on that the Victorian narrative model is no longer appropriate for a world that had changed fundamentally even before Queen Victoria's death in 1901, yet he is at the same time unable to eliminate all aspects of that model from his own fiction. Despite his strong moral sense, James recognizes increasingly the relevance of moral ambiguity in a changing-to-modern world and refuses increasingly, as his career advances, to make moral judgments in his own voice. Yet he can never entirely avoid that voice. Each of his fictions revolves around a moral dilemma, yet James leaves it to his reader to make the requisite judgments. (He cannot imagine that judgment might not be called for.) He understands, however—as contemporary true believers do not—that ambiguity is not necessarily an amoral condition: that it may, in a world of shifting realities and standards, represent the most moral of positions, those which most accurately reflect the actual conditions under which people must live and make their moral choices.[13] Yet, as a rule, we do know where James himself stands regarding his characters' choices. This is why Booth is so comfortable with James.

From the start of his career as a writer of fiction, James is attuned to the nuanced possibilities of point of view as a means of eliciting moral response from his reader. (The same, incidentally, for all its different implications, might be said of Robbe-Grillet.) As his work matures—and this is a prime sign of that maturity—James's point of view makes increasing demands on his reader, enforcing the implied contract between reader and author which he envisioned as the ideal relationship in the state of fiction. It is with James that the active modern reader begins and the passive Victorian reader ends forever in significant serious fiction. This is true even if he is never able entirely to rely on his reader by eliminating his own presence within his fiction.

From the early *The American* (1877), to the mid-career *The Spoils of Poynton* (1897), to *The Golden Bowl,* James's reader is called on increasingly to participate actively in the working out of the art's possibilities. We can trace his progression in these representative works. Near the beginning of *The American,* we are introduced to "An observer" (18), a "discriminating observer" (19), who speaks in the first person of "our friend" (29), speaks directly to "the reader" (34) and calls himself the hero's "biographer" (181).[14] An attempt to distance the author from the action and thus more intimately to involve the reader, our unnamed observer is nonetheless often omniscient, as in his formulaic "the truth is" (41). He even acts as our editor, omitting sections of the story that he finds difficult to communicate to us in such a narrative. His justification is that he is speaking of these events some time after they have taken place (17). And all of the events do center around Newman, the protagonist, even if we do not quite get his unfiltered reading of them. For our supposed "observer" is never realized either as a person or as an independent source; we recognize throughout that he is merely a mask for James, and a transparent mask at that. The point of view is modern only to the limited degree that James attempts to

The Rhetoric of Modernist Fiction

focus on his protagonist's consciousness and so to lessen his own active presence: as a promise, that is, of possibilities to come.

In *The Spoils of Poynton*, Fleda Vetch is a functioning central intelligence/center of consciousness, fully independent as a character and at least partly so as a source, with all of the action seen either through her eyes or, as it were, over her shoulder; but it is apparent that it is James who is peering over her shoulder, relaying to the reader whatever it is that she has seen, as well as evaluations (sometimes hers, sometimes his, often joint) of these events. The sensibility might be either Fleda's or her creator's, but the language is undeniably his:

> In knowing a while before all she needed, Fleda had been far from knowing as much as that; so that once upstairs, where, in her room, with her sense of danger and trouble, the age of Louis Seize suddenly struck her as wanting in taste and point, she felt that she now for the first time knew her temptation. (200)[15]

In his preface to the New York Edition of the novel, James notes that the spoils—the furniture, "the 'things' themselves"—"all conscious of their eminence and their price," "would form the very centre of such a crisis." But "things," of course, cannot serve as a narrative focus, and so he developed his human protagonist/center of consciousness:

> For something like Fleda Vetch had surely been latent in one's first apprehension of the theme; it wanted, for treatment, a centre, and the most obvious centre being "barred," this image, while I still wondered, had, with all the assurance in the world, sprung up in its place.[16]

Explicit in James's comment is his understanding of the need for a human consciousness through whom to reveal his story, one separate not only from "things" but separate also from their author. The contrast with Robbe-Grillet is so stark here that one is almost led to believe that the (perhaps first) post-Modernist theoretician and practitioner must surely have read the (last) pre-Modernist's essays and fictions and decided to respond directly against them. The fact that this is hardly likely makes even more powerful the point that point of view is central both to the depiction of changing realities—psychological and moral, especially—and to the continuing humanistic presence within the novel as a form.

As Jamesians, of course, know, his unsuccessful ten-year career as a dramatist played a significant role in his mature ability to dramatize situations within his novels and thus to lessen the need for him to evaluate them for us: enabling him to dramatize rather than to describe, to show and thus not need to tell. And so, I suspect, James would have approved of the 1972 BBC dramatization of *The Golden Bowl*, which brilliantly resolves the problem of point of view that James himself can never completely solve on the page: by eliminating the voice of James and with it the possibility that there may still be an author present who may, if only he would choose to, make judgments on our behalf. (The line between "author" and "omniscient author" may in this respect be so thin that the terms bear the same functional meaning.) The solution of Jack Pulman, who adapted the novel for television, is the simple, even obvious, yet inspired one—inherent in James's usage—of creating a narrator who can represent James within the action, speaking, as it were, in James's voice, but speaking from personal knowledge as an eyewitness to the events. The actor Cyril Cusack, playing the minor character Bob Assingham, sits in an easy chair in a late Victorian library and speaks to the camera (to the reader, that is), sharing his knowledge of events and people, his observations, his judgments, his uncertainties about the shifting and complex relationships among the four principal characters, between both couples, between individual husbands and wives, between father and daughter, even within each character to the extent that he can conjecture them.

The balance between knowledge and uncertainty is perfect and rich in ambiguity. The knowledgeable reader may see and hear James in Cusack, but no one will consider him as even potentially omniscient. Nor are we likely to think of him as James's reliable spokesman, for we may wish to judge even him. The words, the rhythms, the intonation may be James's, but where those words, rhythms, even intonation on the page may incline us inevitably to think of the author, Cusack on screen remains for us only Bob Assingham, somewhat passive husband to the hyperactive Fanny, a smart, decent enough man, but also a potentially flawed observer. We are inclined to trust him, but may also judge him. If he were less emotionally detached, would his wife find it so necessary to involve herself in the affairs of others? Is he, then, to share responsibility with her for the acts which follow, that calamity, which in perfect Jamesian terms, allows the principals (three of the four of them, at least) to develop their moral sense? As developed by Pulman and Cusack, Bob Assingham is the perfect solution to the Jamesian narrative dilemma, albeit one that James himself can never quite manage, for he seems unable—unwilling, more likely—to let go entirely of his own role within his narratives.

We follow the events of the novel as they develop around two separate centers of consciousness: "The Prince," Amerigo, with additional focus on Charlotte Stant and Fanny Assingham, and "The Princess," Maggie Verver, with an occasional focus on Fanny. As the action proceeds, Maggie becomes increasingly important both as an observer and as a moral judge and actor. She makes the novel's key discovery, and she makes the necessary choices. But she lacks one piece of knowledge that is vital to her: What does her father know about the renewed affair between his wife, Charlotte, and his son-in-law, Amerigo?

At the end, as Adam Verver returns with his young wife to America, it is clear that Charlotte understands nothing of what is happening to her. The reader is confident, however, that Mr. Verver understands everything and that he has understood long before his daughter comes to. We are confident even if we are never made privy to his thoughts. This is James at his most effective.

Omitting Mr. Verver's point of view is one of the signs of James's modernity: There may be little moral ambiguity remaining after Maggie's decisive action, but there is a good deal of ambiguity about who knows what and about when and how he or she may have learned it.[17] This is true although we may be confident that James himself could tell us if only he would. "[W]e have perhaps drawn our circle too wide," James comments at one point in his own voice (105); "we may confess to having perhaps read into the scene," he adds (109).[18] He even at times uses the first-person singular. When the characters speak, they often sound like James; and when they are thinking, contemplating these complex and demanding events, James's voice remains unmistakable. We can find illustrative passages virtually at random:

> That was what, while she watched herself, she potentially heard him bring out; and while she carried to an end another day, another sequence and yet another of their hours together, without his producing it, she felt herself occupied with him beyond even the intensity of surrender. She was keeping her head, for a reason, for a cause; and the labour of this detachment, with the labour of her keeping the pitch of it down, held them together in the steel hoop of an intimacy compared with which artless passion would have been but a beating of the air. (390)

Has anyone but James ever written such a sentence in the whole history of the English language? (For all Joyce's parodying of the development of English style in the "Oxen of the Sun" episode of *Ulysses,* there is nothing there even resembling this.) Its own pitch is perfect, almost a self-parody, yet beyond parody. It cannot be Maggie's prose, yet it offers a very clear sense of the workings of her consciousness at this pivotal point of her life. Anyone familiar with Edith Wharton's comic account of James's oral style will find here none of her amusement at her friend's speech, for we recognize how wonderfully modulated, how subtle, how appropriate this language is. But it is Henry James's language and not some narrator's or character's, and so we may well wonder why he is willing to remind us of his presence if he has been working so hard to eliminate that presence: Why is he unable to step completely from the nineteenth into the twentieth century? The BBC television version of *The Golden Bowl* resolves this conflict masterfully, using James's words without reminding us of his presence. But in the novel as a form, it would require Conrad, through Marlow, a narrator with a character and voice of his own, to move away fully from the old, Victorian forms and realities into the new, what we have since learned to label the Modernist.

*

Where Virginia Woolf is the finest critic among the Modernist novelists, Henry James is surely the most astute and influential theoretician among all novelists. This is no minor artist attempting to justify his art through an exposition of theories about that art—no early-day Phillippe Sollers, for instance—but a master at the pinnacle of his success, looking back and explaining what he has done, writing on behalf of both reader and future novelist. The prefaces of the New York Edition of his fiction are primarily explications of his narrative practice; but they are also an effort to influence future generations of novelists. Because James is a gentleman and because his prose can be convoluted, it is not always easy to note how argumentative his essays can be.

The prefaces are both justifications and dialectics, and they have played a major role in the modern development both of narrative art and of narrative theory. If certain contemporary theorists have failed to take notice of James's continuing relevance—I think, for example, of Gérard Genette—it is likely because his readings, his methods and purposes, are antithetical to theirs. For all the demands which his prose makes on his reader, James is never given to jargon, and—especially if we happen to have read the novels under discussion—he is always precise when speaking of what he has done and why he has done it. These essays of his are not designed for acolytes speaking some private language; they are meant (perhaps unrealistically, to be sure) for the same informed, acute but general reader that the Modernist novelists desired to bring into being. In a significant sense, James helps to make possible the Modernist novel. He also, perhaps less admirably, makes possible critical and theoretical writing about the complex art of telling stories. He would not, I think, have liked the term "narratology," if only because it pretends to a precision that is neither possible nor desirable. He gives us instead that wonderfully imperfect term "point of view."

But James is not a Modernist, not, at least, as I understand that term. For he is unable to make the leap from the nineteenth to the twentieth century that his friend Conrad would so forcefully, almost effortlessly, make: His presence within his narratives militates against that. Nor does he mean to. Although he speaks of himself as an "impersonal author"[19]—a fact possibly missed by Wayne Booth—James neither desires nor seeks, nor is able to attain, the degree of impersonality of a Robbe-Grillet, or even, in truth, of a Joyce or a Beckett.

James makes clear in his preface to *The Golden Bowl* his preference for

a certain indirect and oblique view of any presented action; . . . my preference for dealing with my subject-matter, for "seeing my story," through the opportunity and the sensibility of some more or less detached, some not strictly involved, though thoroughly interested and intelligent, witness or reporter, some person who contributes to the case mainly a certain amount of criticism and interpretation of it.

The Rhetoric of Modernist Fiction

... The somebody is often, among my shorter tales I recognise, but an unnamed, unintroduced and (save by right of intrinsic wit) unwarranted participant, the impersonal author's concrete deputy or delegate, a convenient substitute or apologist for the creative power otherwise so veiled and disembodied.[20]

"Unnamed, unintroduced," even "unwarranted," but also, unfortunately, undramatized. Here is the key to what I see as James's one enduring problem with point of view, the partial failure which persists within his otherwise convincing manipulation of narrative in his last great novels. Because undramatized, the "somebody" never functions as a believable personage separate from his creator, not even as a *persona*: whether he is or is not synonymous with James, he inevitably reminds us of James—especially when we hear coming from (as well as around) him James's unforgettable diction. And James, I have come to believe, wants us to be reminded of him, at the same time that he has worked so diligently against the excesses—and unreality—of omniscience: it would seem that he wants to bestride the centuries.[21]

In his essays on other writers, James rarely speaks directly of their presentation of narrative—and never in detail. He is critical of the technique of Scott (on psychological grounds)[22] and of Maupassant (on moral grounds)[23] and accepting of Trollope, whose technique is so very different from his own;[24] and he has virtually nothing to say of Flaubert's technique, from which he may well have learned at least the need for "impersonality." He is also clearly uneasy with Conrad's technique in the elaborately structured *Chance*. Is this because the several layers of narration separating us from Marlow—and Marlow from whatever truth there might be—are simply too dense? Or is it because of his declared hostility to first-person narrative? ("the first person, in the long piece, is a form foredoomed to looseness, and that looseness [has] never much [been] my affair.")[25] Whatever his reasoning, James is unable to accept for his own practice a strategy such as Conrad's invention of Marlow.

Abjuring omniscience, James nonetheless requires some form which will allow him to maintain "the power to be finely aware and richly responsible,"[26] to sustain, in his adoption of Walter Besant's phrase, "the 'conscious moral purpose' of the novel."[27] In this vital respect, he fully justifies Wayne Booth's regard. This does not mean, however, that he requires certainty, either for himself or for his characters. In his preface to *The Princess Casamassima*, James considers various possibilities of point of view and concludes, "All of which is charming—yet would be infinitely more so if here at once ambiguity didn't yawn."[28]

For ambiguity does yawn in the modern world, inevitably so, and James is among the first novelists to recognize its presence, to use the term itself in his criticism, to manifest it as a force in his art. He understands, of course, its bearing on the moral purpose which is so central to his own art and life, and he knows that its presence need not inevitably undermine morality—that ambiguity does not automatically bring with it amorality. At this point, I think,

Wayne Booth would agree, pointing out that this remains true in James's fiction because we always know where James himself stands in regard to such issues. I would argue, however, that it is possible for a novelist to mask his or her own beliefs, even in regard to moral issues, without compromising morality.

The Modernist reader, so experienced in filling in narrative gaps, should be perfectly capable of recognizing and meeting morality's demands, even in an ambiguous fictional universe. Robbe-Grillet's is not the sole means of managing ambiguity. Joyce, Proust, Mann, Kafka, Woolf, Faulkner, Hemingway, Beckett too, demonstrate throughout their canons the presence and effects of ambiguity in the modern world; manage to mask both their own presence and their moral positions; and enforce the "conscious moral purpose" of their art by inducing their readers to recognize and make for themselves the difficult moral choices: make it possible for their readers to participate actively in what was once the sole province of the (omniscient) author. As I read their fictions, this is not merely not an amoral position; Modernist ambiguity, manifested and explored through an almost endless variety of new points of view, represents an active, even an aggressive, moral stance, one very much in keeping with the moral tradition that is so vital to Booth, and to me as well. And also to Conrad, for all his reliance on dramatized, first-person narration.

Nineteenth-Century European Developments: Stendhal and Flaubert

It would be no great surprise if the elusive Stendhal, hiding behind his two hundred pseudonyms, might also wish to disguise his own presence within his novels. Yet *The Red and the Black* (1830) is filled with evidence of omniscience and of his presence. At the same time, it does attempt to realize individual scenes through the consciousness of a character and is among the very first novels to offer a primitive kind of internal monologue. Virtually all of the classic characteristics of omniscience are here: an author who speaks in the first person ("We must confess with pain, for we are fond of Mathilde," 319), with absolute control over his material ("we have forgotten to say that for three weeks the Marquis had been kept at home by an attack of gout," 286), speaking directly to his reader ("Does the term *hypocrisy* surprise you?" 42), and providing to the reader information unknown to the characters ("Mathilde could not tell Julien of something which she herself did not as yet suspect," 497); in addition, Stendhal offers commentary on manners, a sure knowledge of future events, an ability to correct misperceptions, a mastery of time (which is strictly chronological), and, most egregiously, a clear sense of his own personality, almost as if he too were a character in his novel.[29]

At this stage in the novel's development, such omniscient qualities are hardly surprising. Nor is it surprising that Stendhal's efforts at internal monologue amount to little more than the formulaic "Julien Sorel said to himself" (58) or "thought to himself" (37), a formula applied at times to virtually every one of the characters. (In the C. K. Scott Moncrieff Modern Library translation of the novel, all internal monologue is placed within quotation marks, an awkward practice which nonetheless approximates the effect that Stendhal seems to have wanted.) We never have the sense that we are inside the characters' minds for the simple reason that, in 1830, there were no tools available to Stendhal for taking us there. His effort, however, helped make it possible for subsequent novelists to succeed where he had not.

✳

The conscious narrative revolution to eliminate omniscience—to remove the author as a presence from within his story—begins with Flaubert. Declaring that Emma Bovary was really himself, in perhaps the most famous of all lines of literary attribution, Flaubert set in motion the narrative process that would culminate in Modernism. "Mme. Bovary, c'est moi" refers not to possible autobiographical connections, as some early critics thought, but to point of view—the relationship among the author, his protagonist and the technique of presenting her to the reader.

The critical contention that we are today in an age post-Modernism is another way of declaring that process dead; to contend that we remain under Modernism's sign is to insist that the narrative process begun by Flaubert is not yet complete. (My own guess is that future literary historians will not declare it complete until novelists have learned to incorporate the narrative innovations of *Finnegans Wake* into less ambitious, even everyday novels.) Yet if Flaubert is central to the modernization of point of view, there is still plenty of evidence in *Madame Bovary* (1857)—residue, if you will—of the plain, old fashioned omniscient author. Perhaps Flaubert was less of a purist than he sometimes seems; perhaps he, too, a generation after Stendhal, simply lacked the necessary narrative tools. Yet what strikes us most today is the extent to which he moved away from omniscience and toward the points of view of his characters.

The narrative begins, surprisingly, not with Emma Rouault, destined, it would seem to become his unhappy wife, but with Charles Bovary, and it starts somewhere outside Charles, with an unidentified eyewitness, a classmate just a bit younger than Charles: "We were in study-hall when the headmaster entered, followed by a new boy not yet in school uniform" (3).[30] The classmate is never named, his relationship to an adult Charles and his family never defined. But he does seem to be commenting from the perspective of time—"It would be very difficult today for any of us to say what he was like" (10)—perhaps even from some time after these events have taken place. More or less the same undefined perspective prevails until it shifts almost imperceptibly to Charles himself—or, at least, to Charles as still others perceive him:

Actually, old Rouault wouldn't have been a bit displeased to have someone take his daughter off his hands. She was of no use to him on the farm.....

So when he noticed that Charles tended to be flushed in his daughter's presence . . . he pondered every aspect of the question well in advance. Charles was a bit namby-pamby, not his dream of a son-in-law; but he was said to be reliable. (27)

There are so many different potential points of view here—the old farmer, the unnamed narrator (who has already begun to fade from notice), the omniscient author, public opinion ("he was said to be reliable")—that we might almost call this a communal point of view, or perhaps omniscience. Soon enough, if gradually, the focus shifts to Emma ("Emma herself would have liked to be married at mid-night," 29). The strange result of this new, evolving technique is at once a certain distance—since the characters are approached through a series of other characters' perspectives—and a certain intimacy, as we gradually hone in on Emma Bovary.

Yet Flaubert continues to present her at times as others view her, as when, as she stands in the firelight, "one could see the weave of her dress" (91). Is this merely the grammatical indefinite "one," or does it refer to an actual viewer? In another incident, her dress—"a long-waisted, full-skirted yellow summer dress with four flounces" (145)—is apparently being viewed by the ill apprentice whom she has been tending; the apprentice is Rodolphe's assistant, and the incident introduces him to Emma, an innocent enough beginning to a tragic cycle. We shift now to Rodolphe Boulanger, who will become her lover; "after a time he said to himself: 'Ah, Madame Bovary is much prettier—and what's more, much fresher. Virginie's certainly growing too fat. She's getting on my nerves.'" (147). From this moment on, an early form of internal monologue becomes increasingly the narrative norm for this novel, as Flaubert endeavors—more consistently than any novelist had done before him—to show the workings of Emma's mind.

Flaubert's internal monologue is not much more advanced than Stendhal's, to be sure. Nor, when he focuses on an individual character, would Henry James recognize the result as a center of consciousness: Everything remains a bit removed, objective and outward even when it is meant to be subjective and inward; we might be tempted to label the result omniscient if we did not recognize just how different, ultimately, this is from Stendhal—not to speak of the English Victorians. This is the stuff from which James would build his characteristic point of view and which would lead to the Modernist revolution in narrative technique. *Madame Bovary,* in its own time, was controversial in large part because of its realistic portrayal of a conventional woman's conventional adultery-for moral reasons, that is. The fact that it seems sympathetic to her, that it makes no effort to judge her, merely added to the critical outrage.[31] It was the point of view, we can recognize today—a technical device, but one with the profoundest implications for theme—which made this psychological study so effective and so controversial.

Anton Chekhov

Where Hawthorne attempts, with varying degrees of success, to limit his points of view to his uncertain protagonists—indeed, it is point of view which creates their uncertainty, for each starts out on his adventure with youthful conviction—Chekhov shifts between his characters and their community and from objective to internal views. He may be said to expand the psychological probings of Hawthorne with an accompanying narrative flexibility. Thus Olenka, title character of "The Darling," can provide no consistent point of view because she herself lacks a certain identity; she needs others to provide her focus, and so it is appropriate that they—those whom she loves and the community as a whole, with a few assists from the author—should be the source of her narrative. "She forever loved someone," we read about her emotions, "and could not live without it" (334). As for ideas, "Whatever her husband thought, she thought, too" (337). And how, since "she was unable to form an opinion about anything" (340), do we know so much about her? "[W]hat went on in her house could only be guessed" (339). Even when her words might be her own—

> It seemed to her that she had been dealing in lumber [the business of her second husband] for a very, very long time, that lumber was the most important and necessary thing in life, and for her there was something dear and touching in the sound of the words beam, post, board, plank, batten, slat, lath, slab . . . (337)

—the gently ironic tone is not. Technically, we might label this omniscience, but the narrative lacks any sense of authorial intrusion or control or personality. Like the dramatic technique that Chekhov would later perfect in his plays— as characters speak over the lines of other characters and comment implicitly on them—this functions in essence as the voice of the community, as a chorus, if you will. And for all that it knows about Olenka and her life, it—they—does not know all: Why is it that "her soul submitted" so completely to the little boy whom she adopts? "Why? Who knows why?" (343). The English Victorians certainly could—and would have both done so and told us so.

"The Lady with the Little Dog" opens with what seems another communal voice—"The talk was that a new face had appeared on the embankment: a lady with a little dog" (361)—but quickly shifts to Dmitri Dmitritch Gurov, who will befriend that lady, seduce her (that seems to be his métier, after all) and then, despite himself ("'There's something pathetic in her all the same,' he thought," 363), fall deeply in love with her. Gurov has in the past always been able to maintain distance from his lovers, even from himself and his own emotions; and so he is the perfect point of view through which to witness—and to judge—this surprising affair. At times, his thoughts are unspoken:

> Anna Sergeevna was touching, she had about her a breath of the purity of a proper, naïve, little-experienced woman; the solitary candle burning on the table barely lit up her face, but it was clear that her heart was uneasy. (365)

At times, his thoughts may appear to be offered omnisciently. But they are likely, in the end, to prove to be his own, to come from within him:

> So it had sounded below when neither Yalta nor Oreanda were there, so it sounded now and would go on sounding with the same dull indifference when we are no longer here. . . . Sitting beside the young woman, who looked so beautiful in the dawn, appeased and enchanted by the view of this magical décor . . . Gurov reflected that, essentially, if you thought of it, everything was beautiful in this world, everything except for what we ourselves think and do when we forget the higher goals of being and our human dignity. (367)

There is no ironic tone here.

While Chekhov has not found the narrative means to take us literally within Gurov's consciousness, he comes as close as he can, with the tools available to him—as he offers Gurov's thoughts, "memories," "reveries," "imagination" (369)—to internal monologue. "Closing his eyes, he saw her as if alive" (369). When he does approximate thought, it is likely to be treated as if it were speech, within quotation marks: "'Well, let her cry a little, and meanwhile I'll sit down,' he thought, and sat down in an armchair" (375). Chekhov cannot quite take us within his character and leave us there, by ourselves, to discover that consciousness for ourselves, but he does all that he can to absent himself. Even when he speaks in the third person—"one's breath feels soft and pleasant" in the early Moscow winter (368)—we recognize that this may be Gurov's reflection. Even when he offers expert information—"as in all provincial theatres" (371)—the expertise may be that of his cultured protagonist. Even judgments, he hints, however broad and certain they may seem, however beyond Gurov's knowledge and expertise, are likely to be his:

> And he judged others by himself, did not believe what he saw, and always supposed that every man led his real and very interesting life under the cover of secrecy, as under the cover of night. (374)

Even when the language appears to be Chekhov's, we understand that in Gurov he has created not exactly a surrogate or a reliable spokesman—for we

The Rhetoric of Modernist Fiction

sense that the author, too, distances himself from his character and judges him. But Gurov's sensibility is one that Chekhov may share and that he induces us to share as well. Unlike the omniscient English Victorians or Edwardians, Chekhov's principal purpose in handling point of view is to induce his readers, too, to come close to his character and yet to distance ourselves from him, to judge him as Gurov himself does, from within. He does not expect us, like darling Olenka, to rely on others for our opinions and feelings. That Chekhov is only partially successful is a sign of the times, before the explosions of the modern age would mandate ambiguity, but after the certainty of the late nineteenth century had begun to waver. It is also a sign of the times that he does not yet possess the narrative tools that will make it possible to effect the modern consciousness.

Modernist Intentions and Innovations: The Role of the Reader

As a rule, we approach point of view from the writer's perspective: I know that I first heard the term and learned the concept in an undergraduate creative writing course. But it is far more revealing to regard point of view as it impacts the reader. For what matters most for the construction of the novel is the reader's response to the demands made on him or on her by the novelist. Among the Victorians, those demands are trivial; Trollope even warns his colleagues that no demands at all should be made (other than literacy, of course, although even that may not be necessary if one is listening to someone else's reading). The Victorian relationship is familial, intimate, but by no means equal; Dickens' readers may have attempted to exert some influence on what the great man wrote, but they have virtually no role at all in the novel's true creation: they are told both what happens and what everything means. An occasional, momentary exception aside, they remain, even in Dickens or Brontë, essentially passive participants in the development of the novel.

Henry James ends that cozy relationship by positing an implied contract between author and reader, in which each party is obliged to offer to the other all that he or she is capable of. The reader, in other words, needs to be as active, at least in principle, as the author, for there will be no one present within the novel to guarantee our comfort and understanding. Events may be complex, characters uncertain, meanings ambiguous, and it is our obligation to unravel the possibilities and to decide among them. By failing to eliminate entirely his own voice and presence from his narratives, however, James may be said to have failed to fulfill his part of the contract—although it is probably fairer and more accurate to say that he simply did not fully foresee all of his contract's potential implications.

James Joyce did, and he—and the Modernist novelists as a group—make unaccustomed demands on both themselves and the reader. I am convinced that neither Joyce nor any of his contemporaries thinks of themselves as writing for an elite. Everything that I know about Joyce's career convinces me that he is writing for a general audience, but that he expects that audience to be up to the demands made upon it. *Ulysses* and *Finnegans Wake,* along with many other Modernist masterworks, are efforts to educate and create a new kind of reader. The fact that so many distinguished Joyceans have been, from the start, non-academics, many of them also non-native speakers of English, and that the audience for *Ulysses* continues to expand throughout the world, in dozens of languages as well as English, convinces me that this expectation is not entirely unreasonable.

It is also true, however, that because of these demands on the reader, the Modernist novel precipitates a dichotomy that is new and unexpected in the history of the novel: For the first time, this eminently popular form, whose very origin and rise are tied to the literacy of a newly emergent middle class, breaks down into divergent streams. Where Dickens was both the greatest and the most popular novelist of his age, with the rise of Modernism, serious novels are assumed to be distinct from popular novels. Rare is the reader of Joyce on the subway, returning home from work; and rarely would anyone of my generation teach a novel by Harold Robbins or Stephen King in a modern or contemporary fiction course. Robbins, of course, assumed that since he was the best-selling novelist of his time, he was also inevitably the best—an outrageous assumption that a century ago might not have seemed quite so ludicrous.

If the Modernist novel makes unprecedented demands on the reader—reading a Modernist novel well requires the same intensity once reserved for a Shakespearean sonnet—it also offers to the reader unimagined rewards, not just as a participant in the novel's decipherment, but for what may be considered a kind of co-creation. For these are not just games that the Modernist novelist plays with his reader—although at times a certain gamesmanship does enter in. The most vital determinations—about character, about theme, about the true nature of the world being depicted—are left to the reader of the Modernist novel. If the Modernist novelist is a hero of sorts, as some today would insist, then so, in a certain sense, is the Modernist reader. And I intend this with no hint of irony.

Working our way through, say, Marcel's narrative in Proust's *A la recherche du temps perdu* and discovering at the end the narrator's dual and reinforcing secrets; passing beyond the masks and screens of the searchers in Faulkner's *Absalom, Absalom!,* or Claude Simon's *The Flanders Road,* or Carlos Fuentes' *The Death of Artemio Cruz,* and discovering their beseiged and engaging humanity; turning and returning to the variety of points of view through which Leopold Bloom presents himself in *Ulysses* and discovering not just his humanity but perhaps also our own, the Modernist reader gets to do more than fill in the gaps and maneuver his or her way through a narrative maze—however pleasing such tasks may prove to be. For no one would ever speak in the same sentence of the reader of Trollope, say, and of discovery—no less of self-discovery. While rooted deeply in the novel's long narrative tradition, the novel of the Modernists offers nonetheless a new kind of experience, more demanding and far more fulfilling. The greatest of these demands is in the province of point of view.

Learning What to Leave Out: Joyce's Dubliners

In an early draft version of "The Sisters"—quite similar to the story originally published in *The Irish Homestead* on 13 August 1904—the young James Joyce wrote, from the point of view of his still younger protagonist:

> Three nights in succession I had found myself in Great Britain Street at that hour, as if by providence. Three nights I had raised my eyes to that lighted square of window and speculated. I seemed to understand that it would occur at night. But in spite of the providence which had led my feet and in spite of the reverent curiosity of my eyes I had discovered nothing. Each night the square was lighted in the same way, faintly and evenly. It was not the light of candles so far as I could see. Therefore it had not occurred yet.
>
> On the fourth night at that hour I was in another part of the city. It may have been the same providence that led me there—a whimsical kind of providence—to take me at a disadvantage. As I went home I wondered was that square of window lighted as before or did it reveal the ceremonious candles in the light of which the Christian must take his last sleep. I was not surprised, then, when at supper I found myself a prophet. Old Cotter and my uncle were talking at the fire, smoking. Old Cotter was a retired distiller who owned a batch of prize setters. He used to be very interesting when I knew him first, talking about *faints* and *worms,* but afterwards he became tedious.
>
> While I was eating my stirabout I heard him say to my uncle:
>
> —Without a doubt. The upper storey (he tapped an unnecessary hand at his forehead) was gone—
>
> —So they said. I never could see much of it. I thought he was sane enough—
>
> —So he was, at times, said old Cotter—
>
> I sniffed the *was* apprehensively and gulped down some stirabout.
>
> —Is he any better, Uncle [and the name "John" is crossed out here]?—
>
> —He's dead—
>
> —O. . . . .—
>
> . . . So old Cotter had got the better of me for all my vigilance of three nights. It is often annoying the way people will blunder on what you have elaborately planned for. I was sure he would die at night.

There is virtually none of this in the version of "The Sisters" which opens *Dubliners* for us today: no name for the uncle and not much presence, no absence in another part of the city for the boy, no questioning of the dead man's sanity ("there was something uncanny about him," old Cotter says now), no explicit comment from the boy, evidently remembering past events, "It is often annoying the way people will blunder on. . . ." What we have instead are those pivotal terms, "simony," "gnomon," the dread "paralysis," with all their imagistic and thematic implications for the larger text of *Dubliners*;[32] we also have the clear sense that we are hearing everything in the present, as the boy hears it; as well as the explicit comment that nothing in these events may be made explicit: "I knew that I was under observation," the boy tells us but not his viewers, "so I continued eating as if the news had not interested me." The adults in the story coyly avoid offering before the boy their opinions about the dead priest (although they obviously want to know his views), and he does not trust them with his thoughts or emotions. The key to "The Sisters" as we know it today lies in what is not being said.

In the pivotal final scene of the story, with the boy's aunt and Father Flynn's sisters, we are in this early version told directly what had gone wrong in the priest's life: "It was his scrupulousness, you see, that affected his mind. The duties of the priesthood were too much for him," says his sister. No mystery here and no ambiguity either: merely another Dublin story of a spoiled priest, a little daring perhaps for *The Irish Homestead* in 1904, but nothing that would especially shock or surprise its readers. The final words of both early and late versions of the story are almost the same, describing in both the image of the priest's breakdown in the confessional, "Wide-awake and laughing-like to himself." In the version that we know today, this image "made them think that there was something gone wrong with him," where in the early version, "Then they knew something was wrong." We know nothing for certain today. And so it is fitting that Joyce chose finally to omit the final words of his early version, "—God rest his soul!—"

In the final version of "The Sisters," the one which Joyce wrote after deciding to make of it the first story in a new kind of book of stories, Joyce sets the young boy who is his protagonist and point of view in the center of a society whose hostility he intuits yet never articulates. Yet every event and response in this story is revealed through his limited perspective: limited to what the boy can know, limited by his experience and sensibility, limited in what he will share with his various audiences: limited in ways that Joyce's model, Flaubert, could not himself have imagined. Joyce's surprising discovery—one that, I believe, will prove the key to all of his work, from the remaining stories of *Dubliners* all the way through to *Finnegans Wake*—is what he does not tell us, what he does not say at all, what he knows well enough even at this early stage of his development to leave out. The great master of the vast, encyclopedic Modernist narrative is distinguished most by what he omits; and we, his readers, must not only note in the text what is absent, but be wary about filling in too fully these gaps, for the gaps themselves, the absences in the narrative, may be the point.

There are no absences, of course, in the Victorian narrative. As early as 1904, however, with Queen Victoria newly dead and novelists still writing late Victorian novels (except that now they are called Edwardian)—long before the War to End All Wars and all certainty, before he had an inkling of *Ulysses* or *Finnegans Wake* or even fully of the unity of *Dubliners,* more than half a century before the term "Modernism" would be applied to literature—the young Joyce recognized that the world depicted by the great Victorians no longer existed. A generation before the ravages of the First World War and its aftermath at Versailles destroyed certainty forever, James Joyce understood that reality survived in the interstices alone and not in the writer's depiction of complete realistic surfaces—although from the surfaces of these stories of his, we can indeed recreate a lost way of life in a Dublin long gone. It is the unspoken worlds beneath this surface which constitute reality for Joyce. If we cannot now know all about even our own lives, how better to demonstrate this fact than to hint constantly at possibilities—often banal, sometimes intriguing—and then not allow us to realize them with any certainty at all.

In this Joyce would be followed by virtually every other prose writer of note in the Modernist pantheon: in the sudden silence behind the unlocked door of Gerda Buddenbrooks' bedroom (that door which her husband, despite his suspicions—which, of course, are unstated—will never open); in the moments before Gregor Samsa's awakening on that fatal morning (as well as in those following his death, in his younger sister's still untold story); in the biographies which Hemingway would create for his characters and then carefully omit from their narratives; in the uncertain innocence or guilt of E. L. Doctorow's Isaacsons/Rosenbergs in *The Book of Daniel,* as well as in the mind and meanderings of Thomas Pynchon's Slothrop. A response to the nineteenth-century demand for verisimilitude, this sense of absence in Modernist fiction is as realistic in its way as its predecessor's amplitude: it is reality itself that has changed, and our reading of reality as well. All literary revolutions, as Alain Robbe-Grillet reminds us, are conducted in the name of realism.

The difference between the first and final versions of "The Sisters" is not just the difference between showing and telling, to use E. M. Forster's terms. It is the difference between a narrative art built on and around a passive reader and one demanding the reader's active participation in the working out of the narrative; the difference between a vision of the world in which there are no uncertainties that cannot be resolved and one in which ambiguity is potentially everywhere, in which it is the only certainty; the difference between a Victorian universe striving desperately to remain whole despite the efforts of those eminent Victorians—Marx, Freud, Darwin, Einstein, Frazer—who pointed the way to disintegration and the universe which we have learned since Joyce's time to call Modernist.

Everything that we need to know about the break between the Victorians and Modernism is here on this first page of *Dubliners:* a narrative whose meaning and structures are dependent not on traditional plot and character-ization but upon image and metaphor (looking for the light in the window, for example); a world whose very meaning is ironic (the failure of that light is most evident at the end of "Araby," although it may be reconstituted in the par-tial light at the end of "The Dead"); a vision of modern life at once ambiguous and humanistic, as if fulfilling in a single *geste* the deep desire of Henry Adams' "The Dynamo and the Virgin"; and, most importantly, I believe, a reader who is not coddled like that Victorian lowest common denominator, the young daughter of the family, listening passively to her father's reading aloud from the latest three-decker novel, and an author who is not only not ever-pres-ent but who manifests himself most through what he will not tell us, what he will willfully omit—an author who will impel us through his increasingly elaborate and demanding constructions to suspend disbelief that anyone ever wrote any of these words: certainly not the God of the Creation whom Stephen Dedalus scorns in *A Portrait of the Artist as a Young Man,* but Creation, as it were, of itself, self-generating, the Big Bang of narrative, without the need for an attending deity: the world of the *Wake* is implicit, it seems to me, on this altered first page of "The Sisters."

The Modernist revolution begun so innocently by James Joyce in the pro-cess of revising his first short story consists most dramatically, as I read it, of what is left out: in a world of which we know more and more details and have less and less certainty, a world increasingly unknowable and beyond our grasp: all the innovations in narrative technique by the Modernists, the open-ended conclusions (if we can call them conclusions) to novels and stories alike, the all-pervasive experience of ambiguity: Modernist narrative technique allied to the Modernist worldview: in the great age of expansionist fictions, a sense, somehow, of compression, of an opening for the reader/critic that he or she must nonetheless have the restraint not to fill in completely, since comple-tion may well signal the excess of omniscience, whereas the gap, the omission, may well be the reality. The hardest lesson for the critic, too, is of the need for restraint. As a reticent adolescent has shown us—almost despite himself—in this story from a provincial Irish newspaper almost a century ago, the most important parts of life may be those that we cannot know for certain, precisely because we cannot know them.

Hemingway as Model: In the Path of Dubliners

Where Joyce is acknowledged almost universally today as the most important and influential novelist of the twentieth century, the one who most completely epitomizes the Modernist Age (only Picasso, it seems to me, challenges him as the model Modernist artist), it is not Joyce but Ernest Hemingway who has had the most immediate influence on prose style in fiction: on that pivotal point at which style, metaphor, vision and point of view intersect. Not merely American writers, not only those who began their careers more or less at mid-century: more recent writers, too, even writers in Eastern Europe, have acknowledged their indebtedness to Hemingway.[33] And while his reputation has fallen from its peak (and now is rising again), his distinctively American emphasis on the oral quality of prose (even though it is the appearance of a voice, rather than its sound, that he seeks) can now be heard clearly in a third generation of American novelists. His so-called "Iceberg Theory" (in which seven-eighths of a story's meaning is said to lie beneath its surface) has served for some as a virtual definition of Modernist fiction.

Critics have at times noted the connection between this theory and Hemingway's use of point of view; but none, to my knowledge, has recognized the extent to which this technique—that mix of point of view, image, metaphor and vision of a newly delimiting world—derives from a writer whose technique and worldview seem diametrically different from his. At this vital intersection, I believe, the reticent (if only in his art) Hemingway and the expansive (especially in his art) Joyce quietly meet and join forces. A direct line can profitably be drawn from Joyce's *Dubliners* to the stories and early novels of Hemingway, those model fictions so significant both in themselves and as Joyce's first functioning surrogate.

For all those proposed sources of Hemingway's prose style which critics have advanced—Sherwood Anderson, Gertrude Stein, the Kansas City *Star* and Toronto *Star Weekly*—it is Joyce's *Dubliners*, as I read it, that provides the key to the presence, absence and discovery of meaning in Hemingway's fictions. I mean by this not just the suggestive imagery and powerful metaphors which populate the stories of *Dubliners*—as in the infamous "gnomon," "simony" and "paralysis" of the first page of its first story, "The Sisters"—but especially what is left unsaid, the unstated but certain task of the reader to comprehend and articulate, as in a Hemingway story such as "On the Quai at Smyrna" or "Soldier's Home," or in the opening and closing chapters of *A Farewell to Arms*.

"On the Quai at Smyrna" (1930) seems more a foreign correspondent's dispatch than a short story, and it clearly grows out of the young Hemingway's experience as a reporter covering the Greco-Turkish War of 1922–23 and, in particular, the massacre of the rebellious Greeks of Smyrna (now Izmir) by the returning Turkish army. Only the use of point of view lets us know that this is a fiction and not reportage—although we can assume, even without reading the author's dispatches from the region, that this incident derives from an observed event. The story begins with the unidentified narrator's attempt to distance himself from the horrifying images which he is recording:

The strange thing was, he said, how they screamed every night at midnight. I do not know why they screamed at that time. We were in the harbor and they were all on the pier and at midnight they started screaming. We used to turn the searchlight on them to quiet them. That always did the trick. (87)[34]

The pronoun references are a bit mysterious here. Is the "I" who is speaking in the second sentence the same man who makes the opening comment, or is "he" distinct from that "I," a man speaking now in his own voice, as recalled by the original narrator, presumably at some later date, but without identifying quotation marks. (When "I" quotes himself talking to a member of his crew, he encloses the comments of both within quotes.) Does Hemingway make a mistake here, or is he intentionally blurring the identity of the speaker(s) in order to distance him (and/or himself) still further from these events? The different pronouns, potentially naming two different narrators, compel us to ask such questions and to be conscious of their potential implications. I suspect that what Hemingway is doing, in this early effort to transmute experience into fiction, is borrowing his form from Conrad, who typically introduces Marlow and his narration through some other narrator's reporting of a past narration of his. The fact that at least one of Hemingway's speakers is a ship's officer (and likely a British officer at that) might serve to confirm this identification and narrative echo. (Marlow's comments are also likely to be encased within quotes, sometimes—as in *Chance*—in that multitude and variety of quotation marks which John Barth parodies in his story, "Menelaiad.")

The conversational tone of Hemingway's account, which is not quite two pages long, does little to disguise—perhaps even accentuates—the narrator's horror at these events, which he witnessed at first hand and even, in a sense, participated in (the searchlight to silence the cries of the dying on the quai at Smyrna). His attempt at a distancing irony seems almost juvenile and so lessens the distance still further. ("It was all a pleasant business. My word yes a most pleasant business," 88.) But he is expert enough to implicate his listener/reader, too, in his moral account. Moving from third to first person, we cannot now miss the "you":

> You remember the harbor. There were plenty of nice things floating around in it. That was the only time in my life I got so I dreamed about things. You didn't mind the women who were having babies as you did those with the dead ones. They had them all right. Surprising how few of them died. You just covered them over with something and let them go to it. They'd always pick out the darkest place in the hold to have them. None of them minded anything once they got off the pier. (88)

The blurring of the "thems" is no accident, any more than the multiform "you." At once specific and universal—and doubly specific, as both the narrator ("You didn't mind . . .") and his audience ("You remember . . .")—that "you" implicates us all in one of the century's earliest conjunctions of nationalism

The Rhetoric of Modernist Fiction

and massacre. Even at the beginning of his career, Hemingway understands the possibilities, within narration, of reticence, distance and moral and emotional involvement. This is the central lesson, of course, that he has learned from Joyce.

Joyce's ability to make a forceful statement by means of reticence, of effecting involvement through seeming distance, is his central narrative discovery in *Dubliners,* and he deploys it both through first-person narration in retrospect ("Araby," "The Sisters") and through third-person internal monologue (an almost Jamesian central intelligence but without James, as in "A Painful Case" and "The Dead"). In "Soldier's Home" (1924), Hemingway shows what he has learned from Joyce about the subjective possibilities of a seemingly objective, third-person point of view.

"Soldier's Home" is a story whose background the young Joyce could not have imagined (a soldier returning home from World War I) but which in every other respect he might have written, for the protagonist returns to an almost archetypal Joycean environment: an unconcerned father, an overly concerned mother, and a hometown to which he can never again accommodate himself. Unlike Stephen Dedalus, however, Harold Krebs does agree to kneel down beside his mother in prayer:

> "Would you kneel and pray with me, Harold?" his mother asked.
> They knelt down beside the dining-room table and Krebs's mother prayed.
> "Now, you pray, Harold," she said.
> "I can't," Krebs said.
> "Try, Harold."
> "I can't."
> "Do you want me to pray for you?"
> "Yes."
> So his mother prayed for him and then they stood up and Krebs kissed his mother and went out of the house. He had tried so to keep his life from being complicated. Still, none of it had touched him. He had felt sorry for his mother and she had made him lie. He would go to Kansas City and get a job and she would feel all right about it. There would be one more scene maybe before he got away. He would not go down to his father's office. He would miss that one. He wanted his life to go smoothly. (152–53)

Krebs, "who had been at Belleau Wood, Soissons, the Champagne, St. Mihiel and in the Argonne" (145), has none of the overriding ambition of Stephen Dedalus. He wants only to live easily, "smoothly," at a distance from his neighbors, from his experience, from himself. Without a hint of philosophy, he has reached—he has earned—that distance which Joyce's Mr. Duffy so arrogantly assumes is rightly his. Krebs "had been a good soldier. That made a difference" (148), and we are allowed—we are expected—to extrapolate for ourselves just what that difference might be. Less intellectual, perhaps less intelligent, surely less ambitious and self-conscious than most of Joyce's protagonists—even the adolescents among them—Krebs, a young man of twenty-three or twenty-four years, nonetheless knows exactly how he wants to live:

> He did not want any consequences. He did not want any consequences ever again. He wanted to live along without consequences. (147)

Hemingway, not much older than his protagonist when he wrote this story, understands already that a life without consequences, without involvement, is neither possible nor desirable; he does not need Joyce's "A Painful Case" to discover that basic fact. We anticipate that Krebs will eventually learn this lesson, too, perhaps even more painfully than with the unstated lessons that he has learned in the war. Like Joyce, Hemingway induces his reader to draw such conclusions on his or her own. The purpose of the reticence which he has learned from Joyce, accompanying that of his characters, is precisely to invite us to participate actively in these lives.

Kneeling alongside his mother (he calls her "Mummy," as if he were still her child), refusing to pray with her yet allowing her to pray for him, Krebs unmistakably recalls Stephen Dedalus' refusal to pray with and for his mother, an act of integrity for which he will suffer throughout *Ulysses*. The differences between the two young men are profound, and Hemingway in all likelihood does not expect us to explore them. The character of Krebs and his response to the world derives from Hemingway's own experience and not in any way from his reading of Joyce. But he does intend this scene, I believe, as a sign of his indebtedness to Joyce: for that process by which a character is both revealed and realized through his point of view, his very reticence a factor in our discovery of what he strives to conceal, perhaps even from himself. The third-person but highly personal internal monologue of Harold Krebs in "Soldier's Home," a young man so distrustful of his environment that he must distance himself even from himself—is surely, as I read it, derived from Joyce's practice in much of *Dubliners* and *Ulysses*. The pattern is even clearer in Hemingway's first novel, *A Farewell to Arms*.

Where the battle scenes of *Finnegans Wake* are fought at a remove—in dreams, museum visits and books—and the only such scene in *Ulysses* (Leopold Bloom's encounter with the Citizen) is a hugely comic, civilian parody, Harold Krebs and Frederic Henry earn their distancing directly; their wartime experiences are infinitely more intense and dangerous than anything that Stephen Dedalus and his predecessors have known. Yet the opening of *A Farewell to Arms* (1929), with its suggestive images of mountains and rivers, of diurnal and seasonal cycles, and its powerful metaphors of war and peacetime interconnecting, owes an obvious debt to the openings of such stories as "The

The Rhetoric of Modernist Fiction

Sisters," "Araby," "A Painful Case" and "The Dead."[35] (Hemingway's irony and open-ended conclusions similarly recall Joyce's, although I would not contend that there is any indebtedness here. In these respects, Hemingway would likely have written as he does had he never happened to read *Dubliners* or *Ulysses*.) But it is in his use of point of view, it seems to me, that Hemingway's debt to Joyce is greatest.

The opening descriptions of both *A Farewell to Arms* and, say, "Araby" are objective in form and in language yet are derived from a highly subjective observer. Hemingway notes his presence at the start—"In the late summer of that year we lived in a house in a village that looked across the river and the plain to the mountains" (3)—and then never refers to him again in the opening chapter: yet we would sense his presence, his ironic detachment and yet his involvement, even without the "we." (The "you" near the end of the chapter—"you could not see his face but only the top of his cap" [4]—clearly refers both to "one" and to "I.") The adolescent protagonist of "Araby" is not named explicitly as the source of the description of North Richmond street, which "being blind, was a quiet street except at the hour when the Christian Brothers' School set the boys free," but in a story whose point of view is certainly not omniscient and which just as surely ends with the boy's disillusioned perspective of the Araby bazaar, it is only logical to assume that this initial description is also his—even if he does not perhaps intend the punning irony of his description.[36] And if we read his account as retrospective, we can easily find in the imagery of this street scene that same disillusionment.

It is there at the start of *A Farewell to Arms,* too, in the ironically understated report of the cholera, that "in the end only seven thousand died of it in the army," and in the foreboding image of the soldiers, "bulged forward under the capes so that the men, passing on the road, marched as though they were six months gone with child" (4). Sensing this disillusionment, both foreboding and perhaps also retrospective, recognizing in the "we" and in the "I" of chapter 2 the vision and perhaps also the voice of Frederic Henry, we are hardly surprised at his adventure's end, echoing and expanding that same pregnant image:

> It seems she had one hemorrhage after another. They couldn't stop it. I went into the room and stayed with Catherine until she died. She was unconscious all the time, and it did not take her very long to die. (331)

Where Joyce would never write so potentially melodramatic a line without undercutting it through irony or/and comedy, it works for Hemingway precisely because his point of view follows Joyce's in refusing to articulate his protagonists's feelings. "I do not want to talk about it," Frederic Henry says of Catherine Barkley's death in childbirth (332). And so we are compelled, if not quite to name his emotions, surely to feel them with him. Following Joyce in learning what to leave out—and, thus, in what understanding and feeling his reader must supply—Hemingway provides the narrative model which the next three generations of novelists, even some of those whom we might not name Modernists, would follow.

CHAPTER 4

To Narrate, Narration, Narrator, Narratology

*H*ow difficult the verb "to narrate," with its attendant forms, has proven to be for those even superficially interested in point of view, and what major misunderstandings it has led to. It seems straightforward enough: "to narrate" is a transitive verb, indicating an action which passes from one place or person to another. As I understand it, then, "narration" takes place only when a "narrator" in some form is present, accompanied by an audience which is at least implied. The problems begin when we use the form "narrative" as a synonym for "story," so that every act of fiction (or, indeed, of history, biography or autobiography, and some as well of anthropology and sociology) may also be a narrative. And if we do use that term in that way, we may be encouraged to speak also of a narrator, whether or not there is an act of telling, whether or not there is an audience, identifiable or implied—even an audience to be explicitly rejected—whether someone in the story is present to relate the events: by speaking of them, by writing them down, by planning to write or to speak about them, even perhaps by thinking about them, so long as communication (or its denial) is somehow possible. The indiscriminate use of these forms, as if their meanings were generalizable and not more or less precise, has caused much of the confusion which characterizes so many of the discussions of what we may choose to call narrative technique in the modern and contemporary novel, or what I prefer to speak of as point of view.

It is a bit late, obviously, to rescue "narrative." But unless we can sort out "narration" and, especially, "narrator," we can never hope to appreciate the Modernist achievement in the novel, for it begins with and always return to point of view. In my reading of the Modernist novel, it is defined not so much by its irony, its mythopoesis, its concern for metaphoric structure (the derogatorily so-called "formalism"), but rather by its attitude toward and use of point of view in its myriad manifestations. Thus, critics who cavalierly insert a narrator where such Modernists as Joyce and Woolf pointedly avoided employing one—despite, at times, their providing overwhelming textual evidence to the contrary—have misrepresented that attitude and distorted that use. In the process, will-they, nill-they, such critics have turned Joyce and Woolf into the Victorians whom those Modernists themselves worked so assiduously to reject.

Some Narrators and Their Audiences: Browning, Rossetti, Dostoevsky, Camus

Probably the most accessible illustration of the relationship between a narrator and his audience comes not from a novel or short story but from a poem, Robert Browning's "My Last Duchess" (1842). The prototypical speaker who reveals more than he intends to his listener, the Duke of Ferrara refuses scornfully even to attempt to convince his guest of the purity of his intentions. As a result, this emissary from his intended next duchess will surely advise against the proposed marriage, a course inconceivable to the duke. Or so, at least, we assume, since the emissary never speaks for himself in the poem; instead, Browning skillfully induces the reader to take his place. We are certainly clever enough to recognize what a monstrous husband the duke has been and undoubtedly will be again, given the opportunity, and so we assume a similar awareness from our surrogate in the poem—or have we become his surrogate? It is not simply the poem's pervasive irony which derives from this turn in the narration, but, indeed, its whole purpose: the point of view proves inseparable from the poem's theme of perception. One might, then, make a case for the Victorian Browning as one of the early links to Modernist narrative.[1] Such an attribution—tenuous by its very nature: I would strongly resist, for example, identifying Browning as an early Modernist or proto-Modernist—is made all the more convincing by his early use of wasteland imagery in his poem "Childe Roland to the Dark Tower Came" (1855).

From "My Last Duchess," it is an easy leap to another late-Victorian dramatic monologue, Dante Gabriel Rossetti's "Jenny" (1870), in which another proud man unknowingly reveals himself to another unlikely listener, the eponymous young prostitute with whom he has just spent the night. In envisioning her fall from grace, the seeming subject of his talk, he finds more general fault "somehow in myself.... Ashamed of my own shame" (11. 333, 384).[2] Her innocence despite her profession leads him to acknowledge the contradiction in his own life:

> Well, of such thoughts so much I know:
> In my life, as in hers, they show. (11. 387–88)

Yet he hardly seems the man to open himself so to anyone, even to an audience so unthreatening as Jenny is. And then we realize that she has all along been asleep, so that his monologue is in practice a soliloquoy—in all likelihood, moreover, an unspoken soliloquoy—and all of its revelations remain private, that is, between the speaker and his true audience, the reader.[3] Rossetti builds on Browning's example and takes us one ironic step further from the characteristic Victorian omniscience. In the process, he provides new possibilities (of audience, of reliability, of irony, of internal monologue) for later writers of narratives. (The poem was attacked in its time for its subject and not its technique.)

✳

Perhaps the most intriguing nineteenth-century use of a narrator and his relationship with his audience occurs in Feodor Dostoevsky's *Notes from Underground* (1864). Here, as the title of the novella suggests, the narrator is not a speaker but rather the writer of these revealing notes about his relations with those around him and the intimate feelings which they evoke. There is nothing especially noteworthy about this—we recognize the narrator's disturbed emotions without necessarily identifying with them—until he suddenly exclaims, "But are you really so credulous as to imagine that I would print all this, and let you read it into the bargain?" He goes further, denying not only accessibility but even our presence: "why on earth do I address you as 'gentlemen,' as though you really were my readers? ... I know that I shall never have any readers" (144–45).[4] Yet we are reading his notes, and so we must wonder how we are meant to reconcile this very explicit rejection of our presence with the undeniable fact that we are here, reading them. Dostoevsky gives us no clues. He would have needed only a minor invention to do so—someone coming across these pages before their writer could destroy them, for example. But Dostoevsky makes no effort to resolve the narrative conundrum which he has created. I suspect that this is his tentative experiment to distance us further from his protagonist (who has already admitted, with what seems a most distressing honesty, to being a liar), but that he either did not understand fully the potential use of his little trope or, more likely, that he simply did not have the narrative tools necessary to complete the transaction: a litte distance, a little uncertainty are not quite the same as absolute ambiguity. What might have passed, then, in *Notes from Underground,* as a bit of prescient modernity seems just an opportunity lost—although it is not wise, I believe, to attempt to define just what sort of opportunity (Modernist? pre-modern? post-Modernist?) this might have been. It is not easy even for a Dostoevsky to establish an environment of even relative uncertainty in the midst of a narrative tradition which mandates certainty. And it is all too easy for a modern critic to find glimpses of the modern where none is intended or warranted.

The Underground Man does prepare us for a direct modern descendant, however. This is Jean-Baptiste Clamence, sole speaker in Albert Camus' extended dramatic monologue, *The Fall* (1957). For one of my students, he provided a most effective—even frightening—illustration of the potential power of the bond between a narrator and his audience. The speaker here is a Frenchman, a lawyer, who has settled in Amsterdam, possibly because its canals offer an apt analogy to the circles of Dante's *Inferno*, as well as a comparable need for a guide. His self-appointed task—recalling Coleridge's Ancient Mariner—is to engage appropriate listeners in his tale of moral failure: his unwillingness, some years earlier, in Paris, to intervene in order to save the life of another (a death recalling that of Georg Bendemann in Franz Kafka's "The Judgment"; so much else in Camus recalls Kafka). He now calls himself a "judge-penitent."

His narration proceeds at a lesiurely pace as he subtly, almost imperceptibly, involves his listener—another Frenchman, on this occasion—in his account:

> Covered with ashes, tearing my hair, my face scored by clawing, but with piercing eyes, I stand before all humanity recapitulating my shames without losing sight of the effect I am producing, and saying, "I was the lowest of the low." Then imperceptibly I pass from the "I" to the "we." When I get to "This is what we are," the trick has been played and I can tell them off. I am like them, to be sure; we are in the soup together. However, I have a superiority in that I know it and this gives me the right to speak. You see the advantage, I am sure. The more I accuse myself, the more I have a right to judge you. Even better, I provoke you into judging yourself, and this relieves me of that much of the burden. (140)[5]

Does his unnamed listener even notice the shift from "them" to "you"? Is he so pleased by the confidence that he fails to notice that this, too, is part of the confidence game?

"*Monsieur*," the politely correct narrator at first calls his listener and then, rather quickly, "*monsieur et cher compatriote*," and then, more simply but compellingly, "*mon cher compatriote*." Before the week is over, however, his listener has become "*cher ami*," "dear friend," and finally, in the most engaging manner possible (in both senses of the term "engaging"), the well-named narrator Jean-Baptiste Clamence, both precursor and public acclaimer, has named his willing listener his master, "*cher maître*." And the listener never protests. (He might well protest, if he chose to, for although we never hear his words, Clamence does hear them and frequently responds to them.)

The point is, of course, that each of us is capable of profound moral failings, of acts of omission as well as commission, that in all potentiality, we are comparably all guilty. It is one matter, however, for Clamence to tell this to his listener and quite another for the reader to discover this for herself. For while the speaker's goal is transparent, at least to the reader, the novelist's is more subtle, more telling: Clamence's aim is to involve his listener in his "shames," Camus' to implicate his reader. For my student, this was a painful lesson. She was among the best students in a good Modern European Novel class, and she had chosen to write on *The Fall* for her second essay. (We had discussed Camus' *The Plague* [1948] in class; the assignment was to analyze some other novel by one of the novelists whom we had read for class. We also read that semester Dostoevsky's *The Idiot* and Kafka's *The Castle,* among other, connected texts.) So I was surprised when she called me at home on the night before the assignment was due, to tell me, in tears, that she would not be handing in her paper on time. (This in a class for which lateness was not an option, from a student who was meticulously prompt.) It was not that she would be turning it in late; she had already written the essay but would not give it to me to read. For she had just re-read it, she told me, and she had realized with a shock of recognition that in condemning the speaker, she had also condemned his hearer, and in condemning him—because he so slyly involves his unprotesting audience in his affairs—she had condemned herself.

For such is the effect of this unasked-for confession made to a man who has learned during the past few days to listen closely and to ask telling questions: the same questions that we would likely ask in the listener's place, along with the comments that we would likely make were we present. (We are able to ascertain his words from the narrator's responses to them.) We accept him, that is, as our representative in their dialogue. But we are able to perceive what he evidently cannot: perhaps we can do so because he cannot. As the speaker turns this chance visitor, a countryman, into a friend, a collaborator and, in the end, his master, so we are drawn into the narrative with him—with them both—fulfilling along with him his dramatic role in the monologue: to become involved, to recognize and acknowledge our own complicity. (It may be only potential, but it is nonetheless actual.) In one discomfiting moment, my student had come to recognize all of this. Hers was the most dramatic demonstration that I have witnessed of the power of a skillfully wrought point of view to effect an engagement of narrator and audience. A week afterwards, she handed in an essay on another novel by some other novelist, neither of which remains memorable today. Nor was her second essay, which was competent but uninspired. She never would let me read that earlier, evidently cathartic effort of hers.

Conrad and Marlow

It was Conrad who made the narrative leap which James had refused to, that (symbolic and literal) leap from the nineteenth to the twentieth century, from an insistence on at least the semblance of certainty to a willful acceptance of the ever-present potential for ambiguity. In refusing to turn the full responsibility for presenting his story over to a character—especially not to a character as narrator—James made clear the limits, as well as the limitations, of his narrative technique and worldview alike. He had no need for—indeed, rejected—the absolute certainty of a Trollope. Not for him the role of a manipulative, intrusive, interventionist omniscient Victorian author, unwilling to allow his characters to react and to live on their own. His centers of consciousness go a long way toward shifting the focus from the omnipresent, all-powerful creator to his often vulnerable, morally centered human creations: but not all the way. For James insisted on his own, continuing (if seemingly diminished) role on the fringes of his story, noticeable in his language, peering over the shoulders of his own "centres."

Conrad, however, at about the same time that James was making his resistance definitive—from 1897, with the *Nigger of the "Narcissus,"* to *Chance* in 1913—began to explore and then to develop the very possibilities that James had explicitly rejected: from narration by a first-person eyewitness; to narration by an outside (only partially direct) observer with a variety of sources; to several different, somewhat overlapping, somewhat competing narrators, some of them involved directly in the action, some of them outsiders. In the process, Conrad opened up both the potential for narration (a first-person narrator of a novel before his time was not very different from an omniscient author, with very nearly the same identification and authority) and the ability to realize (and for the reader to perceive) a world of shifting values and even realities. While few of his successors would use narration itself in the way that he had—many would not use narration at all—Conrad's invention of Marlow showed them the way to a new universe in fiction. We may say that Marlow made possible Modernism in the novel.

It seems as easy and natural to trace Conrad's narrative progression as it must have been for him to effect it: there is almost an inevitability about this development as we look at it in retrospect, a sense that Conrad did not so much plan Marlow's role as see the opportunity and then seize it. Certainly, there is nothing at the beginning of the *Nigger of the "Narcissus"* to suggest that here was the germ of a great innovation; there is not only no hint of Marlow here, but no sense of any narrator, except perhaps for Conrad himself. The beginning is totally objective—"Mr. Baker, chief mate of the ship *Narcissus,* stepped in one stride out of his lighted cabin into the darkness of the quarter-deck" (30)[6]—as if Conrad's sole concerns were to establish the imagery of light and darkness and to avoid his own presence. There is only the barest hint that anyone might be observing the scene—"every soul afloat in Bombay Harbor became aware that the new hands were joining the *Narcissus*" (31). Conrad never does say—nor does anyone else—that one of these hands might possibly become our observer within the narrative.

Gradually, however, he does turn out to be one of the crew, although still undefined, without either a name or a specific identity, no more, at first, than a shared, first-person plural pronoun: "Mr. Baker ... kept all our noses to the grindstone" (54), so subtle that only the most atuned reader will notice it on first reading. Eventually, during the pivotal scene in which James Wait, the title character, is saved from drowning, the focus shifts to "[t]he five men" who would rescue him. Four of them are named: the boatswain, Little Belfast, Wamibo and Archie (81), and we are free to suspect that our narrator is the fifth—except, of course, that we have not even thought until this moment that there might be a narrator within the story. We would take him for a Jamesian center of consciousness if we did not know that he might also be telling the story, possibly even (we may begin to suspect—if not necessarily on first reading) in retrospect. It is in this scene that the five turn from "they" to "we": "The boatswain adjured us to 'bear a hand,' and a rope descended. We made things fast to it . . ." (83).

Finally, at the story's conclusion, as if only now had Conrad begun to realize the possibilities inherent in the unnamed fifth seaman, he appears not as one of "them" or even "us," but as "I," a specified observer whom we may be certain will some day sit down to write this narrative that we have just read. There is no explicit metafictional potential in this final scene. Conrad does not revise his novel to account for this presence and does not suggest even at the end that this "I" might somehow be based on his own experience as a seaman who has left the sea for the writing desk. (We know, moreover, that Conrad did not turn directly from able seaman to novelist but was a master at his first trade before becoming one at his second.) But it is impossible, in retrospect, to read this closing scene without some sense that Conrad has discovered here the narrative potential of an experienced seaman who will make a habit of telling those stories of the sea of which he was an observer.

> One by one they came up to the pay table to get the wages of their glorious and obscure toil. . . .
> . . . As I came up I saw a red-faced, blowsy woman, in a gray shawl and with dusty, fluffy hair, fall on Charley's neck. It was his mother. . . . I was passing him at the time, and . . . I nodded and passed on. . . . In the next few steps I came upon Belfast. He caught my arm with tremulous enthusiasm. . . .
> I disengaged myself gently. (167–69)

He does look back one last time at the crew of the *Narcissus,* concludes that "You were a good crowd. As good a crowd as ever fisted with wild cries the beating canvas of a heavy foresail; or, tossing aloft, invisible in the night, yell for yell to a westerly gale" (171), but never says that he has determined to tell their story. "I never saw them again" (170), he tells us, and we are left to recognize—if only in retrospect—that it is likely his tale that we have just read. It is also likely, however, that this possibility would never have occurred to us had it not been for Marlow's appearance the following year in the story "Youth."

Marlow is still not very well defined in "Youth," and we would probably find neither him nor his story memorable had this been his final appearance. But the year after that, 1899, in the far more memorable *Heart of Darkness*, there is Marlow again, now fully formed, telling for the first time the story of another, making use of still other sources and filtering everything through his own experience and consciousness. Marlow is not only an eyewitness to the images of Kurtz's downfall, he is himself impacted by those images, changed utterly, we should assume, by the experience. His experience, of course, is as a master (how ironic the term is in this context) on the Congo, as someone who has actually encountered the legendary Kurtz, as the bearer of Kurtz's African legacy to Europe and, of course, as the narrator of this haunting tale; he, too, he makes clear to us, is haunted by his tale (and so he must tell it, almost like Coleridge's Mariner), and so should we be: we become, in effect, his listeners. Although Marlow never again mentions Kurtz in his subsequent appearances as narrator, it is not unreasonable to assume that the stories that he tells then— of the eponymous Lord Jim and of Flora de Barral in *Chance*—are themselves impacted by this early experience. Marlow's maturity as a narrator, that is, is possible only after he has been to the Congo.

In *Heart of Darkness*, Marlow appears within a frame and with an audience. Five men meet one night aboard the *Nellie*, anchored in the Thames: "Between us there was, as I have already said somewhere, the bond of the sea" (27).[7] The four of them who have already left the sea listen as the fifth, Marlow, "the only man of us who still 'followed the sea'" (29), tells the tale of his Congo experience: "'I suppose you fellows remember I did once turn fresh-water sailor for a bit'" (32), he begins, so "that we knew we were fated, before the ebb began to run, to hear about one of Marlow's inconclusive experiences" (32). What follows is some one hundred pages of first-person narration—quite enough to fill a night's close listening—some of it based on the accounts of others, as they have been relayed to Marlow, all of it presented within quotation marks.

Conrad does not make much subsequent use of this audience; there are occasional interruptions by the outside narrator—"It had become so pitch dark that we listeners could hardly see one another" (59)—but no significant judgment from him after his warning "about one of Marlow's inconclusive experiences." There are possibilities here that remain to be explored: possibilities of distance (why bother, for instance, to shield Marlow by an outside narrator who has so little to say? and why allude to the latter's previous role as a narrator?); of reader involvement (what can those other listeners be thinking about this extraordinary tale?); of moral judgment and ambiguity: some of those very qualities of point of view that would become so central to Modernist fiction. But Conrad still has much to learn about the potential of Marlow as narrator.

✳

In *Lord Jim* (1900), the texture of Marlow's narration has thickened considerably. Marlow is introduced here even more gradually (25, 26),[8] well after we have been introduced to Jim, by a voice at once objective, knowledgeable about the sea and capable of making judgments—a voice, in short, like that of Marlow himself. Late in the narrative, after some two hundred pages of virtually uninterrupted talk within quotation marks, Marlow is again seen from the outside:

> With these words Marlow had ended his narrative, and his audience had broken up forthwith, under his abstract, pensive gaze. Men drifted off the verandah in pairs or alone without loss of time, without offering a remark, as if the last image of that incomplete story, its incompleteness itself, and the very tone of the speaker, had made discussion vain and comment impossible. Each of them seemed to carry away his own impression, to carry it away with him like a secret; but there was only one man of all these listeners who was ever to hear the last word of the story. (242)

Our unidentified outside narrator is presumably that man, and he reads "the last word" in a letter from Marlow, some two years afterwards. "'You alone have showed an interest in him that survived the telling of his story, though I remember well you would not admit he had mastered his fate,'" Marlow writes (243), referring to events of which we have been told nothing. Enclosed with this letter is another from Jim to Marlow, along with one to Jim from his father, likely "the last letter he ever had from home" (245). Marlow concludes his story, again within quotation marks, acting now as a sort of imaginative editor as well as a narrator.

> "I'll put it down here for you as though I had been an eyewitness. My information was fragmentary, but I've fitted the pieces together, and there is enough of them to make an intelligible picture. I wonder how he would have related it himself." (246)

This is perfectly consistent with Marlow's activity as oral storyteller. He has been an actor in some of the events which he narrates, an eyewitness to others and the recipient of confidences not only from Jim but from some half dozen other characters, including Stein, another potential authorial surrogate, and even the infamous Gentleman Brown, villain of the piece. He also, of course, knows all of the rumors and legends that have grown in the East around his subject. But he does not know everything. Some details and nuances escape him; there are problems relating to the veracity of at least one of his sources (Brown), and Marlow is himself on occasion just a bit dense ("'My eyes were

To Narrate, Narration, Narrator, Narratology   55

too dazzled by the glitter of the sea below his feet to see him clearly; I am fated never to see him clearly,'" 173).

And then, for all his desire to unravel this mystery, Marlow is painfully aware of its inherent ambiguities. "'For my part,'" he says toward the close of his oral narration, "'I cannot say what I believed—indeed I don't know to this day, and never shall probably. But what did the poor devil believe himself? ... Both of us had said the very same thing. Did we both speak the truth—or one of us did—or neither?'" (230). And because we ourselves have become so invested in Marlow—despite his avowals of uncertainty, perhaps even in part because of them—because we recognize his commitment to Jim—we find ourselves committed to this tale and its protagonist in ways far beyond anything experienced by the reader of Trollope or Dickens, or even of James. Through his undefined, yet immediate audience, Marlow is confronting us directly when he challenges,

> "What would you have done? You are sure of yourself—aren't you? What would you do if you felt now—this minute—the house here move, just move a little under your chair. Leap! By heavens! you would take one spring from where you sit and land in that clump of bushes yonder." (78)

The commitment, the involvement, is very nearly complete, here in this narrative at the very beginning of the new century. Everything that would follow, in the entire wonderful Modernist revolution in point of view, is at least implicit in Marlow as he functions in *Lord Jim*.

The narrative of *Lord Jim* remains "incomplete" despite its multitude of connections and possibilities, as if incompletion were inherent in the narrative's very form; in *Chance*, Conrad magnifies the possibilities exponentially, as if to prove that incompleteness in itself—the essence of ambiguity—was the point of it all. The author's most ambitious and, during his lifetime, his most popular novel, *Chance* employs Marlow, now retired, in his by now familiar role: telling a story of the sea and its people to a group of old friends. Among his principal sources are young Powell, second mate of the *Ferndale,* and Flora de Barral Anthony, wife of the captain of that ship and protagonist of their various stories. What is new in this narrative is that the sources at times speak to one another, so that we might hear Flora's account as attested to by Powell, who may then speak to Marlow—as well as to an outside narrator known only as "I," who serves also as Marlow's principal audience. "I," even more than Marlow, is also a traffic director of sorts, a director of narratives.

While many of its parts are quite effective, the elaborate whole of *Chance* does not quite work. Taking the kind of risk that James so carefully avoided,

Conrad erects a structure that he cannot fully control. But this, in the end, is what is most admirable about *Chance:* Conrad's conscious effort to take his success with Marlow one step further and to create a narrative structure which, in itself, would suggest the inherent unknowability of the world which it represents. Put differently, Conrad had already developed in Marlow, in *Lord Jim* especially, a narrator fully capable of communicating modern ambiguity; in *Chance,* he is endeavoring to create a structure to replicate that ambiguity in its very nature. The task is not quite within his grasp.

It would remain for Conrad's Modernist successors to effect that ambitious, perhaps even heroic narrative feat. But we must admire his effort, nonetheless, his determination to build on his earlier success, his willingness to assume the risk of failure. In the end, *Chance* is at least a partial failure, but the effort is noble and points the way for those later masters of Modernist narration, Joyce, Proust, Faulkner, Simon and Fuentes in particular, who would erect and control vast narrative structures which in themselves reflect the world which they so realistically depict. Theirs is the most ambitious and powerful narrative feat in the history of the novel, and it is Conrad and Marlow who make it possible.

Oral Histories and Historians: Faulkner and Claude Simon

Engagement effected through narration, it seems, is not just an intellectual exercise; it may prove powerfully emotional as well. In an almost perfect union of function and form, of narrative technique and theme, it may evoke emotion in the reader even when the form seems most extreme and demanding: as when the narrator within the novel is self-consciously involved in a deeply internalized, highly intellectualized narrative search, expecting us to follow him as he winds his tortuous way into the past and within himself. The most famous of such searchers, of course, is Marcel Proust's Marcel, who meanders through some forty years and some four thousand pages in an effort to find himself amidst the accumulated memories and narratives (both written and spoken) of the past (both his own and others'). Only relatively more accessible—and no less moving—are Proust's principal American heir (he is James Joyce's heir as well), William Faulkner, in *Absalom, Absalom!* (1936), and, in an almost magical act of cultural and generational narrative transformation, that joint offspring of Proust, Joyce and Faulkner, the French novelist Claude Simon, in *The Flanders Road* (1961).

In *Absalom, Absalom!* Quentin Compson sorts through the detritus of his family's history and his region's history in an attempt to understand the man that he has become, almost, it would seem, despite himself. His search is his means of assuming reponsibility, although we may question both his understanding of what that means and his response to his discoveries. His sources are mostly oral histories, passed down through generations of Mississippi Delta men and women, some of them his ancestors, some acquaintances, some figures of the local mythology. His narrative, compiled with the active assistance of his principal audience, his roommate at Harvard, Shreve McCannon, is itself an oral history, a complex compound of facts, hearsay, legends, outright fictions and fantasy, a narrative which assumes a life of its own apart from its story and which leads him to the terrifying truth that we cannot escape our histories—or, for that matter, from our need to sort out and tell our histories. Substitute for the proper names in this formulation: *The Flanders Road* for *Absalom, Absalom!*; the character called Georges for Quentin Compson; Rousillon in southwestern France for the Mississippi River Delta; the Jew named Blum (recalling Joyce's Leopold Bloom) for the Canadian Shreve; and a German prisoner of war camp for the dorm room at Harvard, and we have an ideal working description of Claude Simon's compelling novel. The fact that it is so derivative of Faulkner in no way diminishes its power, however.

Each of these narrators, Quentin and Georges, tells a story rooted in history as a means of unraveling the mystery of his own roots. Each radical history delves deeply into the past, progresses hesitantly toward the present, mixes characters and events from different times almost as if to say that time does not matter (or else, that only time matters), that all times in the end are one and that none of its mysteries is, finally, decipherable. Yet the search goes on, perhaps for its own sake, compulsively. In each narrative, the listener plays an active role in the (futile yet somehow fruitful) act of deciphering (futile because no conclusion can be reached, yet fruitful because the narrative process itself gives life to both speaker and listener). Each listener also provides a second narrative voice—since theirs are true dialogues and not just dramatic monologues or soliloquies—a voice that is virtually indistinguishable at times from the narrator's.

> ... and Georges (unless it was still Blum), interrupting himself, clowning, unless he (Georges) wasn't having this dialogue under the cold Saxon rain with a little sickly Jew—or the shadow of a little Jew, and who was not much more than a corpse—one more corpse—of a little Jew—but with himself, that is, his double, all alone under the grey rain, among the rails, the coal wagons, or perhaps years later, still alone (although he was lying now beside a woman's warm flesh), still having a dialogue with that double, or with Blum, or with no one): "There we are: History. I've been waiting for it the last few minutes. I was waiting for the word. It's an odd thing if it doesn't put in an appearance now and again." (139)[9]

But where Shreve may appear amused at the task—it is not, after all, his way of life that is being questioned—for Blum, somehow, the search is a matter of literal life and death. Shreve's disengaged voice is not merely Northern but foreign as well; he exists as an appendage of Quentin, rational complement to his roommate's quixotic personality, the audience that he would have to invent had it not been provided by circumstance. But Blum remains ever-present for Georges long years after his death in the camp; he remains his friend's audience and becomes—in a transformative process blending the narrative act with its goal, function with form—in the end, its principal subject.

When Georges speaks in the present, recounting the story of their search in the camp, he fulfills both roles, his own and Blum's, uncertain seeker and skeptical (but never cynical) questioner, serving within the tale that he now tells as both narrator and audience.

> ... and Georges (or Blum): "I could go on," and Blum (or Georges): "So go on," and Georges (or Blum): "But I must also bring my contribution, participate, add to the heap, augment it by some of those coal bricks), and Blum: "[...] History leaves behind it only a residue." (140)

He is speaking now to a woman, in bed, after lovemaking, telling her the tale of that earlier narration. She, we discover, is his childhood companion and cousin by marriage, Corinne de Reixach, the widow of their former cavalry commandant in the early days of the war, whose suicidal charge (on horseback against a German machine gun emplacement) is the starting point of the search. (Did he discover his wife's unfaithfulness while he was off at war, Blum wonders, and so choose to die in this absurd way?) His death leads them, inexorably, to the death of an ancestor (whose familiar portrait Georges describes in detail to Blum): did he too die, in an earlier war, or returning from it, of an unfaithful wife? (Is suicide part of the family heritage? Is unfaithfulness?) The dead Captain de Reixach and his ancestor play much the same part in this history as Charles Bon does in Quentin's and Shreve's: the pertinent present events coalesce around the mysteries of his past. At this point in the narration, the listening woman departs, in anger, offended not so much by the subject of the story as by its intended audience. For she recognizes before we do—we recognize through her—that Georges all along has been speaking not to her but to Blum, that he tells this tale not to find an answer to some ancient mystery but for the sake of the story itself, to keep the story itself alive and, in doing so, to keep Blum alive. Memory for Simon, as for Proust, is not a phenomenon apart but an integral aspect of narration, and narration may be life.

With the woman's departure, without missing a note of his narrative, Georges goes on speaking, acknowledging as he does his true audience, endeavoring now to reconstruct not just that earlier tale of the absent warrior and the unfaithful wife, but also that earlier effort at reconstruction. Not de Reixach and his unfaithful wife, or the ancestor and his, are his subject, we too now come to recognize, but the young Georges and the long-dead Blum as they strive to sort out those earlier histories. Speaking directly now to Blum, Georges narrates once again the story of their joint search, rehearsing both his own lines as a young man and Blum's. Is this, then, a soliloquoy or a dramatic monologue, as well as a dialogue? The technical terms are obviously inadequate to define the situation. The complication lies less with the narrator—for Georges seems almost an inevitable step forward from Marcel and Quentin—than with his audience. Alive now only in memory and in the act of narration, Blum has become the most multi-faceted listener in modern fiction: being told the story (albeit masked for a time behind a more conventional audience), in which he was at once the listener and co-creator, of a search through the images and themes of the past for the purpose of mastering the present (history's purpose, after all), a story which soon becomes its own justification: to keep alive two desperate men at what seems the deathstroke of civilization. And since the effort fails, it must (paradoxically) be continued, for only in the act of narration can the listener be kept alive. The wonder of it is that so technically complex a narrative can be so compelling and moving.

> The two faceless voices alternating answering each other in the darkness with no more reality than their own sound, saying things with no more reality than a series of sounds, yet continuing the dialogue: in the beginning only two virtual dead men, then something like two living dead men, then one of them really dead and the other still alive (or so it seemed, Georges thought, and judging from appearances it wasn't much of an improvement), and both (the one who was dead and the one who wondered if it wasn't better to be dead for good since at least you didn't know it) caught, enclosed by that motionless and yet moving thing that slowly flattened the earth's surface under its weight . . . : that Olympian and cold progression, that slow glacier moving since the beginning of time, crushing, grinding everything, and in which he seemed to see them, himself and Blum, stiff and frozen, perched booted and spurred, on their exhausted nags, intact and dead among the host of ghosts standing in their faded uniforms all advancing at the same imperceptible speed. (206)

"[T]hat slow glacier" is, it would seem, history, or memory perhaps, bending all before it. ("[C]rushing," he calls it, yet the burden of his story seems difficult but not unbearable, formative far more than destructive.) For the rhythms of Georges' search—of his life and his narration, of his life as revealed and formed by his narration—seem somehow, in the end, redemptive. They involve us, too, the audience beyond the more immediate audience(s), almost despite ourselves, in these lives and these narrative processes and rhythms, offering the affirmation of our own humanity as well as theirs.

The manifold, interconnected, overlapping voices of William Faulkner's *Absalom, Absalom!* become, in the end, a single voice. Although in tone, diction, vocabulary, intent, it may lay claim to authority, this is definitely not the voice of the omniscient author or that of any of his potential surrogates (a reliable spokesman, an invented narrator). The heightened register is that of the historian: not the professional, to be sure, but the dedicated amateur, whose interest lies not in history *per se* (and certainly not in historiography) but in the history of a particular region at a particular moment in time, indeed, of a particular individual whose acts come somehow to represent the region. The history which emerges is thus local, even parochial, yet in a sense universal; temporal, of course, yet reaching from that historical past to the present tense of the narrative and beyond that, too, into the reader's present; realistic, even naturalistic in its details and worldview, yet achieving the quality of myth and of mythopoesis. The contradictions, limitations, overarching achievements are all encapsulated in—and made possible by—that unique, all-pervasive narrative voice.

It is this voice which distinguishes *Absalom, Absalom!* from its narrative *donnée* and model, the voice of Marcel in Marcel Proust's *A la recherche du temps perdu*. Where Proust's character's voice is highly literary and recognizably French in its intonations and rhythms, Faulkner's is unmistakably oral and American. Where Marcel's narrative is a multiple performance in the sense that we hear him, simultaneously, as a young man and as a middle-aged man re-creating the events of his adolescence, his youth, and his early middle age, the narrative of *Absalom, Absalom!* consists of a construct of four speakers separated by age, gender, intellect, experience, even national origin; the fact that two of these speakers are also listeners enhances exponentially the narrative possibilities. Yet while we recognize the differences among the four, it seems increasingly, as we listen, a single voice that we hear. This is Modernist point of view at its most demanding and most successful.

For some three hours on a September afternoon in 1909, an elderly spinster named Rosa Coldfield—her name expressing her destiny—summons young Quentin Compson to her home in order to tell him a story (one which deals, in part, with the reasons for her spinsterhood). "'Because you are going away to college at Harvard they tell me. . . . So maybe you will enter the literary profession as so many Southern gentlemen and gentlewomen too are doing now and maybe some day you will remember this and write about it'" (9–10).[10] Quentin remembers, but he does not live long enough to achieve the distance necessary to "write about it." The best that he can do is retell her story, attempt to comprehend it, strive—with the aid of his father and roommate—to fill in its gaps and interstices: to reconstitute it.

On this evening, though, "It would be three hours yet before he would learn why she had sent for him because part of it, the first part of it, Quentin already knew. It was part of his twenty years' heritage of breathing the same air and hearing his father talk about the man Sutpen . . ." (11). This evening, inspired by his son's unexpected listening experience, Mr. Compson elaborates on those earlier tales of his, commenting as well now on Miss Coldfield's account as shared with him, at third hand, by his son (implicitly, of course, since we never do hear Quentin's version as told to his father). Mr. Compson thus provides the narrative's third point of view, following his still young son, his elderly neighbor and his own earlier, also unheard tales. (Told before this narrative begins—and told frequently, it would seem—these tales of Mr. Compson's become part of this narrative, too, when Quentin does retell them in his words, not many months afterwards, in his Harvard dormitory.)

Some critics have suggested, however, that Mr. Compson is actually the novel's fourth point of view, going on the assumption that the scene with which the novel opens (among others) is being presented objectively, if knowingly, by the author in his own voice:

> From a little after two oclock until almost sundown of the long still hot weary September afternoon they sat in what Miss Coldfield still called the office because her father had called it that. (7)

It becomes apparent as we read, however, that there is little that is objective about this setting and that its source is not the author but his twenty-year-old protagonist. (Technically, to be sure, the novel's protagonist would appear to be "the man Sutpen," who is at the center of the historical events which constitute the novel's principal plot and which provide its theme. To name Quentin the protagonist is to recognize that what *Absalom, Absalom!* is about, in the end, is not the burden of history but the challenge, responsibility, opportunity, onus of storytelling. Narration is at once the novel's core technique and underlying theme, at once its function and form, and so the narrator around whom the storytelling revolves is of necessity the protagonist.)

And this scene in Miss Coldfield's office is demonstrably being presented from Quentin's point of view. There is nothing here that he does not know, nothing that he cannot see or hear or think or feel. (The afternoon, for example, if only for Quentin, is not only "long," "still" and "hot"; it is also "weary." What would be a minor grammatical misuse for an omniscient author is, for a young man waiting to leave home for a new stage in his life, perfectly appropriate.) It would be easier, I suppose, more obvious at least, to assume that since the "they" of "they sat in the office" refers to Quentin and Miss Coldfield, it must be some third party's reference to them; to assume as well that, since the pronoun is in the third person, the account must also be objective; so that, as a result—since there is no one else in the office to view and then to present this action—the voice that we are hearing has to be that of the author. He is not inevitably an omniscient author in the sense that he knows all, tells all, manipulates all, but he is surely—as viewed from this critical perspective—making no effort to eliminate himself from the narrative. Such a reading, I believe, is essentially to turn Faulkner from a Modernist into a Victorian. (In a Modernist context, designed above all else to take the author out of the narrative, this is much the same as calling him omniscient.) To do so is to ignore the elaborate structure of point of view in *Absalom, Absalom!*: of narratives within narratives, the roles of speaker and listener intersecting at times, each level of narration supplementing, supporting, undercutting, enriching another, at once affirming and calling into question its provenance, its audience, its meaning, its significance: a quintessentially Modernist point of view, that is.

The opening setting, then—like all similar settings of present events in the introductory chapters of *Absalom, Absalom!*—is realized here through the memory, sense perceptions, consciousness of Quentin Compson. We do not require the label "Quentin thought," or "Quentin observed" to recognize that these are his internalized responses to the scene, to the storyteller and to her strange, baroque (even mannerist) tale. This is also the closest that we come to hearing directly his narration to his father; we will recognize it again as the background to his account, some months afterwards, to his roommate at Harvard.

On the day on which they learn of Miss Coldfield's death, in mid-January 1910 (Mr. Compson's letter is dated the tenth), Quentin Compson and Shreve McCannon begin their historic collaboration, their effort to reconstitute history: two young men, "both born within the same year: the one in Alberta, the other in Mississippi; born half a continent apart yet joined" (258) at the opposite ends of the Mississippi River Valley (the "Continental Trough"), one so close to the import of these events that he must strive for distance, the other so foreign to them that he reaches for intimacy, yet both romantic seekers after truth. Their speech is colloquial, except for certain heightened moments when it acquires an intensity as if it were history itself speaking and not two bright but naive freshmen at Harvard:

> It would not matter here in Cambridge that the time had been winter in that garden too, and hence no bloom nor leaf even if there had been someone to walk there and be seen there since, judged by subsequent events, it had been night in the garden also. But that did not matter since it had been so long ago. It did not matter to them (Quentin and Shreve) anyway, who could without moving, as free now of flesh as the father who decreed and forbade, the son who denied and repudiated, the lover who acquiesced, the beloved who was not bereaved, and with no tedious transition from hearth and garden to saddle, who could be already clattering over the frozen ruts of that December night and that Christmas dawn, that day of peace and cheer, of holly and goodwill and logs on the hearth; not two of them there and then either but four of them riding the two horses through the iron darkness, and that not mattering either: what faces and what names they called themselves and were called by so long as the blood coursed—the blood, the immortal brief recent intransient blood which could hold honor above slothy unregret and love above fat and easy shame. (295)

Some critics might claim, I suppose, that such heightened diction cannot be true verisimilitude and that, therefore, this must be the author's voice which we hear. But it makes just as much sense to regard this as the voice of history: an abstraction, to be sure, but one perfectly suited to an account filled with ancient, often unidentifiable and sometimes uncertain sources: stories and rumors passed down through generations ("'I have this from something your grandfather let drop one day,'" 49); the observations and memories of the town of Jefferson itself ("Because the town believed that it knew him. For two years it had watched him," 42); a fateful letter which has somehow found its way to the Compson family and somehow survived to tell anew an old tale ("'doubtless knowing no more why she chose your grandmother to give the letter to than your grandmother knew,'" 126).

We read *Absalom, Absalom!* with a growing awareness that much of this is uncharted narrative territory and that the author is justified in his ambitious efforts, even when the results may not be absolutely consistent. It is this narrative ambition that some putative post-Modernist novelists have reacted against in their own work. It is simpler to be consistent when the worldview and sense of profession are simpler and more consistent.

The letter itself is one of the first extended uses of another aspect of Faulkner's point of view in *Absalom, Absalom!,* the use of italics to differentiate among levels of response. At times, the italics indicate unspoken thoughts in the midst of speech:

> *Now you cant marry him.*
> *Why cant I marry him?*
> *Because he's dead.*
> *Dead?*
> *Yes. I killed him.*
> He (Quentin) couldn't pass that. He was not even listening to her; he said,
> "Ma'am? What's that? What did you say?" (172)

At times, italics indicate memories of past speech in the midst of both speech and thought in the present:

> (*Because there was love* Mr Compson said *There was that letter she brought and gave to your grandmother to keep.* He (Quentin) could see it, as plainly as he saw the one [from his father, announcing Rosa's death] open upon the open text book on the table before him. (207)

More often, in the novel's long climactic scene, as Quentin and Shreve strain to reconstruct the events of Sutpen's life, rise, fall and death—and their effect on his family and neighbors—the italics serve to separate event from imagination, thought from speech, character from character, time from time.

"And now," Shreve said, "we're going to talk about love." But he didn't need to say that either. ... [I]t did not matter to either of them which one did the talking, since it was not the talking alone which did it. ... "And now, love. He [Sutpen] must have known all about her before he ever saw her. ... maybe who could know what times he looked at Henry's face and thought, not *there but for the intervening leaven of that blood which we do not have in common is my skull, my brow, sockets, shape and angle of jaw and chin and some of my thinking behind it.*" (316–17)

Are the italicized thoughts—intended to suggest Sutpen's unknown thoughts almost a century earlier—Quentin's or Shreve's? In their process of reconstruction, although they begin by playing distinct roles—the Canadian's aggressive questioning, the Southerner's often defensive responses—in time, their roles intersect, overlap, and so it may not always be possible—even with the aid of italics—to sort them out. Reconstituting history, again, they become together the voice of history.

Each of these narrative tropes serves the larger process of reconstruction— what Proust's Marcel calls *réconstitution*—that lies at the heart of *Absalom, Absalom!* Although Faulkner's narrative invention is in many ways more elaborate and demanding even than Proust's, as an historical process, ironically, it is more in the post-Modernist than in the Modernist (or any previous) vein. That is, it depends not on an objective rendering and evaluation of observed facts, the traditional role of the historian, but is instead a subjective, imaginative, even inventive process of filling in the gaps between the facts and of doing so in a way that values the invention more than the facts. Whatever its value for fiction, it is not, it seems to me, a particularly valuable means of writing history, but it proves powerful and profound as it is practiced by Quentin and Shreve.[11]

Mr. Compson, who has taught his son most of what he knows of history— of Southern history especially—is intensely aware that all the known facts, from all available sources, nonetheless leave basic questions unresolved. "'It's just incredible. It just does not explain. Or perhaps that's it: they dont explain and we are not supposed to know'" (100). He himself effects reconstruction of a sort, but only in lesser matters, in filling in lesser gaps, based on his knowledge of custom perhaps, even more than of human nature: "*He would not have sat; perhaps she would not even have asked him to*" (207). His narrative will be filtered through his son, but it is Shreve, the outsider (who, after all, sounds at times like his father to Quentin), who begins the process in earnest. He does so at first against Quentin's wishes:

"So he got his trump made, after all," Shreve said. "He played that trump after all. And so he came home and found——"

"Wait," Quentin said.

"——what he must have wanted to find or anyway what he was going to find——"

    "Wait, I tell you!" Quentin said, though still he did not move nor even raise
his voice. (277)

But Quentin soon gives way and participates actively in the reconstruction
of events in the lives of three generations of Sutpens, centering around blood
and color and "love and honor and courage and pride" (302), that series of
fateful, tragic and melodramatic events that come to the roommates to encapsulate all there is to know about the South, events which for Quentin add to his
familial failings and hasten his suicide.

> They stared—glared—at one another. It was Shreve speaking, though save for
> the slight difference which the intervening degrees of latitude had inculcated in
> them (differences not in tone or pitch but of turns of phrase and usage of words),
> it might have been either of them and was in a sense both: both thinking as one,
> the voice which happened to be speaking the thought only the thinking become
> audible, vocal; the two of them creating between them, out of the rag-tag and
> bob-ends of old tales and talking, people who perhaps had never existed at all
> anywhere, who, shadows, were shadows not of flesh and blood which had lived
> and died but shadows in turn of what were (to one of them at least, to Shreve)
> shades too, quiet as the visible murmur of their vaporizing breath. (303)

Appropriately, it is impossible to determine with certainty whether the source
of this thought, conceived and expressed and mutually understood, in the cold
Massachusetts dormitory room, is Quentin or Shreve. And is this history after
all, they wonder for an instant, or a fiction of their own: " . . . people who perhaps had never existed at all anywhere. . . ."
    Eventually, under the force of their reconstruction of history, demonstrat-
ing the relationship in this narrative between form and function, the influence
of the act of narration on the narrators, Quentin and Shreve become not just
the re-creators but the original actors:

> So that now it was not two but four of them riding the two horses through the
> dark over the frozen December ruts of that Christmas Eve: four of them and
> then just two—Charles-Shreve and Quentin-Henry. . . . Four of them there, in
> that room in New Orleans in 1860, just as in a sense there were four of them here
> in this tomblike room in Massachusetts in 1910. (334, 336)

They continue with their story, Shreve driving the monologue/dialogue, until
"Shreve ceased again. It was just as well, since he had no listener. Then suddenly
he had no talker either, though possibly he was not aware of this.[12] Because now
neither of them were there. They were both in Carolina and the time was forty-
six years ago, and it was not even four now but compounded still further, since
now both of them were Henry Sutpen and both of them were [Charles] Bon,

compounded each of both yet either neither, smelling the very smoke which had blown and faded away forty-six years ago from the *bivouac fires burning in a pine grove.*" during the final year of the war (351). Their reconstruction, that is, gives them new life. (It will not be long before it takes life as well.)

Quentin and Shreve, incorporating those earlier voices of Mr. Compson and Miss Coldfield, become through their own process of narration the historical characters about whom they speak, whose lives and deaths they are working so feverishly to reconstruct. So at least they believe as they work, for such is the imaginative power of the process. All of the narrative tropes of *Absalom, Absalom!* are in the service, finally, of this reconstruction, whose goal is not so much the understanding of a man or of his region or times—as they are in *A la recherche du temps perdu*—but instead their re-creation: it is the process which matters more here than the result. And where Marcel is restored to life as the result of this process, Quentin will soon be denied it. It is not historical truth, after all, which he and his partner seek, but some truth much more personal and more difficult to define. They never do manage to define it. But we can judge their results nonetheless. The narrators' task as they practice it demands not just imagination, but also a considerable psychic strength and stability, those qualities which Quentin—as readers of *The Sound and the Fury* (1929) already recognize—most surely lacks.

The lives of Thomas Sutpen and of his children and grandchildren, with all their distortion and dislocation, play powerfully and terribly in Quentin's life. The process of reconstruction may appear to be an end in itself as practiced by Quentin and Shreve as we view them in *Absalom, Absalom!* And it may truly be so for Shreve, whom we never encounter again;[13] but its power over Quentin is much more immediate and terrible. Those who know him only from *The Sound and the Fury* are likely to assume that his suicide is the result of familial pulls visualized only in that novel; readers who see in *Absalom, Absalom!* a foreshadowing of the theme of incest—amplified here by the question of race and the hint of a mythic parallel[14]—and thus read this novel as a prelude to that one, are missing the point: the *dénouement* of Quentin Compson's life—both high point and turning point—is here in his role as narrator. These are the events—compounded, of course, by the knowledge of immediate familial relations which we receive in *The Sound and the Fury*—which lead to his death. If there is a positive conclusion to be drawn from them, we must wait for Simon's *The Flanders Road* if we expect to discover it.

CHAPTER 5

(Good Old Fashioned) Reliability and Its Modernist Face, (Potential) Unreliability: Dickens, Fowles, Gide, Ford, and Melville

*T*he first assumption that every reader of fiction makes is that the narrative center is to be trusted. This assumption is so strong that it need never be spoken. In this sense, Trollope was exactly right in his complaints about his contemporaries. As part of this tacit process, we identify automatically with a novel's protagonist regardless of gender—his or hers, or our own—and we assume that, unless proven otherwise, the world which revolves around that hero (from "protagonist" to "hero" is an easy, also unspoken step) is the real world. (Rarely do we pause to question the meaning or significance of "real.") It takes a powerful, sometimes shocking force to undermine that assumption and sever that bond. For the Victorians, this was the natural state of affairs, and narrative omniscience was its inevitable concomitant. That Trollope could criticize Thackeray and Dickens for insufficient omniscience is proof of the power of that assumption; it is another way of claiming that their fictions were unrealistic, the same reasoning later followed by F. R. Leavis. Those brief moments in Dickens when the narrative center is not to be trusted—no matter how accurately the scene is portrayed: the opium den sequence in *The Mystery of Edwin Drood* most notably—must have been especially disturbing to Trollope. It does not follow, however, that any hint of ambiguity should comparably disturb Leavis and Snow a century afterwards. It is not unreasonable to conclude, it seems to me, that the return which they advocated to the trustworthy old order of affairs was, in practice, an attempt to annul modernity: an understandable effort perhaps, given the uncertain nature of the post-war world in Britain, but not one to generate much conviction or sympathy among those who believe that the function of the novelist (as of the critic) is to reflect the world in which we live—and maybe thereby to make life more comprehensible and livable—rather than to ignore or deny or attempt to repeal it.

John Fowles's Daniel Martin

There is an extraordinary opening scene in an otherwise unsuccessful novel, John Fowles's *Daniel Martin,* of a world and of narrative forms in transition. (That the scene is agricultural would seem to link it even more concretely to Leavis, whose rural romanticism parallels that of his American contemporaries, the Southern Agrarians.) The setting is a farm in England on which the work is done with horses and by hand, using ancient implements. Men and boys have been harvesting crops in the field all morning long, and at noontime they pause for their ploughmen's lunch. The language which they speak seems some old dialect of English. To a boy resting in the field, it is a "language so local, so phonetically condensed and permissive of slur that it is inseparable in his mind, and will always remain so, from its peculiar landscapes" (4).[1] A sense of harmony, of timelessness, pervades all. This might be Shakespeare's England and these the fields which he left behind when he went off to London. Or it might be the England of Pope and Swift, the background to their more urbane literary landscapes, or the countryside of Wordsworth. (We are told, in passing, that this is Devon, but it might as easily be Lancashire, still one of the more traditional areas of England, or even the Lake District, so generalized does it seem.) Woolf's Orlando could gaze upon the scene and never guess what county or century he/she had happened upon. And then German planes fly overhead, almost out of sound, on their way to bomb London during the Battle of Britain.

Our shock of recognition is complete. But that shock is not accompanied by a sense of betrayal. For there is no single, identifiable narrative center to the scene—not the unnamed boy, not the all-knowing author (both of whom appear to pass through here), not the perceptions of any other participant or eyewitness: the details are simply present, on the page, open to our eyes and our ears, to be noted at the same moment by us and the characters, as if we were among them. So immediate is the scene that we experience it directly and not through intermediaries: there is no question of questioning its reliability. Our shock is that of the characters, no less but also no more. (On re-reading, we may well come to believe that the boy, "who is already literary" [5] and whom we can now identify as the title character, Daniel Martin, a novelist in his later years, provides the scene's sole point of view. It is impossible to do more than suspect this on first reading—and even that is unlikely. But the adult Daniel Martin is the first-person narrator of at least some of the scenes in this novel, and it is not impossible that he is also the writer/narrator of others, including this opening idyll.)[2] On first reading, however, we can know none of this; we note the dual worlds co-existing and pass quickly on into modernity. In modernity, however, unaware readers—those who have failed to note the new world in which all of us now live, or who, like Leavis and Snow, reject that world—may well feel betrayed. This is not a simple world in which to live, or to read. The unreliable narrator has become one of the surest signs of this new world.

André Gide's The Counterfeiters

In *The Counterfeiters* (1927), by André Gide, for example, the novelist Édouard provides a rare reliable voice among characters who counterfeit not only money but ideas and emotions as well. We are reassured about him from the start, however, because we know that he speaks with the authority of his creator: his comments on culture, on art, on writing novels, especially, appear to derive virtually verbatim from the notebooks of André Gide, such as those appended to the text of the novel. No spokesman could be more reliable, it would seem.[3] And then, quite literally in the last lines of his narrative, we discover that he too is vulnerable: not that he lies to us, or even that he knowingly counterfeits his feelings. But when he says in the very last line of this long account of the falsehoods of others, "I feel very curious to know Caloub" (the younger brother of his friend Bernard, 365), we suddenly realize that he too, whether he admits it or not, like several of the characters with whom he interacts and who, at times, similarly seem to serve as authorial voices in one form or another, may be a pederast. Not that Gide, who courageously acknowledged his own homosexuality to an unsympathetic society and age, would condemn such a quality. But he would condemn—and would expect us to condemn, or at least to judge—all those, homosexuals included, who refuse to admit to the truths of their characters. It is this failing—and not his sexuality—which makes Édouard suspect; and once the spokesman's reliability is questioned, it can never again be reconstituted: once a narrator is viewed as potentially unreliable, even in one, limited respect, then he/she is always potentially unreliable in all. There are no gradations of reliability when we are expected to respond to the facts of a story as told by a narrator or to his/her interpretation. In such a context, "potential" is not a relative judgment but an absolute.

Alerted, therefore, to look more closely at the respective journals of Gide and his putative spokesman, we discover greater gaps than appear on first reading. On 13 January 1921, for example, Gide wrote in the First Notebook of the Journal of *The Counterfeiters*, "This journal must become to some extent 'Édouard's notebook'" (385), and so it seems fitting that it is with "Édouard's Journal" that the novel concludes. "The poor novelist constructs his characters," Gide's Second Notebook comments;

> he controls them and makes them speak. The true novelist listens to them and watches them function; he eavesdrops on them even before he knows them. It is only according to what he hears them say that he begins to understand *who* they are. (410)

"Without exactly pretending to explain anything," Édouard writes in his journal, "I should not like to put forward any fact which was not accounted for by a sufficiency of motive. And for that reason I shall not make use of little Boris's suicide for my *Counterfeiters;* I have too much difficulty in understanding it. ... I accept reality coming as a proof in support of my thought, but not as preceding it. It displeases me to be surprised" (363). Édouard needs control, not the freedom of Gide, and his is not, clearly, the novel which his creator would write; indeed, Édouard never does complete his *Counterfeiters:* he is too involved with the affairs of his life and with playing novelist to be one. At one point, he shows a passage from his notebook to the boy on whom a planned character is based in order to influence his subsequent actions and as a test, for "in my novel it is precisely by a similar reading that I thought of giving the youngest of my heroes a warning. I wanted to know what George's reaction would be; I hoped it might instruct me ... even as to the value of what I had written" (335). What Édouard wants, it would seem, is authorial—and personal—control without the responsibility, not quite the same moral, "true" position as Gide's.

The distance between this novelist and this character as novelist is far greater than we have realized. Re-reading the narrative which we have just so confidently completed, with a different eye for Édouard's actions and a different ear for his proclamations, we discover that *The Counterfeiters* which we have before us is not *The Counterfeiters* which Édouard would write were he ever to complete his novel. The character whom we take at first for a reliable spokesman, in a daring reversal, provides the novelist with the most forceful illustration of his theme of pretense. (In suggesting that false appearance is a greater sin than the presumed "reality" of sin, Gide builds cunningly on Machiavelli's principle that appearance is more important than reality in affairs of governance.)

There are other apparent sources of information and attitudes in *The Counterfeiters* as well: the notebooks of the character Bernard, the book written by Passavant, even a series of letters. Most notable, however, is what appears to be the omniscient voice of André Gide himself, anticipating events ("We should have nothing to deplore of all that happened later if only Édouard's and Olivier's joy at meeting had been more demonstrative," 69); humorously (even self-reflexively) interrupting his own narrative ("Well, we must go on. All this that I have been saying is only to put a little air between the pages of this journal. Now that Bernard has got his breath back again, we will return to it. He dives once more into its pages," 105); attesting to his own narrative deficiencies ("I confess I don't like the word 'inexplicable' and use it only because I am momentarily at a loss," 199). This tendency culminates in the chapter entitled "The Author Reviews His Characters" (202–05). But there are limits to his omniscience; beyond his intrusions and his comments *qua* author, he seems increasingly to turn over his storytelling chores to Édouard and then to undercut him as well. It seems impossible not to conclude that Gide thus uses the various forms and strategies of omniscience—the elaborately constructed reliable spokesman, especially—as a means (one not yet named Modernist in his generation) to destroy both the technique of omniscience and the notions of a secure world which are fostered by omniscience. He is, in this challenging regard at least, a much more significant Modernist novelist than has usually been acknowledged. He reminds us in this regard of his English contemporary, Ford Madox Ford.

Ford Madox Ford's The Good Soldier

An even more dramatic, more ironic re-reading is forced on the reader of Ford's *The Good Soldier* (1914), whose narrator, John Dowell, begins by making an explicit appeal for our empathy: "This is the saddest story I have ever heard" (3), he prepares us for his tale.[4] Naturally, without question, we offer it to him. He is a man who clearly needs our understanding and approval, for he has received little of either, it would seem, from his family and friends. When we meet him—when he begins his narration, that is (for he quickly takes us into the past)—he has suffered a series of personal disasters: the death of his wife, the suicide of his best (and only) friend, the inappropriate re-marriage and moral breakdown of his friend's widow, the irretrievable break-up of the harmonious life which the four of them had lived, side by side, "for nine seasons of the [resort] town of Nauheim with an extreme intimacy." (3). Even worse, as if to prove the malevolence of the universe toward him, Dowell (who might well do better) now finds himself the guardian of his friend, Edward Ashuburnham's, ward, a mentally disturbed young woman whose presence is a constant reminder of all that he has lost. How could we not offer him our empathy?

But as Dowell goes on speaking, he suggests inadvertently that perhaps the foursome was not so idyllic after all: his thirteen-year marriage to Florence was never consummated, we learn, and she and Edward had for long been lovers; Leonora, Edward's wife, proves to be a self-involved shrew, undercutting his ancestral values and driving him to repudiate his most cherished beliefs (about the relationship of an English lord to his tenants, for instance); the mad girl, Nancy, has been driven mad by Ashuburnham's suicide, to which he may have been driven by the scheming of his wife and the refusal of his best friend to become involved. ("I guess he could see in my eyes that I didn't intend to hinder him. Why should I hinder him?" [256])

Dowell begins his narrative speaking in the past tense, convinced that all the sad events of his saddest story have already taken place and that only their telling remains to be completed. But he learns much that he had not even suspected when he began his story, and these discoveries color his narration, for his attitudes change with his knowledge: When he begins his memoir, he has no sense at all of Leonora's betrayal; the affection which he at first feels for her turns rather quickly to hatred. When he begins, he is unaware of Nancy's madness, for it is only in his last two chapters—episodes added as a kind of postscript after his original story has been told—that he is called to Ceylon to bring her home to Branshaw Teleragh, ancestral home of the Ashburnhams, which the wealthy American now owns and where he spends his days and nights watching over the mad girl. "'*Credo in unum Deum Omnipotentem*,'" she declares, words almost savage in their irony. "Those are the only reasonable words she uttered; those are the only words, it appears, that she ever will utter. I suppose that they are reasonable words; it must be extraordinarily reasonable for her, if she can say that she believes in an Omnipotent Deity. Well, there it is. I am very tired of it all" (234). Dowell, it would seem, does not much appreciate irony.

But he does call again on our empathy: "I don't know why I should always be selected to be serviceable. . . . So here I am very much where I started thirteen years ago. I am the attendant, not the husband, of a beautiful girl, who pays no attention to me" (235–36). Now, however, we are less likely to offer it, for we too have learned much during the course of his narrative. Why did he never consummate their marriage? we may ask. Florence's excuse of a bad heart hardly seems tenable in retrospect. We may even decide that Dowell is thus responsible to some degree for her affair with Edward (in which she was evidently the aggressor) and for its eventual consequences—the disruption in his marriage, her death, his suicide. We are not quite so sympathetic to Dowell at this point in his narration as we were when he began. We may even come to see him as the villain of the piece.[5]

"I am writing this, now, I should say, a full eighteen months after the words that end my last chapter" (233). Dowell is no longer the same narrator as at the start, and we are no longer the same, accepting audience. When he tells us now of the final moments before his friend's suicide ("Well, he was a sentimentalist," 241) and of his own failure to intervene, we are much more likely than earlier to be judgmental. And when he comments, in his final statement, that "I also am a sentimentalist" (256), without choking on his words, we are likely to gag on his behalf. How could we ever have offered him empathy? Compelled to re-read his narrative—if only to confirm that we could have been so wrong about him—we are likely to turn against him all those potentially ambiguous statements which he has made: is he merely a fool, too weak and unconcerned to look after his own interests and those of his presumed loved ones? This hardly seems adequate to explain our repugnance. Is he capable of loving others, as he insists that he does? If so, he has a rather lazy, self-centered way of doing so. Is he, perhaps, the prime mover of these events? Some re-readers will surely find that he is, his seeming passivity an active agent in the lives of others. But no one will be able to read his story a second time and to respond to him with either empathy or sympathy; for if we do not absolutely despise him, we surely dislike and disrespect him. He is not only not the reliable narrator that he has insisted he is; he is precisely the wrong person to be telling this story, not so much sad, as we can now see, as reprehensible. That is, he is precisely the right person if the novelist's intention is to use the conventional narrative tools designed to create confidence in the reader—none more guaranteed to work than the first-person narrator who tells of events which he has witnessed and from which he has suffered unjustly—to evoke instead a judgmental distance between the narrator and his audience. This narrative of Dowell's seems so changed on re-reading that it is difficult for us to imagine that it is the same novel.

The distance provided by Ford in *The Good Soldier* is perhaps the best example of that Modernist quality noted, with a certain trepidation, by Booth. While it does make demands on the reader, and it surely does heighten the potential for ambiguity, we recognize easily enough the high moral purpose of Ford's narrative technique: It is Dowell's unreliability which enables us to perceive the truth of the world which he has made for himself and which, if we but allowed him, he would make for us as well.

Not many critics or literary historians have placed the origins of Modernism prior to the First World War. Ford began *The Good Soldier* in December 1913, when few expected war to break out, and no one anticipated a universal war. He evidently did not need the experience of the war (which brilliantly informs his tetralogy, *Parade's End*, 1924–1928) to recognize the ambiguity which would come to encapsulate the Modernist worldview. For those who believe that irony is the most characteristic of the qualities of the Modernist novel, the Ford of *The Good Soldier* must qualify as one of the Modernist Masters.[6] And since that irony is demonstrably a function of the novel's rich and subtle point of view—manifested especially in a narrator for whom "unreliable" seems far too tame a description and from whom we aggressively may distance ourselves—we must acknowledge that this friend of Henry James, collaborator with Joseph Conrad, publisher of James Joyce (he may have provided the name *Work in Progress* for the early *Finnegans Wake*) shares with them the responsibility for that extraordinary development.

Reliability Beyond Narration: Melville and the Question of Confidence

If it is surprising to find Hawthorne mixing in moments of uncertainty in the midst of his more conventional omniscience, Melville's usage is more surprising still—and far more compelling. Near the end of *Billy Budd* (1891), for example—and near the end of his own long career—although he has been obtrusively omniscient throughout ("In this matter of writing, resolve as one may to keep to the main road, some bypaths have an enticement not readily to be withstood. I am going to err into such a bypath. If the reader will keep me company I shall be glad"), Melville turns coyly uncertain.[7] In the novella's key scene, the final interview between Captain Vere and the condemned Billy Budd, he rejects any suggestion of certainty: "Beyond the communication of the sentence what took place at this interview was never known" (358). He is willing to make a guess—"some conjectures may be ventured" (359)—but he appears to prefer uncertainty. We know, of course, that all he need do is walk a few steps further onto the deck, look down through the skylight into the captain's cabin and listen in on the conversation taking place there; he is capable, he has already made it clear, of seeing into the minds and hearts of all of his characters. But here, almost as if he were a fledgling Modernist novelist, he opts for ambiguity, or, at least, for an unusual state of understanding akin to ambiguity, the best that he can manage given the demands and tools of his time. We may not be convinced by this coyness of his, but we can understand easily enough why, in such a demanding circumstance as this, Melville would abjure the omniscience that otherwise came so naturally to him (as to his contemporaries) and choose instead uncertainty. What does the fatherly, condemning captain have to say to the almost Christ-like, condemned common seaman? Or, perhaps, what does he ask of him? Melville recognizes—beyond the limitations (of knowledge, of technique) imposed on the novel by his times—that ambiguity here is both more powerful than certainty and more realistic: precisely the recognition that lies at the heart of Modernist point of view. Even for the Victorians, there must have been moments when doubt seemed, somehow, appropriate and when point of view was the logical tool for effecting that state.

This is never so clear, I think, as in Melville's most under-appreciated work, *The Confidence Man: His Masquerade* (1857). Published six years after *Moby Dick* (itself misjudged for more than half a century) and five after *Pierre*, *The Confidence Man* received the sort of negative reviews in America that might have been expected.[8] (And if English reviewers appreciated the novel, it was largely because they read it as a satire of American mores.) It was the last major work of prose published during Melville's lifetime (*Billy Budd* being published posthumously), and while it enjoyed something of a revival during the heyday of the New Critics (who delighted in resurrecting works misread by their scholarly predecessors), no one, to my knowledge, has ever commented on just how revolutionary its handling of point of view is. For there is hardly a hint here of omniscience: no intrusive author or authorial commentary (except for an occasional passing remark, almost a reflex); no narrator standing in for the author or being supported by some other source of authority (no outside narrator at all, in fact); no secondary or even tertiary source—a manuscript, a letter, the later testimony of someone reliable, what have we—to confirm what we have been told. Every word of text, every image realized on the page, each seemingly picaresque adventure is described in an absolutely objective language—even when a tale is told directly by a character—avoiding all explicit authorial value judgments; described with a sense of immediacy which suggests that the action is taking place as we read about it, with no indication of a backward glance: a mix of circumstances rare, if not unique, in the days before *Dubliners* and Modernism.

The adventures of *The Confidence Man* revolve around a series of confidence men who ply their deceitful art on a Mississippi River steamboat, in the heart of an America spreading both westward and into the Industrial Revolution; it might easily serve as a commentary on the nation as a whole, as Melville obviously intended. (The English critics were certainly correct in this regard.) It is a bit difficult to decide just how many confidence men there are, though, since the line between perpetrator and victim, between representative, allegorical figures (perhaps even including the Devil) and the *picaro* is often rather fine. These figures include a deaf mute; a "grotesque negro cripple" called Black Guinea; a man in mourning named John Ringman; a well-dressed man claiming to represent the "world's charity" (56); John Truman, self-proclaimed industrialist, encouraging investment in his speculative enterprise; an herb doctor; an agent of the "Philosophical Intelligence Office" (P.I.O.), arguing for the essential goodness of humanity; and the "Cosmopolitan," Frank Goodman, the sum of them all, it seems, "'a catholic man; who, being such, ties himself to no narrow tailor or teacher, but federates, in heart as in costume, something of the various gallantries of men under various suns'" (159): he speaks for confidence on all levels, from the most pedestrian to the most lofty.[9] What each of these confidence men sells, then, is confidence: "'Confidence is the indispensable basis of all sorts of business transactions'" (155)—as of moral transactions. Should the novel, therefore, be called *The Confidence Men?* Its current title and subtitle, *His Masquerade,* do offer a hint.

Each of these manifestations of the confidence man is allowed to speak for himself. While the cautious reader may choose to read into his name (true man, good man, frank) as he wishes—to interpret it/them literally or ironically (the date of the action, after all, is April first)—we know nothing about him that he does not tell us. Is he, therefore, reliable, we wonder: of course, he is, he seems to respond, although we may not be quite certain whether this may mean merely that he can be relied upon to attempt to deceive us. But he is never a narrator or spokesman for the author—except, perhaps, ironically; while *The Confidence Man* is not in this sense a conventional narrative, the question of his reliability is clearly connected to the point of view, and we are compelled to consider his reliability as if he were a narrator or authorial spokesman. For Melville makes use of him in ways that remind us of those literal narrators, Gide's Édouard, Camus' Clamence and Ford's John Dowell.

Each episode of *The Confidence Man* is made up largely of dialogue (*cf.* the monologue of *The Fall*), thus obviating the need for authorial commentary. In addition, several of the passengers on board the aptly/ironically named *Fidèle* —including some of the guises of the confidence man—themselves tell tales related to their faith-saving (if not inevitably faithful) profession (recalling both *The Good Soldier* and *The Counterfeiters*, as well as *The Canterbury Tales*). These integrated interpolated tales are themselves either narrated directly, complete with quotation marks, or that narration is paraphrased, albeit objectively and not by an omniscient author. The only signs of a potential authorial presence are an occasional background note (the appearance of the first passenger aboard the *Fidèle* occurs "suddenly as Manco Capac at the lake Titicaca" [11])—suggesting a speaker who has himself seen the world; some of the chapter titles ("Story of the Unfortunate Man, from which may be gathered Whether or No he has been Justly so Entitled" [75]); and a rare remark which appears to be an authorial tic ("But as the good merchant could, perhaps, do better justice to the man than the story, we shall venture to tell it in other words than his, though not to any other effect" [74]—although here Melville may be intruding in order to tell us that he will not be intruding). On the whole, however, the novel is remarkably free of similar intrusions.

Both the novel's title and its rapid transition among scenes and confidence men indicate, it seems to me, that there is but one protagonist here and that these are some of his guises. The singular title and suggestive subtitle are thus to be relied upon—although raising the question of confidence seems a requisite part of the process. If all of this is true, then, it may also be true that the confidence man is the novel's sole point of view, for he is present in every scene and, arguably, the source of all the information received by the reader. He serves, in this formulation, as what James would soon come to call the central intelligence, the character around whom all the action of the story revolves and who serves as filter of all the story's facts—the descriptions of all of the characters, for instance, including his own guises; as well as the narrations (or, in some cases, receptions) of all of the interpolated tales. The central intelligence is the principal Jamesian alternative to Victorian omniscience. In Modernist terms, such a technique would be regarded as relatively conservative: a simple avoidance of omniscience; an objective presentation of the action as it develops around a protagonist; a technique that calls no attention to itself, as either radical or reactionary; more or less what a relatively conservative Modernist novelist—a Mann or Kazantzakis, for example—would do with point of view in most of his novels. The general effect would seem very familiar to many contemporary readers. Even an angry English critic would probably not categorize such a technique as "experimental." But in the context of Victorian America, it is radical indeed. (It is also, to be sure, well within the tradition of point of view in the novel, as it looks both backward—to *Tristram Shandy*, especially—and forward—to the Modernists.) There is no indication that any subsequent novelist ever built upon or even noted Melville's accomplishment in *The Confidence Man*. But it remains, in retrospect at least, one of the most extraordinary narrative acts in the age before Modernism.

Where point of view in *Billy Budd* tends to be so inconsistent as to deflect Melville's theme, in *The Confidence Man* he offers us a fascinating and potentially fruitful paradox: a point of view which is, in its own terms, thoroughly reliable, but with all the reliability of a source whose mission is inherently deceitful: although the deceit is designed to reveal the truths of human behavior. The paradox appears to turn the very concept of reliability on its head: this is betrayal for a moral purpose. (In the tradition of Juvenalian satire, the confidence man's masquerade compels his victims—as well as his audience—to confront themselves in full frontal vulnerability.) We can only imagine how Booth would respond. (Among his several, usually passing references to Melville in *The Rhetoric of Fiction*, none is to *The Confidence Man*.) While the novel's conclusion is open-ended and ambiguous—practices usually reserved for the Modernist novel—and while we may find its morality strange and even at times threatening—it ends with an old man, alone in the dark, accompanied by "the cosmopolitan [who] kindly led the old man away" (294), but where and to what end?—we do recognize the fine fit here between technique and theme. For all its ambiguity, there is nothing uncertain about Melville's vision or about the point of view through which it unfolds. And when he concludes that "Something further may follow of this Masquerade" (294), although we may not be quite certain whether to feel assured or warned, we understand that this ambiguous state is precisely his goal. Does Melville differ so greatly from his English Victorian contemporaries because he is an American, or because his serious, moral efforts were not appreciated in America? That question is unanswerable, but the need to raise it is itself, I suspect, revealing.

What is certain is that Melville perceived that the comfortable vision of life which (in retrospect) appears characteristic of the late nineteenth century did not always suit him and, despite the limited narrative tools available to him, endeavored to devise a point of view that would work to communicate his vision. I would not say that, in doing so, he anticipates the Modernists; I tend to be skeptical of the tendency to find forerunners everywhere.[10] What his example does illustrate, surely, is that the potential for ambiguity in life is not uniquely a modern phenomenon and that the Modernists were indeed working within a well-established, if not yet fully defined tradition. As a step away from omniscience and the world which it so ably defines, the issue of reliability—whether raised by a narrator or spokesman or confident confidence man—serves as a most effective transition.

CHAPTER 6

Narration within Narration
Social and Personal Histories

The Narrative Act in A la recherche du temps perdu

The customary reading of Proust's narrative in *A la recherche du temps perdu* is relatively straightforward: a middle-aged man, unexpectedly recalled to the memory of his past, begins consciously to search through it for meaning. His first-person narrative is essentially chronological, proceeding from adolescence to middle age through volume after volume of reminiscence, with but a single diversion: One of the first stories that he tells is set before his own birth and told in the third person; few actually name this an omniscient diversion, but that, in essence, is what it must be—how else could Marcel learn so intimately about events before his own birth? As I read point of view, this would be a flaw (call it a mere inconsistency, if you insist), but few of us are willing to label so magnificent an achievement as even slightly flawed. Can this problem be resolved, I wonder. It is also not uncommon for readers to identify Marcel with Marcel Proust, a natural response perhaps, but one likely to exacerbate the problem.

In critical histories of the Modernist novel—to the extent that they exist— *A la recherche du temps perdu* is typically considered under the rubric of time rather than of point of view. This fact is emphasized by the title provided for the brilliant, if imperfect, C. K. Scott Moncrieff/Frederick A. Blossom [Sidney Schiff] English translation: *Remembrance of Things Past,* rather than the more accurate *In Search of Lost Time.* Time, of course, is a powerful factor in Modernist fiction: think of the "Time Passes" section of Woolf's *To the Lighthouse* or the whole of *The Waves,* or of the "Circe" episode of *Ulysses* or the whole of *Finnegans Wake,* or of the "Prelude" to Mann's *Joseph and His Brothers,* or of Faulkner's *Absalom, Absalom!* But I am inclined to think of time as a function of point of view and not as an independent technique, and I read point of view in Proust in an unaccustomed way.

As I see it, there is no omniscient inconsistency in the novel, and the narrative is neither simply chronological nor in any sense straightforward. For Marcel's account is actually a narrative within a narrative, an artful autobiography modeled on one less skilled and barely acknowledged, an intermingling of times far more radical than a simple overlapping of present with past. And Marcel's life has little to do with that of Marcel Proust: only the former's account can be called autobiographical, but he, we assume, is not writing a novel. The physical act of narration itself becomes a part, even a determinant of what he writes, and what he writes may, after all, in a final narrative paradox, prove as much a fiction as an autobiography (a life's story, that is, defined by the principles of a novel, and the life itself determined by the same paradoxical needs). Even certainty in *A la recherche* may at times be ambiguous; this huge and rich novel is realistic in ways far beyond the usual. Not merely an account of French society of the so-called Belle Époque, nor even of that nation's grudging movement into modernity, it may serve as well as universal measure of the twentieth century in the West, of the Modernist Age: and all of this from a single insight into point of view with ramifications that probably even promethean Proust did not anticipate from the start.

Proust's insight, available only in retrospect, is initially revealed in the original plan for his novel: that he wrote the final chapter of his final volume, "The Past Recaptured," immediately after completing the opening chapter of his first volume, the exquisite "Overture," suggests a connection, a potential discovery of Marcel's, that Proust clearly had in mind from the start. But this is not likely to be uncovered fully on our first reading; a first-time reader of this four thousand-page narrative is hardly likely to appreciate the conception: He/she is as limited at this point as is the protagonist. We will surely be aware of Marcel's discovery of the inter-connection of life and art, but cannot yet appreciate its ramifications for both the art and the life. But a second-time reader should begin to note the possibilities—much as Marcel himself does. At the end of "The Past Recaptured," Marcel understands for the first time both the pattern and the meaning of his life. And we may now recognize with him that his act of telling his story is the key to that understanding. With all the riches to be sorted through in Marcel's narrative, however, with all the correspondences and connections to note, few critics have perceived the import for his story of his act of narration within the narrative.

We do get a hint of this, however, in an earlier volume, with Marcel's/our rather shocking discovery that the great painter Elstir, who serves for Marcel as a model of artistic integrity, is the same, hapless hanger-on known once as Biche, who, a generation earlier, witnessed the affair-turned-courtship of the *demi-mondaine* Odette by the celebrated Charles Swann. It is this affair, under the title "Swann in Love," which is narrated by Marcel, albeit in the third person, despite the fact that it took place years before his own birth. The discovery that Elstir/Biche was a witness to these events and might well have spoken of them to Marcel—looking back, we can note many details that he might have provided—reminds us that Marcel has other potential sources for his pre-natal knowledge of Swann. As his neighbors in the country, Marcel's own parents know something of Swann (of his character at least, even if they never do appreciate his position in society); as a close childhood friend of Swann's and Odette's daughter, Gilberte, Marcel himself has access to them (if only after the fact, this still offers potential insight into their actions); and Marcel's own life seems strangely to parallel Swann's. We are never told explicitly that Marcel is relying on these and/or other sources for his account of events which he has himself not witnessed, but his frequent use of the term "*réconstitution,*" "reconstruction," suggests strongly that this is precisely what he has been doing.

At the end of "The Past Recaptured," Marcel (who, of course, has a family name, but who never shares it with us—that he is not Marcel Proust is apparent in the fact that he is neither homosexual nor a Jew, although he is sympathetic to both)—comes to the realization, in middle age, that his youthful ambition to be an artist has not been forever lost. He had assumed that in opting to be a (minor) player in the glittering social scene of *fin de siècle* France, he had betrayed his artistic sensibilities. Through a brilliant conflation of metaphor and plot, Proust opens to Marcel the discovery that the two paths need not diverge into infinity, that society and art may indeed come together and that he may thus still become the artist who will memorialize the society which he knows so well and which, with the explosion of World War I, is now a memory only.

At the end of this vast novel, that is, Marcel will begin to write the novel of his life within his society, and we realize with a start that the novel which he will write is the novel which we have just read, whatever he may decide to name it. And that is why we must re-read *A la recherche du temps perdu,* with the understanding now that the Marcel who is writing the novel has already discovered the interplay of art and life that his own character "Marcel" will make in some forty years and four thousand pages. The narrative which flows from that discovery is informed throughout by this realization—even though the character Marcel has yet to reach it. It is a very different novel that we read with this understanding, and the role of the narrator Marcel (the character as narrator, that is) is not at all the simple act of recording that it may once have seemed. (His discovery, we now realize, is something more than serendipity.)

The two different Marcels who should occupy us in *A la recherche du temps perdu* are thus not Marcel Proust and his fictional creation, whether based on his own life or not, but rather Marcel the storyteller within the novel and his character Marcel, whose life story is an honest, yet also constructed account of his creator's life. The presumed autobiography turns inevitably—for Marcel is above all an artist, and he has an agenda of his own—into a fiction: it is his needs, not Proust's, that are served in his story, his failures that can be turned to success in his art. It is always possible, to be sure, that Marcel's obsessive relationship with Albertine Simonet is derived in part from some event (or series of events) in Marcel Proust's life; but the more important parallel, obviously, is to Swann's courtship of Odette.

I would suggest, however, that the parallel is not quite what we have typically assumed it to be: the cycle of jealousy-possessiveness-obsession-loss that characterizes Marcel's relations with his "captive" Albertine is not a heightened replay of the earlier story of Swann and Odette; it is yet another source for Marcel's reconstruction. The story of Swann and Odette, that is—an affair that the narrator cannot know at first hand—is based in some part on events which he knows all too well: the story of himself and Albertine. Marcel's narrative, I suspect, is in part an effort to come to terms with this terrible failure in his own life. How natural it is, then, for him to tell the tale of "Swann in Love" near the beginning of his own life story, as preparation for the greatest drama and most profound mystery of his life, as a potential step toward an understanding not just of an older friend's misadventure but of his own.[1]

As fiction, Marcel's search does have its models, moreover. The most notable of these is the autobiography of Mme. de Villeparisis, the elderly friend of his grandmother, who has been exiled, as it were, from polite society because of her own youthful indiscretions. Her writing about them presumably serves for her as vindication and for society as reaffirmation. We never do get to read her memoirs, but Marcel indicates several times that he has. Since we know that he has done so before he sets out to write his account, it is not unreasonable to conclude that he has made some use—positive and/or negative—of her example.[2]

There are further implications for the narrative when we identify Marcel as its creator. The narrator who offers freely his comments on life, love and social mores is thus not "Proust's narrator," as he is typically called, but rather Marcel's: it is his voice, his values, that are heralded here. And so not only is there no omniscience in this novel, as such comments might incline us to believe (or if there is, it is not Proust's omniscience but Marcel's), but the distance between Proust and his several creations is far greater than we have realized. Proust does not turn this distance into irony, as Joyce does with Stephen Dedalus, but it nonetheless allows the reader as well to step apart from Marcel when he "imprisons" and persecutes Albertine, and so also to appreciate the deliciousness of the irony when he learns that she may have been unfaithful to him after all (and with a woman), but with her accidental death can never uncover the truth. We like this aspect of Marcel's story no more than he likes

The Rhetoric of Modernist Fiction

to recall it, but the distance allows us both to bear it without rejecting him and to respect him (the middle-aged narrator, that is) for his willingness to recount this sad tale with what seems a certain basic honesty. In *A la recherche du temps perdu*, almost uniquely among novels (I can think only of *Tristram Shandy* and *Finnegans Wake* as possible parallels), not only is the novelist distanced from his own creation, but that character-as-narrator is also distanced from his.)

Finally, the recognition of Marcel's (self-)recognition and (narrative) role makes possible another surprising discovery about the narrative itself. For the story that Marcel will tell—now that he has made his pivotal discovery toward the end of "The Past Recaptured"—will probably come to be called, self-reflexively, *A la recherche du temps perdu*. Having made the discovery that he can yet turn his life into art, he is committed to do so. (His position is analogous to that of Stephen Dedalus at the end of *Ulysses*, who has at last discovered his subject in Bloom and who now must set out to write his story, very likely to be called *Ulysses*.) There is none of the narrative gamesmanship here that we have learned to associate with such self-reflexive fictions as Borge's "Pierre Menard, Author of the *Quixote*," or Italo Calvino's *Once on a Winter's Night a Traveler*, or John Barth's *Lost in the Funhouse*. Naming Proust's novel (or Joyce's) "self-reflexive" does not in itself provide new understanding of the novel. But it does remind us that continuity in the modern novel is greater than some may have realized, and it enables us to note that the self-reflexive—or simply the reflexive, or metafictional, as it has also been named—is also a function of point of view.

My own earliest lesson in point of view took place outside the schoolroom, when I was still in grade school, on a day when I stayed home with some childhood illness and listened, will-I, nill-I, to my mother's unavoidable radio programs. Was it Don McNeil and the early morning Breakfast Club, or Art Linkletter later in the day? One of my mother's favorites played a game with the audience in which several participants were chosen and all but the first sent off to separate rooms. The first was then told a story which he/she was asked to repeat to the second participant, who would then tell it to the third, and so on. Only the final narrator would return to the microphone to share the story with the audience. Invariably, that story had little in common with the original narrative. The studio audience always loved the alterations, and so, at home, I must admit, did I. In those days, however, the only serious conclusion that I could draw from this entertainment was that oral testimony was not always to be trusted. Perhaps that is why I decided about this time to become a lawyer. Today, well out of law school and the law, I recognize in the experience a far more apt lesson: narration within and enriched by narration is exponentially more problematic than simple tale-telling and thus may prove far more promising as a narrative technique: means to suggest not merely ambiguity but the richness of modern life as well. The Modernist novelists certainly understood this.

Every narrative source outside the author brings with him/her/it an almost infinite potential for deviation from certainty. It is for this reason that the Victorians generally avoided human narrators: God—the omniscient author—was so much more reliable, so much less likely to raise hints of uncertainty. Even the best intentioned and most conscientious character as narrator—think of Nelly Dean in *Wuthering Heights*—will inevitably raise questions of confidence in the mind of the reader, even of the most passive Victorian reader. In a Modernist novel, with its less clearly defined, more ambiguous reality, a simple narrator within the novel—even one as reliable as Marlow—is bound to shake the reader's certainty at times. It is no accident that Conrad created Marlow as the first conscious step toward developing a distinctly Modernist point of view. Then, too, as Conrad demonstrated in *Chance*, progressing geometrically, there may be narrators within narrators.

On the simplest level, like that of the morning radio game, a narrator who recounts another's story is bound to get some facts wrong (or at least different). Everyone who has ever told a story or a joke and then heard it repeated by someone else—whether immediately or at a distance in time—has noted the changes (and probably resented them). The second teller may not have heard the tale perfectly, may have decided to improve it, may merely alter the emphasis or the wording: No one can tell a tale well without imposing his or her own personality upon it. And that change will inevitably change the tale itself. How much more dramatic those changes may be when a narrator has a private agenda, or even when the reader suspects that he or she may have one. Once shattered—by changes in the narrator or the narrative technique or in the world—certainty can never be established anew.

Patrick Chamoiseau, *Oiseau de Cham* and Texaco

In Patrick Chamoiseau's *Texaco* (1992), a man has told the story of his life to his daughter, who after some time writes it down in a notebook and, years afterward, re-tells his tale in more or less her own words. She seems, in fact, to tell the tale at least three times, first to a wise old man named Papa Totone, then to an unnamed urban planner, then again to a writer (who also corresponds with the planner).[3] On each oral occasion, she adds to her father's story the story of her own life. (A literary friend of hers, Haitian by birth and experience, seems also to have heard or read or commented upon or edited at least parts of her written tale. The epigraph which opens the first episode of *Texaco* derives from him: "Ti-Cirique's Epistle to the Shamefaced Word Scratcher" [9], it is titled.)[4] Her narrative, then, while seemingly straightforward, is inevitably touched by these other listeners, readers and potential voices. It is even possible that the version which we are reading in *Texaco* is already being retold here by the writer within the narrative, whom the speaker refers to periodically by what seems a variant of his name, Oiseau de Cham. This is also the name used by the author's persona in an earlier novel by Patrick Chamoiseau, *Solibo Magnificent* (1988).[5]

In *Texaco*, too, he calls himself "Word Scratcher"; the speaker he names "The Source" or "my Source." He attributes to himself some of the qualities which we find in Chaucer's persona, especially his uncertainty about his art—his ability to represent adequately this story which he has been granted. Is the text's final section, the seeming afterword entitled "Resurrection (not in Easter's splendor but in the shameful anxiety of the Word Scratcher who tries to write life)" (383), the product of Patrick Chamoiseau or of his *persona*? If the former, *Texaco* may be a work of oral history only—recalling Steven Spielberg's Shoah Project and the modern disciplines of some American universities—and not of fiction. But if the "I" of "Resurrection" is the persona—so that this section is part of the novel rather than the author's Afterword—then everything here is a fiction, even if rooted originally in some sort of historical reality.

Was there, in Martinican history, a Marie-Sophie Laborieux (by whatever name) who spoke to Patrick Chamoiseau? Is there an urban quarter called Texaco of which she was the founder and protector? Is there a Schoelcher Library in Fort-de-France, Martinique, in which the Notebooks of Marie-Sophie Laborieux and the correspondence between Word Scratcher and Urban Planner (by whatever names) are deposited? This last would be easy enough to determine, the earlier questions not very much more difficult. But these are all issues of background and not of narrative technique. Their answers are relevant, surely, to our understanding of Chamoiseau as a novelist, but they are not relevant to his novel per se. As the editor of a scholarly journal, with its interest in historical and biographical background and in archival evidence, I would be delighted to publish an article on Chamoiseau's sources. But as a reader and critic of the novel, I need know none of this. And I am confident that this is a novel and not an oral history if only because Chamoiseau induces me to ask such questions: as such, whatever their actual provenance, they become an essential part of the fiction, whose purpose—whose vision of the world and narrative technique— is advanced by our asking. For the reader must take an active role in this tale. Perhaps when I am next in Martinique, I will spend a day in Fort-de-France (which has some fine French-Creole restaurants) and look up the Schoelcher Library, Chamoiseau and Marie-Sophie. To appreciate the novel's accomplishment, however, I need know only this text and the vital, evocative, disturbing yet affirmative world which it creates—as well as the point of view which makes that world viable. The reality of the novel is not in its (potential) sources but in its various voices, of narrators functioning knowingly as narrators, inspiring the creativity of their audiences and perhaps being affected by them: of narrations within narrations.

On the primary level, *Texaco* is a history of the author's native Martinique, from the days of slavery to its contemporary development, even a certain prosperity, as a *département* of France. Highlighted historical events are the abolition of slavery in 1848, the destruction of the city of Saint-Pierre by volcanic eruption (with some thirty thousand deaths) in 1902, the establishment of a Vichy government in 1939, the election of the poet Aimé Césaire as Communist mayor of Fort-de-France in 1945, the achievement of departmental status in 1946, the visit of Charles de Gaulle in 1964. Juxtaposed against these events are others rooted in more local history, in particular those related to the quarter of Texaco, founded and nurtured by the novel's principal narrator, Marie-Sophie Laborieux. While typically indirect and requiring at times some knowledge of modern Martinique, the historical theme—amplified frequently by local socio-political considerations (related largely to the survival of Texaco as a community)—provides a major part of the narrative's surface. Balanced against this is the life of the narrator, seen (heard) from childhood to old age, beginning with the life of her father from the time of slavery. Aside from what we are told (rather, what our surrogate audience within the narrative is told) there is little dramatized character development.

Book I, "Around Saint-Pierre," is the story of the narrator's long-dead father, Esternome, as he told it, years earlier, to his daughter, who seems to have been (by her own account) alternately attentive and uninterested. She rarely raises the question of her own reliability, but it remains, unspoken, if only for minor details; she certainly feels no ambiguity about her father's character or about the value of his life. There is no doubt that this story of a former slave who endeavored to conquer the capital city and failed is intended to be representative. It is through him that we trace the early modern history of Martinique. Esternome is also the source of wise social and political advice to his daughter—advice which she never questions and does not expect her listener to: about the relationship of race to economic and political power, in particular; about City as the seat of all possibility. Chamoiseau's epilogue suggests that the story originated with an old woman whom he met in the district on the edge of Fort-de-France known as Texaco (from its location on the site of the tank farm of the oil company of that name): "my Source: an old câpresse woman, very tall, very thin, with a grave, solemn visage and still eyes. I had never felt such profound authority emanate from anyone" (387). The Author's Acknowledgements at the end of the volume indicate that at least some of the characters' names have been altered from their originals—assuming, of course, that this too is not part of his fiction.

Chamoiseau is technically a French novelist—his citizenship is French, since Martinique is considered to be part of mainland France; his novel has won the French Prix Goncourt; he is widely ranked in France among the leading French novelists of his generation—but it is evident that his French novelistic tradition is different from that of, say, Claude Simon. Not that he is uninfluenced by Proust and his narrative innovations, or even by Simon and his; but the narrative tradition embodied in *Texaco* includes as well the idiosyncratic local storytelling tradition. The resulting union of indigenous American and borrowed European sources recalls that of the so-called Boom in Latin American fiction of the 1970s and 1980s (sometimes conflated, a bit too easily, as Magic Realism).[6] One major difference, however, is that Chamoiseau is fluent in Creole, where virtually none of the novelists of the Boom knew any of the Indian languages whose unique way of viewing reality is a primary ingredient of Magic Realism and of the Boom. Where they are thus at a certain remove from both the local and the European and North American sources of their art, Chamoiseau seems immersed in both: attuned not only to the French but to his native idiom as well and committed to maintaining its oral tradition—"oraliture," he calls it (389). One of Chamoiseau's primary concerns is that the oral tradition of his island is now dying out. Marie-Sophie herself is proud of her ability to speak French as well as Creole, as of her (rather limited) knowledge of French literature (Rabelais and Montaigne among her favorites).[7]

The conflict between these two cultures, one of them literary and at least partly borrowed, the other oral and indigenous, is at the core of her narrative. She feels it strongly, and so does her listener: The relationship between the novelist-as-character and his native source, only occasionally articulated, provides much of the narrative tension in *Texaco*. In order to compose Marie-Sophie's story—to provide its structure, to order its language, to undertake and make use of his oral research—Chamoiseau/Oiseau de Cham (the novelist as character, that is) is compelled to reach out to the Caribbean island's oral tradition; yet he is at the same time constantly falling back on the learned French literary tradition and its formal and scholarly tropes. Is this an accurate reflection of Patrick Chamoiseau's position vis-à-vis Martinican culture, or is it another fictional construct, an aspect of his narrative strategy? It can, of course, be both.[8]

✳

From its start, the narrative threatens to break its bounds, as the (as yet) unidentified speaker begins to explore the tangents raised by her strange opening image of sharks visiting Texaco. But she quickly draws back—"let's not lose the thread here—let's go back to the story stitch by stitch, and if possible one stitch before the other" (11)—and so she re-introduces the opening scene as it was viewed by various eyewitnesses. (On re-reading, however, we may conclude that this is Chamoiseau's re-ordering. He has not yet been introduced, but neither, for that matter, has Marie-Sophie, nor her father.) Yet we know that if she allowed herself to (or if he allowed her), she could tell us tales (off

Narration within Narration 87

the subject) that would delight us, about the courtship of the parents of one of her witnesses, for instance. "[B]ut a detour would be risky" (14).

From the start, then, we are advised that narration itself is a central theme of this narrative. In an oral culture, especially one whose predominant concern is its own survival, point of view may serve as a metaphor for life:

> In other words, with her in our Quarter of Texaco, a life without witnesses, like life downtown, was a difficult wish. All was known of all. Miseries shouldered miseries. Commiseration intervened to fight despair and no one lived in the anxiety of extreme loneliness. (19)

Many of Marie-Sophie's stories, which seem almost like interpolated tales unrelated to the main action of her (and her father's) life, derive from a common popular source—"a diarrhea of gossip . . . how people like to talk" (283). No lives in such an oral culture are lived unwitnessed—unattested to—and the narrator is free (commissioned by the culture, as it were) to tell the stories of others in her own words. Conscious of her sources and of her audience, viewing herself as a Creole communal Scheherezade—

> —Little fellow, permit me to tell you Texaco's story [. . .] That's probably how, Oiseau de Cham, I began to tell him [the City Planner] the story of our Quarter and of our conquest of City, to speak in the name of us all, pleading our cause, telling my life (27)

—she knows well the inherent dangers for the storyteller of telling stories of deeds which she has not herself witnessed ("I've heard the story so often that I sometimes doubt my own absence when I start telling it," 22) and the persistent fear of proving unreliable ("I know only too well that my memory no longer attends to certain details. . . . And if it didn't happen like that, that doesn't matter" (25, 27).

From about 1823 to 1902, Marie-Sophie tells the story of her father, Esternome, as she remembers his narrating it to her, or else, perhaps, as she reconstructs it. She speaks at times in his voice—without quotation marks (neither two sets nor one)—with herself as his audience. ("Allow me not to go into details about the dungeon, Marie-Sophie, because you see those things are not to be described. Lest we ease the burden of those who built them," 36.) She understands that he, too, as narrator, may have had an occasional tendency to exaggerate: "I suspect my Esternome rebuilt his memories a bit so as to oppose his stories' need for contraband" (54). She also understands that there are limits to what a father may wish to share with his daughter; thus, as to the first time that her parents make love, "that was altogether another story. Alas, I never learned it" (66). Less personally, there are other details that the old oral historian would not share with his daughter: "The mountain that razed Saint-Pierre.

That, my Esternome did not want to describe. He covered it with the same stubborn silence he had kept his whole life concerning the old days in chains" (149), thereby explaining why his account begins with his personal progress toward emancipation. Even when she speaks of her own life, in Book II, Marie-Sophie frequently reminds her listener of her father's earlier narration. His true audience, she senses, was not only his dead wife, Idoménée, "but rather himself, frantic that his life should end in muddy waters" (169). We may intuit a similar need in his daughter. It is not only educated Europeans and North Americans who may feel compelled to justify their lives by telling of them.

Proud of her (incomplete, we assume) mastery of French, she is capable at times (as when speaking of France, the "goodly mother" of Martinique) of a heightened diction. She is also capable of direct, pungent, almost poetic prose: Speaking of the death of her African maternal grandmother, whom she never knew, Marie-Sophie writes, "She was quickly buried. Even wrapped in its strange cloth, the little body thwarted fervor: it wasn't from here, never had been, it came from a great rumor still unknown to us and it was carried like a rock broken off from the moon following a crime" (117–18).

From the grave of that old African woman grows a tree "not from here" (118), an African tree. We think inevitably of Magic Realism, somehow at work in Martinique, a generation after the great period of Latin American narrative play with verisimilitude.[9] There is said to be a similar tree growing from the remains of Saint-Pierre, her father's beloved City. But Marie-Sophie undercuts the possibility that she has raised:

> I've never gone there to see it myself, because you know, Chamoiseau, these stories about trees don't interest me. If I tell you this it's because you insist ... if these things are to be written, I would have noted different glories than those you're scribbling. (118)

She understands, though, that he will not only pick and choose among her tales but that he will re-write her words in his book. But what kind of book does she expect him to write—a novel, history, biography or sociological text?

They need not be so very different. As the French term *histoire* indicates, such a narrative may contain at least a dual component. Esternome has taught his daughter about their interplay:

> Oh Sophie, darlin', you say "History" but that means nothing. So many lives, so many destinies, so many tracks go into the making of our unique path. You dare say History, but I say histories, *stories*. The one you take for the master stem of our manioc is but one stem among many others. (88)

Marie-Sophie is, almost literally, a born storyteller, her father's true daughter. Native to her island's rich oral tradition, she nonetheless bridges the gap, in her notebooks, to written narrative. The next step in the progression, presumably, is the work of Chamoiseau—the novelist as character—perhaps even in *Texaco* itself, assuming that this novel is the work which he will produce from her narratives.[10] Is this a leap to be applauded or decried? While neither narrator raises the question directly, the reader may perhaps sense the novelist's own preference for the oral tradition, even as he is by profession committed to the written language. (There is much the same sense of a preference for the Creole in the contest between the native tongue and the French.) But the novelist remains conflicted: "writing is to be fought," Word-Scratcher writes to The Source; "in it the inexpressible becomes indecency" (202). But at the same time, Marie-Sophie adds, in great books "writing becomes the sorcerer of the world" (216).[11] If there is a resolution, it would seem to be in a new form of writing offered by Marie-Sophie:

> Oiseau de Cham, is there such a thing as writing informed by the word, and by the silences, and which remains a living thing, moving in a circle, and wandering all the time, ceaselessly irrigating with life the things written before, and which reinvents the circle each time like a spiral which at any moment is in the future, ahead, each loop modifying the other, nonstop, without losing a unity difficult to put into words? (322)

So The Source questions her writer, the novelist/biographer of her own words. Telling her father's story along with her own, with his narrative and its sources within hers, with her many sources and audiences (and potential audiences), some of whom may in their own turn become narrators, this old wise woman with her finely tuned ear and richly turned tongue, with no suspicion that in the world outside Martinique there is a phenomenon named Modernism and a concept called point of view, produces/makes possible a novel (does she know even that term?) which builds on some of the central narrative techniques of Modernism and advances them into a new, perhaps post-Modern world. Marie-Sophie and Chamoiseau succeed in *Texaco* where Conrad failed honorably in *Chance*: creating, in their narratives within narratives within narratives, a viable, coherent (if at times still ambiguous), convincing world and worldview.

The Rhetoric of Modernist Fiction

CHAPTER 7

Narrative Invention:
Critics Inventing Narrators

*I*n 1979, I was invited to lecture on modern British fiction at several Scottish universities. My title, designed, naturally, to be provocative, played on that of one of the most influential works of recent English novel criticism, F. R. Leavis' *The Great Tradition:* I labeled my talk, "The Ingrate Tradition: An American Looks at the Modern British Novel." More provocative by far than my title, however—if only for this audience—was the talk's major premise: that the three most important and influential British novelists of the twentieth century were all outsiders, James Joyce, Samuel Beckett and Virginia Woolf. My selection of Joyce surprised no one, I suspect, although in 1979 the only work of substance being done on Joyce in the British Isles was being done either by foreigners (Australians and Americans especially) or outside the university; my listeners were bothered, though, by the thought that it was the Irishman Joyce who had made the most forceful and effective use of our (more or less) joint language, a suspicion which they had evidently held for some time and which I merely helped to confirm for them. My choice of Beckett was something of a surprise, since most of these professors and graduate students of English had consigned Beckett to French departments and assumed that they needn't be concerned about him; I trust that I shook at least a few of them out of that complacency, since Beckett, like Joyce before him, regardless of the language in which he was writing, clearly had developed within the joint, if also separate, British and Irish novelistic traditions.

The most controversial aspect of that lecture by far, however, was my insistence on including Woolf in that rather select number. Since she was the sole one among them actually to be English, since she appears to have come out of and to have helped form the English literary establishment, it was my turn to be surprised by the intensity with which many in my audiences rejected my selection of Woolf. I will never forget the comment made to me after my talk in Edinburgh by three women graduate students: "They don't teach Woolf here, but we want you to know that we read her," surely the most damning comment I have ever heard about academic canonical practices. Woolf is, without doubt, the most important writer for women who are interested in writing; she is also among the very few greatest novelists in the great Modernist age of the novel. And today, some two and a half decades afterwards, she is at last being taught and written about throughout Great Britain, albeit still somewhat grudgingly at times, I gather. This would seem proof that virtue wins out, or at least that the power of a hostile critical establishment to prevent the reading and discussion of an individual author is limited (particularly when so many critics from a sister establishment—in this case, the American—insist on discussing that author).

The irony of my little tale is that today it is Woolf's own admirers, both American and English, who are most actively—if unintentionally—limiting her import and denying her most basic intentions. They are doing so, moreover, in the same way that certain Joycean critics have been acting unwittingly to delimit Joyce: by inventing a narrator where none is present. As best as I can understand it—since virtually no one seems concerned to justify the usage—this is an unthought-through solution to a problem of narrative which creates, in its own turn, a far greater problem: one which would convert two of the most original of the Modernist novelists into the very Victorians whom they had worked so hard to repudiate. The presumed "narrators" whom critics have invented to resolve potential problems in both Woolf's and Joyce's fictions, if allowed to continue operations, threaten to distort our understanding of some of the major works of art by some of the most important artists of our century. The problem is relatively straightforward in Joyce, somewhat more complex in Woolf—although the results are identical.

The Presumed "Narrator" in Joyce's "Telemachus"

Virtually every critic who has written about *Ulysses* has spoken—sometimes in awe, sometimes in bewilderment—about the inventive and varied narrative strategies employed by Joyce in the eighteen episodes of the novel. For many readers, these strategies provide the initial and, frequently, the most difficult hurdle which they must cross on their way through this now famed but once notorious masterwork. For some, the term "stream of consciousness" encapsulates everything that we need to know about point of view in *Ulysses;* of the many misuses of that term (and it is more often misused than applied appropriately), its association with *Ulysses* is likely the most egregious. For where Joyce surely perfects the technique in *Ulysses*—providing a model for all novelists to follow—it is by no means the only, or even necessarily the dominant point of view which he employs. Nor are the so-called "styles" of the separate chapters, listed for us in the novelist's own charts, adequate to explain

Joyce's actual practice. There are times when those techniques are so straight-forward—and no less revolutionary for being straightforward—that fanciful titles for them are both unnecessary and potentially destructive. Speaking of a "narrator" where there patently is none is one potent example. We see this especially clearly in "Telemachus," the novel's opening chapter.

The opening words of "Telemachus" are by now known to many who have themselves never even opened the novel: "Stately, plump Buck Mulligan came from the stairhead" (1: 1).[1] Written in the third person and the past tense, they have induced many critics of the novel to conclude that they are spoken by a narrator. (To some, the step from "third-person narration"—itself a useless term in describing narrative function—to "narrator" can be made without transition or thought.) Yet no one has ever attempted to identify this narrator. There are other chapters in *Ulysses* in which narrators demonstrably operate: Stephen Dedalus himself sometimes functions as a narrator (in the "Aeolus" episode, for instance, when he tells the notoriously ineffectual Parable of the Plums, as well as in the "Scylla and Charybdis" chapter, when he tries desper-ately to convince his listeners of the cleverness of his Shakespeare theory). The most notable narrator in the novel is, of course, the exceptionally clever and malicious unnamed fellow—we later discover that both Leopold and Molly Bloom know something about him—who tells us all of the happenings in "Cyclops." So why does no one even attempt to identify the presumed narra-tor of "Telemachus"? Why has no one—at least to my notice—even asked this question?

The answer, as I see it, is simple: There is no narrator to identify. If a narra-tor must be an individual and a narration a tale told to an audience, then it is obvious that there is neither tale, nor audience, nor narrator in "Telemachus"; the events are presented to us directly, immediately, as they occur; the fact that they are presented in the third person and past tense is the only proof that any-one has ever adduced for the existence of a narrator here. (Indeed, "adduced" is far too strong a term: "assumed" would be more accurate.) Nor is this an assumption without implications. For if we invent a narrator when there patently is none, we are not simply denying the term "narrator" has a literal meaning; we are inserting an intermediary between the events and the reader; we are saying, in effect, that the author himself is telling us this tale, that he is, in other words, acting omnisciently. Now, no one would dare to call Joyce an omniscient author: it is obvious to everyone that the Modernist revolution which Joyce led in the novel was directed primarily against the operations of the omniscient author in a closed universe. To call Joyce omniscient would be to deny the very heart of his work. But the effect of the invented narrator is essentially the same: it is to call Joyce omniscient. (Nor does it help to speak of an "implied narrator": Why would a novelist such as Joyce need to imply a narrator when he can easily create one? Rather, we might speak of an "inferred narrator," a creation of the critic not content with the novelist's creation.)

This is not only foolish but absolutely unnecessary, for the point of view of "Telemachus" is readily apparent to anyone willing to read it: and not even to read beneath the surface; the evidence is on the page—on the first page, repeatedly—for those willing to note it. When Buck Mulligan climbs the stairs to the roof of the tower which he shares with Stephen Dedalus and turns his morning shave into a mock Catholic Mass, he is initially alone—but not unnoticed. As he himself notices almost immediately (on the eleventh line of the novel), he has an audience. "Then, catching sight of Stephen Dedalus," he turns up his performance. Stephen, climbing the stairs, may well have seen from below his towermate's opening gestures, has almost certainly heard his profane song, and has probably witnessed earlier performances. There can be no doubt that he is present and serves as the point of view for everything else that occurs here: Joyce makes it explicit: Buck Mulligan "skipped off the gunrest and looked gravely at his watcher," and then, in the event that we might somehow have missed the clue, Joyce repeats it six lines further on: "Stephen Dedalus . . . watching him still."

Recognizing that Stephen has been the point of view from the start of "Telemachus," we can understand that those opening words, "Stately, plump," are not some simple, objective description; seen from Stephen's point of view—our recognizing, that is, that they are his words—they are filled with attitude: how incongruous they are together, "plump" aggressively undermining "Stately." The tone is clearly ironic, and it derives not from James Joyce, not from some objective, tone-deaf narrator, but from the character who will react similarly to young doctor Mulligan every time they meet during the course of this day, his towermate. There is not a single image or word or thought or memory in "Telemachus" that could not be derived from Stephen. It is through his sense perceptions ("Buck Mulligan frowned at the lather on his razorblade" [4: 64]), his memory ("Silently, in a dream [his mother] had come to him after her death" [5: 102–03]), his consciousness ("The ring of bay and skyline held a dull green mass of liquid. A bowl of white china had stood beside her deathbed holding the green sluggish bile which she had torn up from her rotting liver by fits of groaning vomiting" [5: 107–10]) that we learn of these events. The invented narrator would lessen or even eliminate Stephen's involvement in these events and, similarly, would lessen or eliminate our involvement with him and, through him, with these events. The effect would be no different if we were to call him not a narrator but the omniscient author.

The implications of this reading of point of view are significant not just for "Telemachus," its opening chapter, but for *Ulysses* as a whole. For it puts us on notice from its opening words that this is a new world which we are observing and that we are observing it in a dramatically new way. The prevailing critical theory that *Ulysses* begins as a more or less conventional narrative and only about halfway through turns revolutionary—a theory dependent upon the invented narrator—collapses when he is removed, and we are able to recognize how logical, how inevitable, yet how extraordinary Joyce's point of view is from the start: how prototypically Modernist it is. The disrespect toward Modernism which has been manifested in recent years by various post-Modernist critics and theoreticians is dependent upon just such misreadimgs as this one. Buck Mulligan's "watcher" puts us on notice—from the very first page of Modernism's very best and most influential novel—that this is no aberration in the history of narrative; that there are no needlessly, foolishly "heroic" gestures at the heart of this enterprise; that point of view in the Modernist novel is practical, realistic and very much within the tradition: no less revolutionary for all that, but revolutionary in essentially the same ways that the novel has traditionally developed.

The Would-Be Narrator in Woolf's The Waves

Woolf and Joyce are forever linked in both literary history and the popular imagination, yet no one would ever mistake her work for his. In sensibility, in language, in characterization, social setting and plot, in particular in their handling of point of view, their work could hardly be more distinct. Yet their goals are similar enough to warrant their union. Each recognizes the obvious truth that their world has changed irremediably, and each accepts the literary truism that a new age demands a new approach in the novel; nowhere is this more evident than in point of view. Joyce has little to say specifically about the subject, however; his critical comments tend to be reserved for the work of earlier writers. (We must never confuse Stephen Dedalus' theorizing for Joyce's: a simple matter of narrative distance.[2])

And so it was left for Woolf, the wisest and most experienced critic among the Modernist novelists, to speak for them all. Ironically, the result was to damn both Woolf and Joyce with almost willful misunderstanding. Woolf's own early caustic remarks about Joyce surely exacerbated the critical situation, as the opponents of Modernism used them against both novelists.[3] The post-World War II English rejection of the Modernist novel—and especially of Woolf and Joyce—makes use, rather cyncial use, as I read it, of these several misunderstandings. With their tendency to invent narrators where there palpably are none, Woolfians and Joyceans alike have in recent years added their own unfortunate fillip to the mix.

When Woolf writes, in her essay "Modern Fiction" (1919),

> If a writer were a free man and not a slave, if he could write what he chose, not what he must, if he could base his work upon his own feeling and not upon convention, there would be no plot, no comedy, no tragedy, no love interest or catastrophe in the accepted style, and perhaps not a single button sewn on as

the Bond Street tailors would have it. Life is not a series of gig lamps symmetri-
cally arranged; but a luminous halo, a semi-transparent envelope surrounding us
from the beginning of consciousness to the end,[4]

she is quite consciously challenging virtually every aspect of the conventional
novel as it was practiced by the great Victorians and their lesser successors, the
Edwardians. (We tend to forget that in that so-called *annus mirabilis*, 1922,
when Joyce published *Ulysses*, Arnold Bennett, still going strong, published his
own novel, *Riceyman Steps*.) And the Establishment responded as she might
have expected it to: in defense of tradition, convention, realism, plot, characterization, morality and omniscience; and in assaults, often vitriolic, against
those who would threaten those qualities. That uniquely English critical form
of offense as defense continues, perversely, almost to the present day. And so
we find John Bayley—who should surely know better—writing half a century
later, "'What is it, life?' Virginia Woolf is continually asking. . . . She creates
because she is unable to be, and her creations cannot therefore, to most persons, appear as an adequate representation of being."[5] Or Malcolm Bradbury,
usually so perceptive as critic and novelist, claiming that Woolf "not only tends
to poeticize modernism, but also to feminize and domesticate it."[6]

I would like to believe that no critic of Woolf today would be quite so foolish
or irrelevant: Woolf's demands both for a new fiction and a new respect for the
writer of fiction who happens to be a woman—all the more dangerous because
they are so elegantly expressed—have long since been heard and, in varying
degrees, responded to. If our understanding of Woolf today is threatened, it is
more by the invented "narrator" in her novels, the creation not of her enemies
but of her own adherents. This misunderstanding is even more fundamental in
Woolf studies, I suspect—and thus more destructive—than it is with Joyce. The
invented narrator, without identity or function, roams freely throughout her fictions, serving only to reconstitute that cozy, easily knowable world constructed
by the Victorian novelists, that world which Woolf worked so hard to upset.

In "Mr. Bennett and Mrs. Brown" (1924), her best known essay, Woolf
blames her Edwardian "elders and betters" for not providing her and her fellows with narrative means other than the external and superficial—"'Describe
cancer. Describe calico,'" they respond to her request for a point of view to
delve within a potential character's psyche[7]—why would Woolf herself create a
functionless narrator incapable of or uninterested in looking inward?

The "luminous halo" posited by Woolf as critic, the "semi-transparent envelope surrounding us from the beginning of consciousness to the end," are, as
I read them, not some vague "poetic" deviations from realism, but a specific
injunction to develop a point of view that is capable of depicting realistically
the new world of "consciousness": for that is the key term in Woolf's statement,
and this is her definitive statement about the connections between narrative
technique and authorial vision.[8] Outside narrators may be able to describe—

from outside, of course—what appears to be consciousness, more or less as well and as immediately as an omniscient author can. But a narrator cannot take us inside a consciousness. Woolf, to be sure, rejects the direct, even aggressive methods that Joyce developed for the realization of consciousness on the page. But I believe that what has been characterized as her "narrator" is not only a misnomer but is actually her own indirect and suggestive means of realizing consciousness. Her practice is at once least evident and most effective in her greatest novel, *The Waves*.

✳

To be sure, the need for a narrator may seem clearcut on the surface. The narrative formula of *The Waves* appears almost to mandate her/his presence: virtually every passage in the novel is accompanied by the name of one of the six protagonists and the past tense of the verb "to say"; hence, "said Louis," or "said Susan," or "said Bernard"—usually near the beginning of a passage. For many readers—perhaps most readers—the past tense and the third person are *prima facie* proof that a narrator must be operating here: someone capable of reporting what each of the characters has had to say over a lifetime of intense inter-relationships. Some critics have even endeavored to give the narrator a name: most popular is Bernard, the novelist in the group and therefore a potential reliable spokesman for Woolf. No one has yet dared to argue, so far as I know at least, that such a narrator, whether named or anonymous, a surrogate for Woolf or but one of her characters, however knowing, is in practice another form of omniscience. But it is. It is also based on a misreading, and an unnecessary one at that, for the evident inconsistencies which it is designed to ameliorate are not at all inconsistent. We have simply not accommodated ourselves to Woolf's narrative needs and practices.

What matters when Woolf writes, "said Neville," or "said Rhoda," or "said Bernard," is neither the name nor the verb, but rather the fact that although the passage which follows is set off by quotation marks, seeming to indicate that this is a character's dialogue, it is not actual speech. It also functions not in the *pro forma* past tense but in the very strongly felt present:

> "He is dead," said Neville [referring to Percival, their friend]. "He fell. His horse tripped. He was thrown. The sails of the world have swung round and caught me on the head. All is over. The lights of the world have gone out. There stands the tree which I cannot pass. (128)[9]

Or,

> "There is the puddle," said Rhoda, "and I cannot cross it. I hear the rush of the great grindstone within an inch of my head. Its wind roars in my face. All palpable

forms of life have failed me. Unless I can stretch and touch something hard, I shall be blown down the eternal corridors for ever. What, then, can I touch? What brick, what stone? and so draw myself across the enormous gulf into my body safely?" (135)

Or,

"I became, I mean, a certain kind of man, scoring my path across life as one treads a path across the fields. My boots became worn a little on the left side. When I came in, certain rearrangements took place. 'Here's Bernard!' How differently different people say that! There are many rooms—many Bernards. . . . What I was to myself was different; was none of these . . . existing in the midst of unconsciousness." (223–24)

While each of these passages is unique to its character, none attempts to replicate a particular character's actual speech patterns. The images, the ideas, the emotions—these may relate to a single actor only; but the words might belong to any of them. Moreover, Woolf makes no effort to differentiate the separate voices of the putative speakers: We are told frequently, for example, that the Australian-born Louis is self-conscious about his accent, but we never hear what it sounds like or how it might differ from any other accent. Nor do we find here any suggestion of general speech rhythms, such as we hear in Hemingway's fictions; there is no sense at all in which Woolf's "said" is meant to convey human speech. And so whatever activity is being depicted here, we must conclude that it is something other than speech.

Woolf's essays make it as clear as she can that it is the inner voice which she seeks: not those varied voices of interior monologue which Joyce strives to replicate in *Ulysses*—the differing rhythms of the coldly intellectual Stephen Dedalus, the hotly emotional Molly Bloom, or that marvelous mix of mind and emotion that is Leopold Bloom. Nor does Woolf seek for the different forms of interior monologue which Joyce adapts to these voices: the pure stream of consciousness—the flow of the unfettered mind as it incorporates sensory perception, when Stephen walks along the strand in the "Proteus" episode; or the re-creation of the preconscious state of mind as Bloom orates in "Circe"; or the dizzying blend of voices and identities which characterizes various interactive moments (as identities may blur) involving Stephen and Bloom, Bloom and Gerty MacDowell, the denizens of the Ormond Hotel, the promenaders through Dublin. The spectacular narrative effect which so appealed to Joyce and which, more often than not, he controlled with such self-discipline (and which called such attention to itself): this was decidedly not for Woolf. But this is not to say that she abjured interior views: She simply sought for them more subtly and indirectly.

A passage marked "said Louis," then, is likely to be his interior monologue, that is, his unspoken speech, consisting of his feelings, sense perceptions, ideas, memories, fears and desires; his responses to his own experiences, present and past, as well as to those of his fellows and to the nature which surrounds them all; a sense at once of his own, individualized identity and of the community of which he has for his entire life been an integral part. Much the same might be said as well of a passage marked "said Neville," or "said Rhoda." This is an interior monologue, however, with none of the usual trappings or signs which we are accustomed to reading in that familiar Modernist mode. Woolf's awareness of Freud is evident in each of these passages, yet none is an effort to replicate the precise processes which govern the unconscious mind. It is the conscious individual mind that interests Woolf in *The Waves*, yet even here her goal is not to re-create its processes but to suggest them. Freud functions here without the flash of "Circe" but with comparable effect.

It might also be said, I think, that Woolf was equally aware of what Joyce—along with Proust and Mann—was doing with interior monologue and had opted to use her own very different form as more appropriate to her interests and abilities. That we have not recognized her technique for what it is—that so many of Woolf's admirers have tacitly assumed that Woolf had made some sort of mistake which could be rectified by speaking of a narrator—suggests how seriously we have misread her interests and undervalued her abilities.

Beyond this individual interior monologue, because of their lifetime of shared experiences, the six protagonists of the novel may be said to form a community; this explains both why they seem to share a language and why they may in other ways appear interchangeable. Each is an individual, and as adults they lead separate lives, yet they are joined—not just by experience but by sensibility and even consciousness. Although they come together only occasionally as adults, their childhood experiences together ensure that, in a very real sense, they will always remain one—and this one may suggest at times a collective unconscious. "'We suffered terribly as we became separate bodies,'" says Bernard (207). And he elaborates, "'For this is not one life; nor do I always know if I am man or woman, Bernard or Neville, Louis, Susan, Jinny or Rhoda—so strange is the contact of one with another'" (242). Thus, while he appears to be the only one among them to merit a biographer, Bernard understands that his is but part of a larger life and that no biographer can tell the story of his life who does not know the others. (*The Waves*, therefore, just a bit self-reflexively, may prove to be their one true—joint and individual—biography.) Not just the novelist Bernard, moreover, but each of them is capable of speaking for them all. Each is at once protagonist and chorus.

In the late essay "Anon" (1940), written almost a decade after the appearance of *The Waves,* Woolf provides the perfect analogue for her unique point of view in that novel, an identity, if you will, for that joint yet individual, intimate yet somewhat distant speaker implicit within the formula "said Neville," or "said Susan," or "said Bernard." It is almost as if she set out in "Anon" to explain point of view in *The Waves.*

Intended as the opening chapter of what Woolf would call her "Common History book—[its program] to read from one end of literature including biography; and range at will, consecutively," the essay attempts to account for—and give a name to—the voice implicit within early (and perhaps also late) English literature. The book itself, left incomplete at her death, was clearly intended to build on Woolf's own greatest, complementary strengths, as a writer and as a reader, and to explore both their inter-connections and, in the words of their editor, "the emotions embedded in the human psyche and shared, however unconsciously, by the community as a whole."[10] Anon, in this conception, is at once the creator of the great early English texts (the Popular Ballads, *Le Morte d'Arthur*) and the audience which kept them alive (who would become the Elizabethan playgoing groundling: "Indeed, half the work of the dramatists, one feels, was done in the Elizabethan age by the public.")[11]

Condemned frequently as an elitist, Woolf is positing here one of the most egalitarian of all theories of English literary history: This is a literature which emerges from and is sustained by what would in another context be called "the folk," that oral, anonymous creative force at the core of all pre-literate cultures destined in time to construct great literatures.

> [D]uring the silent centuries before the book was printed his was the only voice that was to be heard in England. Save for Anon singing his song at the back door the English might be a dumb race.[12]

Woolf never does address in "Anon" the literature of her own age—she can hardly have defined it as essentially "popular"—but it must be equally clear that, observing from her own silent station somewhere behind or alongside Anon, she was not writing for some self-selected elite. The voice of Anon, for Woolf, is the ideal manifestation of a literate, yet still oral people, breeding ground as well for the new reader demanded by Woolf and her Modernist fellows. In his/her anonymity, his/her emergence from and place as part of the collective folk, his/her dual position as creative voice and active listener, Anon evokes both the individual and the group voice, the identity both personalized and unknown.[13] His/her presence is most evident in the contemporaneous novel *Between the Acts* (1941)—in the communal play performance in particular. But it serves as well in *The Waves,* in which just such a voice operates as organizing principle.

The historical presence of Anon, Woolf proclaims, did not end with the end of oral culture: "Nor is Anon dead in ourselves."[14] The voice is alive still in Bernard, Louis and Neville, in Susan, Jinny and Rhoda, in the reader who shares intimately their revelations and (self-)discoveries. It serves as bridge between them and the reader, between the life revealed in literature and daily life. It does not distance us from them, as would an invented narrator, but links us together, firmly and irretrievably. This is an internal monologue which emerges from and reaches deeply within both the characters and their society.[15]

CHAPTER 8

The Creation of Consciousness on the Page
Forms of Internal Monologue

Individual Consciousness: Mrs. Dalloway and Mr. Bloom on City Streets

"The literature of townsmen"—Frank O'Connor's phrase to describe *Ulysses*—would serve well as a description of Modernism at large and especially of the Modernist novel.[1] We remember James Joyce's explanation for setting his most influential novel in Dublin: for while his hometown was small enough to be widely accessible, it was nevertheless a city, and thus the representative venue for its century. Stream of consciousness, in much the same manner, similarly has been proclaimed the representative Modernist narrative technique. And even if that term has been used carelessly, with little precise sense of what it actually entails in practice, it does seem appropriate to use city scenes to illustrate its workings and to help to define its borders, to determine just what it does and what it does not do. My representative texts are two of Modernism's most popular, Woolf's *Mrs. Dalloway* (1925) and Joyce's *Ulysses* (1922), with two of the novel's most enduring characters, afoot in two great cities, unaware, on the cusp of profound change: Clarissa Dalloway in London, in the aftermath of the Great War, a decade or so before the city will be changed forever by the Second World War; and Leopold Bloom in Dublin, in its final decades as an imperial city. The revolutionary points of view devised to depict them are wonderfully appropriate to their personal and historical circumstances.

We first encounter Clarissa Dalloway, "stiffened a little on the kerb, waiting for Durtnall's van to pass, . . . waiting to cross, very upright." In this first glance at her, as she stands on a street corner in London, we appear to be seeing her through the eyes of a neighbor, Scrope Purvis, whom she does not notice ("never seeing him"). And then, almost imperceptibly, we shift to her consciousness:

For having lived in Westminster—how many years now? over twenty,—one feels even in the midst of the traffic, or waking at night, Clarissa was positive, a particular hush, or solemnity; an indescribable pause; a suspense (but that might be her heart, affected, they said, by influenza) before Big Ben strikes. There! Out it boomed. First a warning, musical; then the hour, irrevocable. The leaden circles dissolved in the air. Such fools we are, she thought, crossing Victoria Street. For Heaven only knows why one loves it so, how one sees it so, . . . creating it every moment afresh; . . . In people's eyes, in the swing, tramp, and trudge; in the bellow and the uproar; the carriages, motor cars, omnibuses, vans, sandwich men shuffling and swinging; brass bands; barrel organs; in the triumph and the jingle and the strange high singing of some aeroplane overhead was what she loved; life; London; this moment of June. (4–5)[2]

All of the forms here are in the third person—"Clarissa was positive," "one feels," "she thought," "they said," "[i]n people's eyes," "why one loves it so," "was what she loved." Yet we understand intuitively that none of this is objective. For we are clearly somewhere within Clarissa's consciousness, even to the point that we sense already what she cannot even begin to articulate until near the very end of this long, representative day: that as her own life is threatened by heart disease, so may be this city life that she loves so well and so deeply. Notice also the silent, yet profound intimacy of "or waking at night," as if preparing us for the "Time Passes" section of *To the Lighthouse* (1927).

How are we to label the point of view of this passage? To call it "third person" and leave it at that is so obviously inadequate that it seems ludicrous. To invent a "narrator" as the source of this information about her is equally fallacious, for no one outside Clarissa—not even this fabricated substitute for the omniscient author—could possibly know her so well, yet be so reticent about her, and at the same time open her up so potentially (if not firmly) to the reader's sensibility, allowing us that sense of discovery and intimacy that is never possible from an outside source, whether in omniscience or through a narrator: that sense of discovery that is at the heart of all Modernist narrative technique.[3] For we surely understand that we are now seeing, now feeling, now judging as Clarissa Dalloway does. The point of view is obviously hers; we are clearly within her sensibility and consciousness; what we cannot understand or articulate is what she cannot yet—or will not yet—understand or articulate (although we may already have a sense of her hesitancy). But should we merely label this as the general "internal monologue" or insist on the more specific term, "stream of consciousness"? Or is it wiser simply to describe what is happening in this scene and to evaluate its effect on our reading and thus to avoid labels completely?

The problem is confounded by a comparable scene near the start of *Ulysses*. Leopold Bloom is walking to the butcher shop at 8:00 A.M. on another June morning of an earlier generation, in the Empire's second city.

Baldhead over the blind. Cute old codger. No use canvassing him for an ad. . . .

Stop and say a word: about the funeral perhaps. Sad thing about poor Dignam, Mr O'Rourke.

Turning into Dorset street he said freshly in greeting through the doorway:

—Good day, Mr O'Rourke.

—Good day to you.

—Lovely weather, sir.

—'Tis all that.

Where do they get the money? . . . On the wholesale orders perhaps. . . .

How much would that tot to off the porter in the month? Say ten barrels of stuff. Say he got ten per cent off. O more. Fifteen. He passed Saint Joseph's National school. Brats' clamour. Windows open. Fresh air helps memory. Or a lilt. . . .

He halted before Dlugacz's window, staring at the hanks of sausages, polonies, black and white. Fifteen multiplied by. The figures whitened in his mind, unsolved: displeased, he let them fade. The shiny links packed with forcemeat fed his gaze and he breathed in tranquilly the lukewarm breath of cooked spicy pigs' blood.

. . . .

He took a page up from the pile of cut sheets: the model farm at Kinnereth on the lakeshore of Tiberias. Can become ideal winter sanatorium. Moses Montefiore. I thought he was. Farmhouse, wall round it, blurred cattle cropping. He held the page from him: interesting: read it nearer. . . .

He walked back along Dorset street, reading gravely. . . .

He looked at the cattle, blurred in silver heat. Silverpowdered olivetrees. Quiet long days: pruning ripening. Olives are packed in jars, eh? I have a few left from Andrews. Molly spitting them out. Knows the taste of them now. Oranges in tissue paper packed in crates. Citrons too. Wonder is poor Citron still alive in Saint Kevin's parade. And Mastiansky with the old cither. Pleasant evenings we had then. Molly in Citron's basketchair. . . .

A cloud began to cover the sun slowly, wholly. Grey. Far.

No, not like that. A barren land, bare waste. Volcanic lake, the dead sea: no fish, weedless, sunk deep in the earth. No wind would lift those waves. . . . Brimstone they called it raining down: the cities of the plain: Sodom, Gomorrah, Edom. All dead names. A dead sea in a dead land. . . . It bore the oldest, the first race. A bent hag crossed from Cassidy's, clutching naggin bottle by the neck. The oldest people. Wandered far away over all the earth, captivity to captivity, multiplying, dying, being born everywhere. It lay there now. Now it could bear no more. Dead: an old woman's: the grey sunken cunt of the world.

Desolation.

Grey horror seared his flesh. Folding the page into his pocket he turned into Eccles street, hurrying homeward. . . . Well, I am here now. (47–50)

There is no better illustration in all of literature of Freud's idea of free association.

As a simple matter of verisimilitude, then, this passage from Eccles street to Dorset street and back to Eccles street is quite extraordinary. But the passage is also so much more, as Bloom moves among sensory perception, imagination and memory; the present and the past, both his own and the imagined past of his people; from conjecture to hope to fear to the need to escape (both his past and his present) and to reach his home. Much of his personality is revealed here in virtually our first glimpse of him; here also are all of the novel's major themes as they relate to Bloom. The narrative technique is perfectly maintained, its role in the development of the theme unmistakable. This scene, I believe, not the more famous so-called "nightmare" sequence in "Circe," is the most representative example of Modernist mastery of point of view. But how are we to characterize it?

From the first word and image to the last, we are lodged firmly here within Bloom's consciousness. Where Clarissa Dalloway is introduced to us through the perspective of her neighbor, Bloom, in a sense, introduces himself. Although others do see him—O'Rourke the pubkeeper ("curate"), Dlugacz, the Hungarian (probably Jewish) pork butcher—it is not until later in the day that we learn directly from his neighbors what it is that they see when they view Bloom—and much of that is through conversation, probably as it is overheard by Bloom. The only consistent points of view which present a direct vision of Bloom are those of the anonymous narrator of the "Cyclops" chapter and of Molly Bloom, as she lies awake after her husband has fallen asleep. Most of what we learn about Bloom in *Ulysses*—both directly and from what we infer—is thus through Bloom himself; in this early morning scene in "Calypso," he is our sole point of view.

His initial stimuli here are sensory: all of Bloom's senses, but especially the visual, are engaged as he walks to and from the butcher shop. The images of his senses lead instantaneously to the workings of his mind: to his business sense ("No use canvassing him for an ad"), his senses of community ("Stop and say a word"), of his own Jewishness ("Montefiore. I thought he was"), of his sensuality (the hanging meats, the olive and citrus trees in Palestine—omitted from this passage are the "vigorous hips" of the girl on line in front of him and his urge to watch them as she walks from the store).[4] Much of Bloom's sensibility is revealed here as well: his practicality, his sense of tradition ("The oldest people"), the mix of pessimism and optimism which underlies so much of his thought; we sense from all of this his desire to belong and yet his isolation, the vulnerability and strength that lie just beneath the seemingly placid surface of his personality.

The result is at once naturalistic and metaphoric; the stream of imagery, the flow of the mind, the sensibility and vision of life revealed in the process: by taking us immediately into Bloom's consciousness, Joyce endows us with a power and opportunity that earlier readers of novels could not even imagine. There would be flashier, more dramatic demonstrations of the possibilities of Modernist point of view—some of them in this same novel; but the great leap is here, between Eccles and Dorset streets. And yet it seems so logical as we read it, inevitable almost. And how are we to classify it? Can it be stream of consciousness when so much of what transpires in Bloom's mind is under his control? Can it even be internal monologue when so much of what we see on the page is the product of Bloom's senses before it even turns to thought? Just where is the line—if there is one, or several—between internal monologue and stream of consciousness?

The same broad, general terms might be used to describe Bloom's point of view in the "Calypso" chapter of *Ulysses* and Clarissa Dalloway's at the start of her day: Alert to the life of the cities around them, each progresses from immediate sensory perception to thoughts of his or her own life to thoughts of the nature of life. Woolf, who had read Freud as closely as had any artist, makes no effort to replicate Freud's understanding of the workings of the mind in free association (or in any other form). At what almost seems a distance from Mrs. Dalloway's mind—that distance which has misled many critics to imagine that someone else, some narrator perhaps, or maybe Woolf herself, is presenting her observations—we are able to follow the workings of that mind and to appreciate that sensibility. What seems at first distant and controlled is revealed to be intimate and even passionate.

Joyce's technique is in a sense more obvious, almost as if he—who denied that he had read Freud—were endeavoring to replicate Freud. There are also more layers to Joyce's approach, as various forms of human observation interact and meld. If Woolf's delving into consciousness is perhaps more suggestive than literal, Joyce's seems at once literal and suggestive, a representation both of the workings of the conscious mind and of what may lay beyond. In both cases, it is the conscious mind on display; in both also, the physical senses are an integral part of the process. Both Woolf and Joyce in these city scenes create forms of internal monologue; but there is only a suggestion of the flow of the mind in *Mrs. Dalloway,* where in "Calypso" we are ourselves caught up in that flow, that stream, if you will, of consciousness.[5]

There are almost as many ways to define internal monologue as there are novelists who seek to enter the minds of their characters. Most definitions become uncertain, however, when it comes to stream of consciousness, internal monologue's most specialized—and spectacular—form. But if I am correct when I tell my students that there are no right or wrong answers in literature, but only good or bad answers based on our readings of texts, that ours is not a discipline that lends itself to true-or-false questions (or even to short-answer questions), then we must be wary of misapplying our definitions. It is not the job of the critic to make works of art fit some preconceived system; we must use definitions—if we use them at all—not to delimit discussion but to make it possible.

The growth in recent years of so-called "narratology," with its wealth of definitions and technical terms, has made the process, I believe, not easier but more difficult, has tended to place the critic/theoretician before the novelist. If I have myself learned anything from reading Wayne Booth and *The Rhetoric of Fiction*, it is that we must allow novels to speak for themselves and not restrict them to the parameters of our terminology. "Stream of consciousness" is at once the most potentially liberating and the most dangerously delimiting of all narrative terms.

Stream of Consciousness/Monologue Intérieur (Ulysses)

Some years ago, I had an argument with a French friend over whether to label a passage in *Ulysses* as "stream of consciousness" or merely as the more general "interior monologue." I no longer recall the passage in question, but I do remember that our discussion was lengthy and just a bit heated. And then, at least as the moment survives in my memory, we together recognized—as if in a Joycean epiphany—that we were really in agreement about the label, although we had been using conflicting definitions: for our discussion was in English, and the French term for "stream of consciousness" is *monologue intérieur*, which he had translated literally. We had a good laugh about the confusion, as I recall, and I doubt that the incident even remains in my friend's memory today. But to me it has always seemed important, even symbolic. For the most misunderstood of all literary terms, I suspect, the most readily misused, is that seemingly easy one, "stream of consciousness."

I had encountered the term long before I knew with any precision what it might mean; reviewers and critics appeared to use the term casually, familiarly, as if to say that, of course, we all understand this defining term. And that is the problem: It continues to be used in so loose a way that it stretches meaning and invites confusion. For many, "stream of consciousness" refers to any presumably "experimental" internal transmission of individual consciousness, especially if it is associated with free-wheeling language and revealing, preferably sexy thoughts. Inevitably, it is associated with Joyce's *Ulysses,* an association which has in recent years acquired legal implications: the James Joyce Estate, in a copyright infringement suit which it initiated, has apparently specified stream of consciousness as a particularly Joycean property, almost as if it were one owned today by Joyce's litigious heir.

Joyce himself knew better, to be sure. He attributed the invention of stream of consciousness to Édouard Dujardin, although I suspect that this generous gesture also functioned as a public relations smoke screen for Joyce, designed to raise the issue in public discourse and, in the process, to aggrandize his own, unique accomplishment. Some literary historians attribute the invention of stream of consciousness to Dorothy Richardson in her monumental, if somewhat tedious thirteen-volume novel, *Pilgrimage* (1915–1938, 1967), but anyone who has read both Joyce and Richardson will recognize that his practice is infinitely more varied and accomplished and owes nothing to hers. Indeed, anyone who has read Dujardin's *Les Lauriers sont coupés* (1888) will be aware that while in broad, general terms its method appears comparable to Joyce's, the differences in practice and result are so vast that we are dealing in effect with totally different phenomena.

I am reluctant, as always in such cases, to attempt to offer a precise definition of my own, in the fear that it would prove as delimiting as most other literary definitions. And the term "stream of consciousness," as one form of interior or internal monologue, does speak quite literally for itself: Its locus is the conscious mind, not the unconscious, and its distinguishing quality is the free flow of its language and imagistic stream. The closest psychological analogy is to free association, but the literary construct is likely to be much more sustained, much more rich and complex than our everyday practice. Its ramifications on the page appear limitless, its sources virtually untraceable, its end point always potentially revealing and its process as significant as its result. The subjects of free association in our daily lives, on the other hand—despite Freud—are typically trivial: the question, why did I happen to think of that at this moment? is one common manifestation. In Modernist fiction, the process of stream of consciousness leads almost always to epiphany.[6]

Stream of consciousness, moreover, is rarely pure in the sense that only thoughts are involved: present sensory perceptions are likely to merge in it with thoughts and with memories and to become part of the stream, generating new associations of thought and image and memory. The challenge for the novelist is to maintain verisimilitude (of a venue far more difficult to reach than that of Virginia Woolf's Mr. Bennett) and, at the same time, to reveal the inner, often hidden core of a character (as Woolf wished to do with her Mrs. Brown: Woolf discovered, of course, that a suggestion could be as dangerous to her reputation as a definition). Despite the protestations of some of the other Modernists—Joyce prominent among them—there can be no doubt that it was Freud (and the currents which made his work possible) who made stream of consciousness possible, even inevitable, in fiction. But it is a literary, not a psychological development, and it must be judged by literary and not psychological (or, perish the thought, psychoanalytic) criteria. For its goal is the familiar one which Hawthorne spoke of as "the truth of the human heart" and which Henry James called, in speaking of his own first novel, "the drama of . . . consciousness."[7]

If there is no easy, general definition of stream of consciousness—and if it may be dangerous to offer one—it is because there is more than one stream of consciousness technique: even within *Ulysses,* supposedly the epicenter of the form, there is no single, characteristic approach, so that no single description will suffice for every episode in the novel. More pertinent still, in only a few of the eighteen episodes of *Ulysses* does Joyce even use stream of consciousness to reveal his characters. The characterization of *Ulysses* as a stream of consciousness novel is, as a result, rather misleading. What we need, then, as I read the problem, is not another attempt at definition (knowing in advance that it will likely fail) but, instead, some descriptions of practice, always keeping in mind that in each of the other chapters of *Ulysses*, to varying degrees, Joyce develops other forms of interior monologue, usually in combination with seemingly external points of view. Thus, in "Telemachus," the opening episode, in which there is no stream of consciousness, virtually every act is viewed through the senses of Stephen Dedalus, and we move only momentarily—if vitally—into his mind. For example,

> Buck Mulligan suddenly linked his arm in Stephen's and walked with him round the tower, his razor and mirror clacking in the pocket where he had thrust them.
> —It's not fair to tease you like that, Kinch, is it? he said kindly. God knows you have more spirit than any of them.
> Parried again. He fears the lancet of my art as I fear that of his. The cold steelpen.
> ... Cranly's arm. His arm. (6)

The presumably objective description of Mulligan's actions and words, while it might at first seem to come from someplace outside Stephen, perhaps even from an omniscient author (or the notorious "narrator" invented for the purpose), proves on examination to be Stephen's own sensory perception of the event. The adverb "kindly," however—Stephen's unspoken, (uncharacteristically) un-ironic acknowledgement of his tower mate's intent—is purely subjective, the word interspersed amidst Mulligan's spoken words.[8] The first-person comment which follows ("my art," "as I fear") is obviously Stephen's private judgment, to be shared only with the reader; the third-person comment which follows that, "Cranly's arm. His arm," as the reader of *A Portrait of the Artist as a Young Man* must recognize, is even more personal than the preceding first-person comment, for it assumes that we know that Stephen has tagged his college friend Cranly as his betrayer, and it notifies us that he expects nothing different from Mulligan.

These subjective, internal comments prove demonstrably that the seemingly objective, accompanying description also functions internally and that Stephen is also their source. To argue otherwise is to make of Joyce, the most meticulous of Modernist artists, an inconsistent craftsman, turning from one technique and source to another, sans transition or purpose, within the same passage. Consistency comes only when we acknowledge that Stephen is the sole source of every single observation here, sensory as well as intellectual or emotional, and that everything displayed on the page—every word, every act, every thought and emotion, whether silently expressed or simply implied—is equally internal and subjective.

Still, only the "Parried again" passage, along with "Cranly's arm. His arm," can literally be termed internal monologue. We are close in these words to the surface of Stephen's mind; no emotion or expectation is openly expressed; the association of images and ideas is controlled, not free: he knows their implications, and since he is his sole audience, he need not be explicit about them (thus leaving the reader, in the best Modernist manner, to discover meaning for himself). It is eight o'clock in the morning; Stephen is alert and generally in control of his faculties and emotions, responding to the stimuli around him. There is no occasion in "Telemachus" to probe more deeply, no need—either for him or for us—to explore the stream of his consciousness. Since every event in this chapter, I would argue—every observation, every reaction—takes place in or is filtered through Stephen's consciousness, everything here is potentially internal monologue in its effect. But not a word of this is stream of consciousness. Reminiscent of Flaubert's so-called free indirect discourse, point of view in "Telemachus" goes far beyond that precursor.

Three hours later, however, in "Proteus," as he walks along Sandymount Strand on his way into Dublin, with no especial interest in the natural world around him, Stephen contemplates what does interest him: his own sensibility and situation, the images of his reading and memories; when he does turn to nature, it is more likely to be as an intellectual construct than as an aesthetic source. (His sometimes poetic prose may mask the fact that he has little interest in nature *per se.*) "Proteus" is the most intellectual of all the chapters in *Ulysses* and to my mind the least engaging (for Stephen's intellectual interests are very different from mine, at once more philosophical and abstract, and—at this point in his life—less mature). And from the very first words of the chapter, Joyce shows us the ways in which Stephen's mind will work during his long walk. All of this is stream of consciousness.

> Ineluctable modality of the visible: at least that if no more, thought through my eyes. Signatures of all things I am here to read, seaspawn and seawrack, the nearing tide, that rusty boot. (31)

That telling phrase "thought through my eyes" advises us that the stream of Stephen's consciousness will consist as well of his sensory perceptions and of what he will make of the images that he perceives ("seaspawn and seawrack, the nearing tide, that rusty boot"). There can be no doubt that we are lodged firmly now in Stephen's mind.

At this point, he goes on to think of Aristotle and the philosopher's reading of the natural world, to offer (for his self-edification) his response and his own reading, to evaluate both readings and to link them—within a matter of seconds—to a vast variety of images, from the most eclectic of sources: Shakespeare, Gilbert and Sullivan, erotic hymns to the Mother Goddess in ancient Anatolia, Swinburne, Alexander the Great, the midwife who delivered him (Stephen, that is, although the confusion with Alexander is not entirely accidental), Blake, the Kabbalah, Irish mythology and his "consubstantial father's," Simon's, reactions to his uncle, Richie Goulding. He refers to himself in the first person, as part of a metaphysical experiment ("Open your eyes now. I will"); as a character in literary myth ("Like me, like Algy, coming down to our mighty mother"); as a man of action ("I mustn't forget his letter for the press"), one with practical matters to consider ("Am I going to Aunt Sara's or not?" 38–39). He then goes on to visualize the prospective visit with his uncle's family (or perhaps to remember a past visit, most likely to conflate imagination and memory).

Through all this—although there is no mention of time elapsed or space encompassed—Stephen has progressed over two pages of text, perhaps ten minutes of a mid-June morning, half a mile or so of the beach at Sandymount, a suburb of Dublin. The ever-shifting, well-named "Proteus" episode is our true introduction to stream of consciousness in Modernist fiction, as I read it. But it is essential to be aware of its multiple associations and frequent shifts, to note, for example, that in this intense, immediate, revealing, highly subjective account, Stephen refers to himself not only in the first but also in the third person, and even in the (imperative) second:

He had come nearer the edge of the sea and wet sand slapped his boots. The new air greeted him, harping in wild nerves, wind of wild air of seeds of brightness. Here, I am not walking out to the Kish lightship, am I? He stood suddenly, his feet beginning to sink slowly in the quaking soil. Turn back. (37)

First, second and third persons here are equally subjective in practice, outer world and inner world the same world, merged in the consciousness of a young man poised for (self) discovery. Joyce never hesitates to break the supposedly self-evident boundaries of form when his subject demands that he do so, never confuses prescribed definitions of narrative form ("he" is supposedly an objective pronoun, after all, the subjective presumably reserved for "I") with his own narrative needs (Stephen's perception of himself as a model for ours), never allows himself to be limited by the limits of his critics. It is vital, of course, that we read such passages carefully, considering all of their potential human sources, along with their forms. But it would be destructive for us to attempt to confine them—and their author—within some narrow, preconceived critical framework and phraseology. It is not the point of view's name that matters, but its source and function. "Proteus" is all stream of consciousness, that is, but even for intellectual Stephen, it partakes of sensory observation and language that might otherwise seem omniscient.

The closest general parallel to the technique of "Proteus," ironically, is that of "Penelope," when we find ourselves in the mind of Molly Bloom, Stephen's antithesis. Characterized by feeling rather than intellect, with an entirely different vocabulary and sentence structure, Molly's unspoken, free-flowing soliloquoy is the perfect embodiment of her personality (" . . . that longnosed chap I dont know who he is with that other beauty Burke out of the City Arms hotel was there spying around as usual on the slip always where he wasnt wanted if there was a row on youd vomit a better face there was no love lost between us thats 1 consolation . . ." 629). The transitions between her thoughts are provided not by past reading but by experience, her memories (in both their origins and their expression) always sensuous, if not sensual, always true to her sense of herself. As with Stephen's thoughts in "Proteus," Molly's here are altered at times by physical phenomena and by reactions to them—the dog which Stephen sees on the beach and which he fears may attack him, the chamber pot which Molly gets out of bed to use. But Molly maintains no distance at all from herself. Joyce may be suggesting here that such distance is a function of intellect, even for so self-involved a character as Stephen; Molly is incapable of thinking of herself as anything other than "I." While it is possible that Molly may be falling asleep as "Penelope" ends, it is important to recognize that she is fully awake throughout the episode: There is not only no dream here, no unconscious state, but also no preconscious condition between wakefulness and dream. Her mind is perhaps a bit freer to roam than during the daytime, but there is little of the liberty here— or of the indirection—of dream.[9] It is also possible that at the end of "Ithaca," the preceding chapter, which leads directly into this one—although it was written immediately after "Penelope"—Leopold Bloom does fall through the preconscious into dream. The mythic images which close that chapter may suggest something of this sort. It is even possible that the final question of "Ithaca," "Where?" (607) begins to be answered in the dream world of *Finnegans Wake*. But it is aggressively not answered in "Ithaca."

Nor is it answered in "Circe." The most spectacular of all the episodes of *Ulysses* —and, indeed, with the possible exception of *Finnegans Wake,* the most spectacular in all modern literature—the "Circe" chapter is everywhere cited as the pinnacle of stream of consciousness writing. Yet Freud, I suspect, would not have acknowledged it as an accurate depiction of the workings of the conscious mind. It is surely not very scientific, not even in Freud's some-what loose terms. Joyce's insistence that he had not read Freud is not merely a common novelist's lie, I would guess, but a claim for his own originality in "Circe" in depicting the intricacies of the human mind under great physical and emotional stress.[10] Stephen is tired, drunk and out of control in "Circe," subject to his deepest fears and desires; even Bloom is less in control of his thoughts and feelings than we have come to expect of him. Here Joyce hews close to Freud. But the psychic world that Joyce endeavors to create in "Circe" goes well beyond the individual consciousnesses of his principal characters. If this is indeed stream of consciousness—and I know no better term to describe it—it is surely more advanced than what even "Proteus" has led us to expect from the form.

The lack of control—by Stephen, by Bloom—is, naturally, the starting point. The free associations which have characterized earlier ventures into their consciousnesses have in "Circe" become anarchic. Even the physical page, with its look of the playscript, is a bit disorienting; even the opening passages, which take place in public, as Stephen and Bloom are (separately) walking through the Nighttown section of Dublin, seem more phantasmagoric than realistic: They do more than prepare us for the breakdown of consciousness which will take place at Bella Cohen's establishment—they suggest that breakdown has already occurred and that its source is somewhere beyond the individual trau-mas of the protagonists.

THE CALL

Wait, my love, and I'll be with you.

THE ANSWER

Round behind the stable.

(*A deafmute idiot with goggle eyes, his shapeless mouth dribbling, jerks past, shaken in Saint Vitus' dance. A chain of children's hands imprisons him.*)

THE CHILDREN

Kithogue! Salute.

THE IDIOT

(*lifts a palsied left arm and gurgles.*) Ghahute!

THE CHILDREN

Where's the great light?

THE IDIOT

(*Gobbing.*) Ghaghahest.

The Creation of Consciousness on the Page   113

(They release him. He jerks on. A pigmy woman swings on a rope slung between the railings, counting. A form sprawled against a dustbin and muffled by its arm and hat snores, groans, grinding growling teeth, and snores again. On a step a gnome . . . A crone . . . A bandy child. . . . Figures wander, lurk, peer from warrens. . . . (350–51)

Only then does a recognizable character appear, and we can never be quite certain why she should be here—or, indeed, who is seeing her, or even that she is here in her flesh. (The play form allows Cissy Caffrey, whom we have recently encountered in the "Nausicaa" episode, to appear on the stage without needing to identify it: is it a naturalistic stage? an imaginative one? one created by an individual viewer? or by the potential audience as an entity? The play form barely disguises the most basic questions of point of view.) It is one thing to say that the sources of this scene are the *Walpurgisnacht* from *Faust,* or the first scene of *Lohengrin* or *The Flying Dutchman,* or that there will soon be an echo of the Easter Mass; but the sense of unease raised by the setting's opening images will persist and magnify until the very end, when Bloom, seeking to control Stephen's disorder, will himself experience the most phantasmagoric of all of his images, the vision of Rudy, his son, born deformed and dead eleven years earlier at eleven days of age, and now, in imagination, "a fairy boy of eleven, a changeling, kidnapped, dressed in an Eton suit with glass shoes and a little bronze helmet, holding a book in his hand. He reads from right to left inaudibly, smiling, kissing the page" (497), preparing for his bar mitzvah, evoking a future image of adolescent Stephen as Molly will remember him, as if, somehow, in the Blooms' collective imaginations—although they will likely never discuss this—the infant and the struggling young artist were the same.

The street scene at the start is naturalistic, a slice of life cut on the bias; it is also dreamlike. But it cannot be a dream, for there is no possible dreamer here. Neither Stephen nor Bloom has yet appeared on the scene, and very few events in *Ulysses* take place without at least one of the three protagonists present to serve as point of view. (Molly, of course, is home now in bed.) Is this, then, a glitch in Joyce's technique, or is he trying to suggest at the beginning of "Circe" that something special is taking place here, that the sort of consciousness which he would explore here is other than that of the individual actor? The closing image of Rudy appears to be as Freudian as anything that Freud ever evoked, yet our discovery of Stephen/Rudy in Molly's stream of consciousness, some time after Leopold has fallen asleep—a recognition that only the reader makes fully—takes us somewhere beyond Freud, beyond science, beyond naturalism or even realism, into a realm of Joyce's own devising, a consciousness that might almost be termed universal. Joyce's drama is surely different from that of Hawthorne or Henry James, and it is played on the stage of a point of view that should be named "stream of consciousness" but that looks and feels more like a river or that flows into an estuary or bay: perhaps the Dublin Bay within which *Finnegans Wake* opens.

Universal Consciousness/The Unconscious (Finnegans Wake)

"Universal consciousness," as I use the term here, is not quite synonymous with C. G. Jung's term, "the collective unconsciousness," but there are certain similarities. First of all, of course, we need to note the difference between consciousness and the unconscious and to remember that most Modernist efforts to probe the human psyche are content to reach into consciousness only—or, perhaps, no further than to Freud's so-called preconscious state—and then to probe no further. In this regard, the Modernists are at one with virtually all previous psychological explorations in fiction, from Sterne and Hawthorne to the aggressively non-"experimental" modern (but not Modernist) Iris Murdoch. (Efforts in the novel to employ dream imagery, while they may seem an evident exception to such a claim, are themselves almost always descriptions of dreams, as if from the outside, after the fact, rather than efforts to depict the dream state itself.) While the Modernists will almost surely know Freud, while their points of view may be much more varied and adventurous than those of their predecessors, and while they are far more likely to want to show the working processes of the mind, they are likely to probe no more deeply beneath the mind's surface than did their forebears.

Moreover, their concern is almost always with the state of mind of the individual, even when, as in Faulkner, their theme is the history of an entire region or people. Benjy Compson, to be sure, is an idiot, and so the stream of his consciousness is likely to seem to us, somehow, closer to the psychological depths, perhaps even to those of humankind in general; but it is still more or less the near-surface of his own, rather singular mind which is explored in *The Sound and the Fury*. It is the level of Benjy's language, syntax and intellect that may astound (or bedevil) us—his mind's workings, that is—and not the (shallow) depths at which we approach his thoughts and emotional responses. Virginia Woolf, most notably in *The Waves* (but as early as *Mrs. Dalloway*), does attempt to suggest the unconscious links that may bind individuals together, but she does so more by creating a subjective impression of linkage (of Clarissa Dalloway and Septimus Smith, of the six schoolmates who grow to adulthood) than by penetrating deeply into their minds. Even Woolf, who almost alone of the British novelists of her generation admitted to reading Freud, recognized that it was not possible for a novelist to do more than hint at the depths of the unconscious.

Even in that most famous of all Modernist psychological renderings of the human mind, the "Circe" chapter of *Ulysses*, Joyce's concern is not with the unconscious—whether individual or collective—but rather with the consciousnesses of Stephen Dedalus and Leopold Bloom, along with the latter's preconscious. (Stephen's disturbance when he sees the ghost of his mother—and drunkenly destroys the whorehouse lampshade—may be a sign of guilt-ridden neurosis, but we need not plumb his depths in order to understand its sources.) We might argue, perhaps, that the uncanny connections between Stephen and

Bloom—connections that cannot be logically explained—are proof of some deeper, more generally shared aspect of consciousness or, indeed, of the unconscious; but Freud would not likely accept such a reading as scientific. (Nor would he accept as science that mystic union with Nature that takes place at the end of *The Waves*.)

Even the Surrealists' efforts to replicate the dream state and thus to capture the unconscious directly—I refer, of course, to Surrealist literature and not painting—are more suggestive than realistic. Perhaps the most successful of such efforts are Roger Vitrac's plays *Free Entry* (1922), with its sequential yet overlapping enactments of dream, and *The Mysteries of Love* (1924), which alternates dream sequences with those of presumably objective reality.[11] Yet even on the stage, such efforts demand the suspension of our disbelief: these are not dreams *per se*, but enactments—and enactments not of actual dreams but of what dreams might be if they neatly met certain literary criteria: in Joyce's terms, they are more memories of dreams than dreams themselves. In *Finnegans Wake*, however, Joyce does aim to create the universal consciousness, or unconscious, as it may be at work during the dream state.

We know, of course, of the connections between Joyce and Jung: The psychoanalyst for a time treated Joyce's daughter, Lucia; Joyce's patron, Mrs. Harold McCormick, urged that he meet with Jung to be analyzed; his refusal to do so may have led to the end of her patronage; and Jung wrote a biting, even scornful assessment of *Ulysses*, failing completely to recognize the similarities between Joyce's understanding of myth and his own.[12] Had Jung been more open to the possibilities of *Ulysses*, he might also have been able to appreciate the even greater extent to which *Finnegans Wake* attempts to create a state very much akin to the collective unconscious: what I am calling here universal consciousness.

*

One of the most common critical clichés about Joyce is that just as *Ulysses* is the book of the day, so *Finnegans Wake* is the book of the night. As the novelist told a friend, "A nocturnal state, lunar. That is what I want to convey: what goes on in a dream, during a dream. Not what is left over afterward, in the memory. Afterward, nothing is left."[13] The problem that Joyce sets for himself in his final novel is unprecedented for a writer of fiction: how to represent in words, on the page, the largely visual imagery that populates our dreams. Joyce's resolution of the problem is twofold, with each aspect overlapping and reinforcing the other: the creation of a universal language, consisting both of his so-called "portmanteau" words (a designation that trivializes Joyce's accomplishment) and of the images of world history, geography, literature and culture. Joyce will employ vivid new words, in other words, to create the literary equivalent of the vivid visual imagery of our dreams.

It is, of course, an impossible task, requiring on the part of the reader yet another suspension of disbelief: we must be willing to read these new words of his not as representations of the dense, clustered images which populate our dreams, but as those images themselves. Yet when we consider all those other demands which the *Wake* makes on its readers, this one does seem relatively simple to meet. (Any serious reader of *Finnegans Wake* will insist, to be sure, that the rewards for doing so—in delight, as well as in instruction—more than justify the demands.)

The English language and Irish history and culture are the starting point of Joyce's *Wake,* but some dozen and a half other languages quickly join in, along with the broadest, most encyclopedic range of images of human experience that have ever been gathered for a literary project: all this to enact the supposition that, as both Freud and Jung assured us, the dream of each individual plays a vital role in the drama of the universal dream as it is evoked in myth. The *Finnegans Wake* dream is at once individual and general; that is, although there is but one dream, there are at least several dreamers, a family of dreamers, as it turns out: all five Earwickers—Humphrey Chimpden Earwicker, the father, a Protestant pubkeeper in Catholic Dublin, known widely as HCE; Anna Livia Plurabelle Earwicker, Catholic wife and mother, the most marvelous and musical of modern earthmothers, also ALP; and the twin sons, the artist figure, Shem the Penman (Stephen Dedalus' successor), and the man of affairs, Shaun the Post, bitter enemies and rivals, both in life and in dream, for the love of their sister, Iseult, or Issy. The family servants, especially Kate but also possibly Sackerson, may also join in and play the parts of dreamers.[14]

As the start of the first full sentence of the novel makes clear—most readers know by now that the novel begins in the middle of the sentence with which it also ends—the individual and familial experience of the Earwickers' dream immediately becomes universal:

> Sir Tristram, violer d'amores, fr'over the short sea, had passencore rearrived from North Armorica on this side the scraggy isthmus of Europe Minor to wielderfight his penisolate war.[15]

Tristram immediately invokes Iseult and their forbidden love, as well as the connections between Ireland and England and between the British Isles and the Continent (the two channels crossed in two different versions of the myth; there is also an echo here of that great, betrayed fighter for Irish independence, Charles Stewart Parnell, his flight to America after his fall—for a sexual affront to his society—and his triumphant return home, after his death). He has both "not yet" and "once again" rearrived on his perpetual journey, this violator of loves and mores, who will both "fight again" (German *wiederfichten*) and fornicate again (German *wiederficken*). My favorite pun (the word already seems so inadequate) in this passage is his "penisolate war," with its echoes of the

Peninsular War between Napoleon and Wellington, the battle that the isolated artist must wage both with his public and with himself, the war of/with/for/by the penis, which may or may not have its own consolations (Latin, *solatium,* "a payment for injured feelings"—Tristram is castrated in one version of the myth, healed in another; don't forget that third channel also involved here): a fertility myth turned sour, yet still with potential.

Even this incomplete reading provides a sense of the riches of the text, as well as its attraction to those who love solving puzzles or filling in spaces— crossword puzzlers, stamp collectors, collectors of words and phrases—mildly anal types all. What is relevant here, however, is the notice in these early lines that the family dream will invoke not only the innermost desires and fears of its immediate members but the whole spectrum of human experience, with love and war and creativity at the fore. Among all the efforts to delve into consciousness, almost uniquely in *Finnegans Wake,* Joyce turns to and begins to explore the unconscious. This is not quite Jung's collective unconscious—there is no sense here, for instance, of our pre-human ancestry cluttering our experience still further; but it is as close as we have ever gotten, I suspect, in any artistic medium, to the point of view of the universal.

It is not surprising that the *Wake* has had so little direct influence on subsequent novelists, however. This is surely not the death of the novel that some have proclaimed (actually, they began to do so with *Ulysses,* which has proven an extraordinary source of inspiration for later novelists). But it is clear, as I read the history of the novel's development, that no further great leap is possible until our novelists learn how to make use of *Finnegans Wake* and its quite wonderful, demanding, rewarding—individual, yet universal—point of view.[16]

Disintegration

The literary creation of consciousness leads inevitably—and naturally—to its disintegration. We might almost argue, indeed, that the Modernist novelists were interested in creating consciousness on the page precisely so that they might immediately begin to deconstruct it. (For those critics and novelists who distrust Modernism, it sometimes seems synonymous with the creation and disintegration of consciousness.) Both perpetrators and detractors appear to agree that the individual consciousness in ruins represents the disorder of modern civilization at large; critics such as F. R. Leavis and C. P. Snow, novelists such as Kingsley Amis, William Cooper and John Wain—those, in England, who spoke out most forcefully against the Modernist novel while it was still in its prime—while recognizing the presence of Freud and the stresses and strains of modern life, do seem to fear the effects of depicting consciousness realistically—that is, from within—as if this were especially threatening to whatever stability remains to us in our time. Virginia Woolf, in her poetic yet forthright way, expresses best the expectations of both camps: "Mr Wells, Mr Bennett, and Mr Galsworthy," she says of her predecessors, "are materialists."

> It is because they are concerned not with the spirit but with the body that they have disappointed us, and left us with the feeling that the sooner English fiction turns its back upon them, as politely as may be, and marches, if only into the desert, the better for its soul.

And she goes on, in what is for some one of the most infamous claims from a Modernist novelist, "life is a luminous halo, a semi-transparent envelope surrounding us from the beginning of consciousness to the end."[17]

The contest could hardly be more charged: "materialism" and "the body"—the traditional Realistic novel—as opposed to "the spirit," "the soul," "life [as] a luminous halo." No wonder her enemies leaped on this statement to ridicule and vilify Woolf and her fellows. Reading "Modern Fiction" at a distance, however—and I do not necessarily mean here the distance of time; it is enough just to step back a bit from her metaphoric prose—Woolf is asking merely for the obvious: in the era after Freud, a legitimate subject for the novelist is human consciousness, from its beginning to the end; no subject could be more legitimate, more self-evident, one would think. In fact, what Woolf is asking for is no more than novelists have always done: remember Freud's comment about artists discovering the unconscious; remember Hawthorne's division between the novel/objective realism/the events of everyday life, on the one hand, and the romance/what might be called subjective realism/the events of the life of the mind, on the other. Metaphors aside, what Woolf is demanding in "Modern Fiction" is a recognition that, in the era post-Freud, the reality of the mind is as valid and viable as that of the body.

But to Woolf's English enemies after the Second World War, her insistence that the First War had created a new world and that novelists needed to respond to it in new ways—by turning from the goods of the draper's shelves, as she puts it in "Mr Bennett and Mrs Brown," to the stock in trade of the widow's consciousness—was proof that the Modernists were the enemies of reality as they knew it and of the novel form as they were accustomed to read it and as they preferred to write it. It was the new novel forms that they feared most, I believe, more even than they feared the new reality: not so much consciousness, then, or even its disintegration—in, say, the aftermath of the battles of World War I—but in its depiction on the page.[18]

It is no accident that the (chauvinistic) English enemies of Modernism tended to link the new ways with the obviously immoral French: Flaubert, of course, had first created their problem; even Snow's beloved Proust was not exempt (reading Snow on Proust, one gets the decided impression that the critic/novelist/reviewer is doing his best to turn Proust into an Englishman); and they simply knew that the so-called Nouveaux Romanciers of the 1950s and 1960s had to be engaged in some immoral activities. As William Cooper put it at the time,

> not only are these anxious, suspicious, despairing French writers nullifying the novel, but they are weakening the intellectual world as a whole, by bringing one part of it into disrepute. The impulse behind much Experimental Writing is an attack from the inside on intellect in general, made by intellectuals so decadent that they no longer mind if intellect persists—in fact some of them sound as if they would be happier if it didn't.[19]

"Experimental" in this context (post-World War II English novel criticism) always refers to non-traditional (that is, aggressively non-omniscient) points of view and is always a pejorative. And Cooper makes it clear, as I read him, that efforts to display consciousness from within are the principal experimental evils ("an attack from the inside on intellect in general").

Although Cooper—like his mentor, Snow, and like Snow's enemy, Leavis—seems to have no suspicion that there might be another way to write novels and offers no indication that he has actually read any of the novels of the contemporary French *"avant-garde,"* he would surely have felt vindicated had he managed to read any of the novels of Michel Butor, among the best known and best practitioners of the so-called Nouveau Roman. For they are case studies in the disintegration of individual consciousness, and they make use of points of view that both capture and seem to embrace the process. I can envision a review of Butor by Cooper: It would in some ways recall Wayne Booth's objections to Robbe-Grillet, with moral complaints at the fore (albeit with none of Booth's acknowledgement of the technical accomplishment). But Butor is no Robbe-Grillet: his agenda is more limited, his technique less (if I may risk the pun) single-minded, his thematic concerns far more tradtional (that is, humanistic).

Where Robbe-Grillet sets out to overturn the Modernist novel by using its narrative tools, Butor seems merely to be writing novels of and for his time, using the tools of his time. It is not unreasonable, then, to consider him a conservative, where his compatriot Robbe-Grillet is surely a revolutionary. He is also a better novelist, I believe, than Robbe-Grillet, more likely to engage his reader in the lives of his characters. For Butor's point of view accommodates emotion and affirms humanity, where Robbe-Grillet's is designed to deny emotion and negate the human center of the novel.[20]

"An attack from the inside": The Narrator Self-Deconstructs: Michel Butor

In *L'Emploi du temps/Passing Time* (1956), his first mature novel, Butor plays with the interleaved possibilities of point of view and time that erupt when

The Rhetoric of Modernist Fiction

a disturbed journal keeper attempts to decipher a mystery only to find that his efforts have caused far greater disturbance.[21] Jacques Revel, so revealingly named, a Frenchman on assignment in a northern English industrial city, keeps a journal in which he details his efforts to solve the attempted murder of a mystery writer whom he has befriended. The body of narratives and images which make up his journal—the characters in a novel written by the victim, the characters in a film that Revel recently has seen, images from a tapestry in a local museum and from a window in the cathedral, mythic tales that seem to parallel this one—blend together, enrich the possibilities of discovery and lead, in the end, absolutely nowhere.

The journal itself, meant for discovery, becomes a party to the confusion, one major problem its dual time scheme—Revel begins writing several months after his arrival in England and endeavors to keep a simultaneous log of both the present day's events and those of a day several months earlier. The technique turns treacherous as the mystery unfolds. Revel becomes, in the end, as incapable of distinguishing present from past as of sorting through the characters and images of the mystery/myth which he has been constructing. He is saved from the inevitable disintegration inherent in his project only by departing from England (and only because his one-year contract there has ended).

Threatened by the calendar and saved by the calendar, almost certain victim of the presumed voyage of discovery which he has mapped out yet reprieved by its coincidental abandonment, Revel serves as warning of the potential perils of journal-keeping among the Modernists. The promise of Rousseau's *Confessions*—the reconciliation of body and spirit, of the individual and Nature, the integration of the individual consciousness within the universe, and, above all, the knowledge of oneself—has been betrayed by the simple fact that there are today too many possibilities and too little certainty. The journal-keeping which served so well for Jean-Jacques is a deadly trap for Jacques Revel, from which he is saved through no virtue of his own. His aborted journey serves as a warning for those who would follow him.

Pierre Vernier, the narrator-journal keeper-historian-ironic hero of Butor's *Degrees* (1960), unfortunately, has not learned that lesson. Journal-keeping, for him, turns deadly, the narrative itself—his effort to impose order on disorderly modern life—the cause of his quite literal disintegration. He has simply uncovered too many possibilities to juggle—the multiform, overlapping relationships among his students, relatives and neighbors—and his effort to keep them all in the air of his journal, as it were, is too much for his skills (psychological as well as journalistic). We observe his gradual, growing dissolution until, toward the end, he suffers a nervous breakdown. But his journal, unlike Revel's, is not merely an internal document; much of it is directed to "you," and we gradually become aware that this is not some undefined second person, that he definitely does not mean us, the reader. His audience, we learn, is his nephew, who is also one of his students, and this journal is to be his gift. Even after Vernier's hospitalization, however, the journal-keeping persists, directed still to the same "you": this is another uncle writing now, on the other side of the family, devoting himself both to the journal and to its (unreachable) goal. "Your Uncle Pierre will not write any more. . . . I am writing; I am taking up where he left off; I shall shore up this ruin a little" (330). We expect much the same result for him, of course. But his disintegration is off the page and in the future, open-ended, even if it does seem to promise the same result for all those who would impose narrative order on modern life.

In both *Passing Time* and *Degrees,* the protagonist's disintegration is the direct result of his narrative project: Butor seems to be saying that there are too many possibilities open, in the modern age, to the Modernist novelist; that constructing narratives has become a dangerous business. Long before the coining of the theoretical term, "deconstruction"—that effort to supplant New Critical "close reading" by a more fanciful term—Butor had demonstrated deconstruction at work: not merely of the text, but of the psyche. (It may be no wonder, then, that he himself stopped writing novels at the height of his career.) But in a journal, the psyche is revealed, in a sense, only at second hand: it is what we might call an external narrative. In his other major novel, the perfectly named *La Modification—A Change of Heart* (1957), Butor takes us directly into the disintegrating consciousness, into what we might label an internal narrative.

While not a literal narrative, with a speaker (or writer) and his audience (whether explicit or simply implied) and an attempt to communicate a story from one to the other, *A Change of Heart* does offer a narrative of sorts. That is, there is a "you" here, too, although it is a very personal second person: when he thinks of "you," the protagonist is referring to himself: "Standing with your left foot on the grooved brass sill, you try in vain with your right shoulder to push the sliding door a little wider open" (1), the novel's opening image. From the start, then, Léon Delmont seems detached from himself. As his adventure proceeds—he is traveling on the overnight train from Paris to Rome in order to bring his mistress with him, at last, to Paris—the "you" becomes more intense, its detachment and objectivity less certain, the confusion—his disintegration—increasingly evident. As the traveler grows weary, as the reality of this tiring train trip blurs with those of past journeys which he has made and of a book which he is reading, he is less and less able to differentiate among images and selves.

At one point, he is questioned by a figure "whose features you can't make out clearly, wearing the same clothes as yourself but in better condition, and carrying a suitcase like your own; he looks a little older than you. . . . 'Who are you?'" he demands. "'Where are you going? What are you seeking? Whom do you love? What do you want? What are you waiting for? What are you feeling? Can you see me? Can you hear me?'" (219). He can answer none of his questions, of course, uncertain as his train draws into Rome after a sleepless night of just who "he" or "you" or "I" really is and of what he will do next. But as he

The Rhetoric of Modernist Fiction

debarks from the train, his mind begins seemingly to clear; the long, treacherous night has brought to the fore all of his unacknowledged uncertainties, and, even if he is not yet able to define completely his own identity, he has at least learned to ask some of the right questions. Tracing the consciousness' disintegration, Butor makes clear in *A Change of Heart*, need not be for its own sake, as a sign of disintegrated times; it may sometimes lead to re-integration as well. William Cooper, it seems, need not have worried so for the sake of civilization.

Novelists, in any event, do not so much cause change in society as reflect it: A retrograde narrative technique will not bring back some desired (and likely imagined) past, any more than a radical technique will destroy it. The very few, very greatest novelists may perhaps note societal change before we others have had the vision to notice it. But they do not cause change—except, of course, in the ways that novels are written. (And the greatest of their works, such as *Finnegans Wake*, do not always accomplish even that.) There are likely as many ways of constructing narratives of the disintegrating consciousness as there are apt modern stories. But the final step in the process, as I read these novels, is not so much disintegration *per se* as the possibility of re-establishing consciousness, of re-integration, if not within society, that traditional goal, at least within itself.

As a representative of all those Modernists who have deconstructed the individual psyche—and he is a more useful representative, I believe, than is Robbe-Grillet—Butor illustrates that this narrative goal, too, along with the tools to bring it about, is consistent with the novel's core tradition, the next, inevitable, necessary step in the novel's progression as our principal artistic form of revealing our selves to ourselves. And I would go further and argue that the Modernist narratives of consciousness, however they reveal it and whether they display it as whole or in fragments, externally or internally, in the daytime or during the night, leaving it in ruins or offering the potential for reintegration, are not only a positive development in verisimilitude and form, but are inherently humanistic. Robbe-Grillet's effort to deny humanism through such narratives is one sure proof of that fact; a more telling one is that we read the narratives of Butor and Simon and care about the consciousnesses which are their subjects and sources. Wayne Booth need not have worried so.

CHAPTER 9

Omniscience

Late Modern Revivals

The strangest literary phenomenon of modern times—and this has been a century of strange phenomena—is the reversion to omniscience which took place in England after 1945. The reasons remain obscure, but it is undeniable that in the aftermath of losing its Empire, England experienced in the novel an unprecedented nostalgia for the kind of art and attitude which had populated Victorian and Edwardian times. Although the term itself almost never arises in the heated critical discussions of the time, the key to this reversion was authorial omniscience. In its place, a series of coded terms appeared, the most prevalent (and heated) of which was "experimental." Used aggressively, even derisively, it was intended as an attack on those forms of point of view which the Modernist novelists had developed to replace omniscience and to reflect modern realities. Invariably, "experimental" as used by English novelists and critics from 1945 to about 1980 was a pejorative and was accompanied by those other key, hallowed words "realism," "morality," "humanist" and "English."

Led by the critic F. R. Leavis and the critic/novelist C. P. Snow, an entire generation of English novelists repudiated Modernism as, at best, a temporary aberration; it was as if the greatest epoch in the history of the novel had never even occurred. Joyce, Woolf and Beckett were simply written out of the English tradition which had nurtured them and which they had so brilliantly advanced: almost never written about, never taught in English universities (except, in the case of Joyce, by occasional American or Australian professors). Foreign, especially French, Modernists were simply dismissed as, well, foreign, or, even worse, French. As Snow wrote jingoistically in 1953, "Looking back, we see what an odd affair the 'experimental' novel was. . . . [B]etween *Pointed Roofs* [by Dorothy Richardson] in 1915 and its successors, largely American, in 1945, there was no significant development." And Snow goes on, "In fact there could not be;

because this method, the essence of which was to represent brute experience through the moments of sensation, effectively cut out precisely those aspects of the novel where a living tradition can be handed on. Reflection had to be sacrificed; so did moral awareness; so did the investigatory intelligence. That was altogether too big a price to pay and hence the "experimental" novel ... died from starvation, because its intake of human stuff was too low.[1]

Thus decisively, Joyce, Proust, Mann, Kafka, Woolf, Faulkner, Hemingway and others are written out of the history of the novel. Can Snow have actually read the Modernist novels that he decries: no "reflection" in his supposedly beloved Proust? No "investigatory intelligence" or "moral awareness"? It is obvious that, to Snow, these powers can reside only in the omniscient author—certainly not in the reader, as created and induced by the Modernist novelist.

Snow's disciple, the novelist William Cooper, goes even further in attacking French culture in general (this is also the time of the so-called Nouveau Roman), as if "Experimental Writing" were another form of the French pox: "Aren't the French wonderful," he says. "Who else in these days could present a literary *avant-garde* so irredeemably *derrière*? *Avant-garde* —and they're still trying to get something out of Experimental Writing, which was fading away here at the end of the thirties and finally got the push at the beginning of the fifties."[2]

Cooper himself is a most mediocre novelist, and it is perhaps unfair to posit him against the Modernists (even if he did not himself hesitate to do so). But more talented writers, such as Kingsley Amis and John Wain, clearly agreed with him, and they too wrote novels that are comparably anti-"experimental," i.e., omniscient.[3] The result is the least interesting and effective fiction written anywhere in the world during this period (this at a time when poetry was lively in England and the theatre was beginning a new, very nearly golden age).While the generation that came to maturity before the war—Graham Greene, William Golding, Anthony Powell, Anthony Burgess, among others—continued to write novels acknowledging the Modernists' presence, the next generation claimed to know better The few young novelists, such as B. S. Johnson, who persisted (unlike Tom Stoppard) as novelists, were never allowed to forget that they were squandering their talents. Some even saw Johnson's suicide as a commentary on the sort of fiction that he wrote. All this in the name of "tradition."

Unfortunately, Leavis and Snow and their adherents had forgotten that the tradition of the novel has always embraced change: especially changes in form to communicate changes in the world outside. There is obviously more than one way to characterize the history of the novel as a form: tracing the development of point of view is, to my mind, the best of them. Tracing the movement out of omniscience is surely, as I understand it, the most useful clue to the emergence of the Modernist novel. That almost an entire generation of English novelists and critics should rebel against Modernism by moving back to omniscience, with such disastrous results, is ironic proof of point of view's power.

There are some interesting addenda to this brief history. The following generation of English novelists, recognizing the deadend that Snow/Leavis imposed on the novel and unable, or unwilling, to return to the example of such second-generation English Modernists as Graham Greene, Anthony Powell and William Golding, turned instead to English history as an appropriate venue for the modern (but not Modernist) novelist. In this, they were following the example of such American novelists as E. L. Doctorow, John Barth, Robert Coover and Thomas Pynchon (whose work, I have argued elsewhere, must be considered within the context of Modernism, even as itself Modernist).[4] Avowedly post-Modernist contemporary American novelists, however—notable among them Walter Abish (in *How German Is It* [1980]), Gordon Lish (in *Peru* [1986]), Lawrence Thornton (in *Naming the Spirits* [1995] and William T. Vollmann (in *Argall* [2001])—have made use of demonstrably Modernist points of view in their aggressively post-Modernist histories. Whatever one thinks of their work, they have at least recognized that the way to go forward is not to turn back.

Margaret Drabble

When Margaret Drabble suddenly declares about a character, in her own voice, in the midst of her novel *The Realms of Gold* (1975), "Remember him, for it will be some months before he and Frances Wingate meet again" (51), we are compelled either to wonder whether some powerfully ironic, perhaps self-reflexive, putatively post-Modernist force is comically at work here, or else to conclude that she has consciously chosen Trollope and Thackeray as her improbable models.[5] The novelist lets us know soon enough, however, that she is deadly serious; there is neither irony nor humor here: "They had never met, and were not yet to meet" (99), she goes on to advise us, and then, in an intrusion that seems almost incomprehensible in the late twentieth century, she adds, "The truth is that David was intended to play a much larger role in this narrative, but the more I looked at him, the more incomprehensible he became, and I simply have not the nerve to present what I saw in him in the detail I had intended. On the other hand, he continues to exist, and meanwhile he will have to speak, as it were, for himself" (176). The reader who has read Woolf and Joyce—if no further than the early *Jacob's Room* and the first few stories in *Dubliners* —and who has noted their turn toward a new dimension in point of view, will surely wonder in what literary century he has suddenly found himself.

When Melville changes his mind early in *Moby Dick* about the novel which he is writing and so decides to kill off the character who originally would seem to be his protagonist, we may be a bit bemused. But we give Melville the benefit of the doubt, if only because he is writing in the mid-nineteenth century, when the principles of novelistic structure are still rather loose, and, after all, we have come in our time to recognize the measure of his accomplishment in *Moby Dick*. But Drabble in the late twentieth century is another matter. For her reversion is no accident but a highly self-conscious, almost symbolic repudiation of the Modernist novel, and one that goes to the heart of the entire Modernist endeavor: to innovation in point of view. Drabble aggressively returns to Victorian conventions in point of view, as if, somehow, such an act would in itself restore Victorian certainties.[6]

✷

That there were other possibilities, other ways of responding to the Modernist example, is obvious—even other ways of making use of omniscience. Not even every Modernist novelist was centrally concerned with point of view. It is hardly, for example, the first subject that we think of when we think of Kafka (although his irony would not have been possible in an omniscient world) or of Kazantzakis (although he shows a keen awareness at times of point of view's potential in his world, at once contemporary and timeless).[7] To some Modernists, as to some of their successors, it was not necessary to develop new forms of point of view in order to communicate their sense of a new world; it was enough simply to avoid omniscience and its implications. (Such a position was made possible, of course, by the awareness that Joyce and others had developed many new forms of point of view undermining omniscience and its attendant reality.) For the presence of an all-knowing, all-powerful, manipulative author was in every respect anathema to the Modernist vision of a world not only in flux but inherently ambiguous. If we need a single symbol of resistance to the Modernist novel, we will find it not in some supposedly post-Modernist invention (since most of the inventions claimed for the post-Modern novel will prove, on examination, to be rooted in Modernist practice—if not direct fruit of the Modernist flowering), but in the reappearance of omniscience in the English novel post-World War II.

Recent playing with omniscience, then—whether we name it Modernist or post-Modernist is essentially irrelevant—offers a neatly ironic commentary on this supposed commentary. It may also work, paradoxically, to expand the possibilities in point of view that are available to novelists today. To such contemporary writers as José Saramago and Carol Shields, omniscience is not a weapon to be wielded against "experimentation" but a surprising and playful means of reinforcing Modernist insights into the nature of modern life. When Saramago turns to the Portuguese Modernist poet Fernando Pessoa as his model and Shields for hers to the father of all Modernist writers, Lawrence Sterne, omniscience, ironically, turns Modernist.

At Play in the Fields of Omniscience: José Saramago

Where Drabble is deadly serious in her omniscience, so that her novels are deadened by its presence (for who in our ambiguous time can accept a worldview which includes such imposed stability, such unthinking certainty), José Saramago uses omniscience to precisely the opposite purpose: in *The Year of the Death of Ricardo Reis* (1984), he plays with omniscience as a means of establishing the world's instability, along with the instability of his protagonist and even of his story. That playfulness is apparent even before the story begins: The first of its three epigraphs is from Ricardo Reis himself, as if the fictional poet/protagonist were an historical figure whose supposed observations can cast light on present events (who exists, that is, both within and before this book about him).

That epigraph, "Wise is the man who contents himself with the spectacle of the world," serves as ironic forewarning that Ricardo Reis will not accept his own sage advice. It even prepares us for the novel's principal "spectacle," the source of its third epigraph, the most important of twentieth-century Portuguese writers (beyond even Saramago himself, who won the Nobel Prize for Literature in 1998), the poet Fernando Pessoa. It is Pessoa's recent death which has drawn Ricardo Reis back to Lisbon after many years in Rio de Janeiro, and Pessoa's frequent appearances on the streets of Lisbon and in Reis' room at the Hotel Braganza and then in his apartment punctuate and give form to the returnee's final year in his homeland. There is no suggestion in the novel that these appearances, seen from Ricardo Reis' point of view and absent comment from an omniscient source, are anything less than—or more than—actual, that is, physical and not merely (if that is the right word) imaginary. Yet we recognize early on—we have been warned by the title—that this is the year of the protagonist's disintegration and death, and we may view these appearances as sign, or as source, of that condition. They may prepare us for an omniscience which, similarly, will upset our sense of certainty.

The Lisbon to which Ricardo Reis returns is the gray, closed capital of the dictator Salazar, who (in comparison to Mussolini, Hitler, and Franco, presumably) seems a mere benevolent despot. The dictatorship, the beginning of the Civil War in neighboring Spain, the rise of Fascism throughout Europe— forces which we follow as Doctor Reis reads about them in his daily newspaper and about which he offers no comment—serve as background to the mundane surface events of his daily life. (We never do uncover his politics, if, indeed, he has any—if his current self-obsession will allow him such interests.) His desultory affair with a hotel chambermaid, his unsuccessful courtship of a middle-class woman with a crippled hand, his temporary takeover of another doctor's practice seem so pedestrian, as viewed from his perspective, that we may wonder why he has bothered to return to Lisbon. (Can this dull man be the poet whose potential was once so praised by Pessoa, or, so at least, he tells us?) Only his encounters with the dead poet engage and enliven his imagination. They begin and end in the perversely named Prazeres (Pleasures) cemetery;[8] Reis appears to take more pleasure in meeting Pessoa than in lovemaking or courtship or practicing medicine. Do they signify a breakdown on Ricardo Reis's part? He himself cannot tell us (either because he does not know the truth, or because he cannot acknowledge it, or because he is simply too reticent or fearful to do so), and the omniscient author whose voice we will soon hear evidently will not tell us. That there is an omniscient voice here is another of the novel's surprises.

The narrative opens in the third person and promptly turns to the second and first persons; it begins descriptively and soon becomes judgmental. The opening setting is Lisbon as seen from the sea, as if viewed by a passenger about to disembark from the *Highland Brigade*, leaving behind him the "homey atmosphere" of the ship as he enters the "somber," "gray," "colorless city" (1–3).[9] We may sense an echo here of Conrad's anonymous sailor departing from the *Narcissus* as it berths at last on the Thames (to which the Tagus is explicitly compared). But there is also a hint of omniscience here: "No one by choice or inclination would remain in this port" (2).

"He is accompanied by a porter whose physical appearance need not be described in detail, otherwise we should have to continue the examination forever" (4). Is this aggressive reticence—recalling Drabble's commentary in *The Realms of Gold* but with a suggestion of authorial humor—that of Ricardo Reis himself, we may wonder. It is surely his internal monologue which we overhear (as it were) in the taxi, his dialogue with the driver which is recounted, at a remove, sans quotation marks, as if part of the action, objectively: "The driver informs him, The hotel is that one as you enter the street. . . . You'd better ask first if they have any rooms," 7). His internal monologue is similarly indirect, almost as if there were no difference between monologue and dialogue, suggesting Ricardo Reis' customary thought processes (a sort of controlled free association) rather than his actual words, his tendency to stand at a distance not just from those around him but also from himself.

Meticulously, for the remainder of this first chapter, Saramago provides us with the varied shifts and nuances of his protagonist's point of view, but always with the hint of a presence in the background, perhaps Ricardo Reis' *persona*, perhaps the author himself. Throughout, we sense a disturbing mix of the most intense self-involvement and a dispassionate distance. We may almost wish that this were omniscient, so potentially upsetting is this movement to and fro, devoid of transition or explanation. *Viz,*

The man did not say these words but that was how one might have interpreted the look on his face. (8)

Do you like the room, the manager asked with the voice and authority of his profession but ever courteous, as befits someone negotiating a rental. It's fine, I'll take it. How long are you staying, I can't tell you, much depends on the time it takes to settle my affairs. It is the usual dialogue. (9)

We cannot explain how he [the hotel porter] knew, for he had not seen the register of arrivals. The fact is that the lower orders are every bit as shrewd and perceptive as those who have been educated and lead a privileged existence. (11)

They must be regular clients, perhaps the owners of the hotel. It is interesting how we forget that hotels have an owner. . . . Such details you notice when you pay attention. The girl sat in profile, the man with his back to Ricardo Reis. (15)

The [newspaper] editor did not add these comments [tell me, dear editor, what should I do. In reply to your question, dear reader], nor did Ricardo Reis, who is thinking about something else. (18, 19)

Ricardo Reis falls asleep while reading this newspaper article about mad dogs eating their own young. "A sudden gust of wind rattles the windowpanes, the rain pours down like a deluge. Through the deserted streets of Lisbon prowls the bitch Ugolina slavering blood, sniffing in doorways, howling in squares and parks, furiously biting at her own womb, where the next litter is about to be conceived" (19). We assume, naturally, that this is his dream, and we may as easily conclude that all of these observations and comments, both objective and subjective, have all along derived from his point of view; but perhaps we will wonder as well what this may have to do with cannibalizing one's own pro- duce. If the point of view is that of the protagonist, why does Saramago tempt us—bedevil us—to think of it as potentially omniscient? In the second chapter, however, the point of view appears to turn truly, unambiguously omniscient.

When Doctor Reis first meets the chambermaid Lydia, who will become his mistress and the mother of his posthumous child, he takes care to remember her name, "in case he should need to call her again. There are people who repeat the words they hear, because we are all like parrots repeating one another, nor is there any other way of learning. This reflection is inappropriate, perhaps, since it was not made by Lydia, who is the other interlocutor and already has a name, so let us allow her to leave, taking her mop and bucket with her" (34). Ricardo Reis—he is almost always presented in the formal third person—then falls asleep and has a familiar, disturbing dream set in Rio de Janeiro.

Let us say that it was because he slept so little the previous night that he slept so soundly now. Let us say that they are fallacies of doubtful depth, these inter- changing moments of enchantment and temptation, of immobility and silence. Let us say that this is no story about deities and that we might have confidentially told Ricardo Reis, before he dozed off like any ordinary human being, What you are suffering from is a lack of sleep. (35)

The second-person "you" is unquestionably the subjective, self-centered pro- tagonist; the implicit "I" speaking to him is presumably José Saramago or his *persona* —or someone else's *persona,* perhaps. Of course, this "I" ("Let us") may prove functionally no different from the "you" or the "he," for each of them refers to Ricardo Reis, and each may be his creation. For it may prove impossible to sever this seemingly omniscient voice from the surrounding internal monologue.

Falling asleep "without first undressing" is the first sign of Ricardo Reis' dis-integration, for even in the tropics, he "has always observed the code of civilized behavior, the discipline it requires." (36). This judgment, however, out of context, even without hindsight, might derive from either the poet returned home or the omniscient author awaiting him there. The chapter which follows, however, goes aggressively out of its way to affirm the author's presence, using many of the old tropes of omniscience and inventing some new ones as well: "We shall soon learn," "The observant reader," "we hasten to add," "we are witnessing," "we are speaking," "These contradictions walk through the mind of Ricardo Reis," "Perhaps it is the language that chooses the writers it needs," "When one idea is drawn from another, we say that there has been an association," "I am speaking," "we already know," "Here is an association of ideas for you, then," "let us say," "which is why we can see" (43–53).

There can be nothing accidental about such tropes; Saramago, who has demonstrated in the previous chapter his ability to create original and varied forms of internal monologue, is demonstrably functioning here as an omniscient author: not merely intruding, but, by his self-declared presence as author of these words and events, suggesting strongly his ability to control the life of his protagonist—or so, at least, it would seem. The chapter concludes, in the event that we may have missed the point, with a sort of summation—of narrative method as well as of events: "It is Ricardo Reis's thought," the author insists, "let him do the explaining" (63), and then we are presented with what passes for that explanation. Not a commentary at all, as the term "explanation" might suggest, but an account, at once objective and subjective, of the central event of the novel—objective because presented in the third person, through the sense impressions of a character; subjective because we understand from the event described that something more than sensory knowledge is involved here: this is the first appearance of the dead Fernando Pessoa before the dying (although neither he nor we yet appreciate this fact) Ricardo Reis.

In that most closely observed of all fictional narratives, *Ulysses,* Joyce demonstrates that images and events which appear beyond rational explanation may naturally co-exist with both objective and subjective experience in a novel. There is simply no way to rationalize some of the shared images of Stephen Dedalus and Leopold Bloom—images which not even they come to recognize that they share—beyond declaring that this is but one further proof of their linked sensibilities.[10] Even saying this, however, one must acknowledge that this claim too is incapable of proof, that it smacks of mysticism (to be scorned, one assumes, by any rational being), that it seems thoroughly at odds with the vision of life expressed in the remainder of *Ulysses* and, indeed, throughout Joyce's canon. But there it is, nonetheless. Why can't Saramago create similarly, we may well ask.

The topics of Ricardo Reis' conversations with Fernando Pessoa range from the personal to the poetic: The dead poet cannot help but observe his friend's dalliance with the chambermaid Lydia, and he comments knowingly—and sometimes critically—about his poetry: "I know your poetry by heart, both the poems you have written and the poems you will write" (313); "your odes, my dear Reis, if one looks at them closely, might be considered a paean to law and order" (288), the latter not, presumably, a compliment for a poet. These seem precisely the conversations which the two men might have had were Pessoa still alive, and although there are no narrative markers to indicate that they are anything but actual, it is hardly unreasonable to question whether they might not, in fact, be imaginary, the products of Ricardo Reis' heightened awareness (even if he will not acknowledge it) of a crisis in his mid-life, issues which he might have rehearsed over and over in his mind as the *Highland Brigade* crossed the Atlantic before this story begins. Rehearsed or spontaneous, imaginary or actual, marked or not, Doctor Reis' encounters with his dear friend seem surely to signify his increasing loss of stability now that he has returned to his homeland. The frequent tropes of omniscience, paradoxically, serve to intensify the uncertainties of his personal situation. Because they appear to promise certainty, the resultant uncertainty may seem to us—as to Ricardo Reis—even more destabilizing than internal monologue might be.

If we cannot take seriously such tropes, if the apparent presence of an omniscient author cannot guarantee certainty about the most vital issues in a character's life, if neither the advice of a much-admired poet nor the presence beyond him of a long and stable tradition of authorial stability can provide personal stability, perhaps they may serve instead to undermine it—or, at least, to make us aware both of that character's deep need and of his failure to find what he seeks, what he needs. The fact that Ricardo Reis is himself an author may magnify our awareness of his predicament. His personal reticence may similarly add to our suspicions about his reliability, since he is, after all, this novel's predominant point of view, and he gives us no hint even of why he has returned after so many years to Lisbon. (Visiting the recent grave of a dead poet, however great, however admired, may not seem adequate cause to throw over a secure way of life an ocean away.) Nor does he think to comment on the cause of his original departure, years earlier, to Rio de Janeiro. We might easily conclude that the signs of omniscience are Reis' own creations, designed to mask his uncertainty, that he has himself conjured up this would-be omniscience in order to form a protective facade of certainty, as if to convince himself (as well as his audience) that all will be well in his life. Such programs never work, it seems.

But Ricardo Reis does indeed have an audience, and he is—or so the text assures us—an author, perhaps even "the author of the work" we are reading (119). "I Ricardo Reis," he writes, "you my reader" (259), as if to suggest that this fiction is not merely (or not even) omniscient, but metafictional, a Portuguese variant of that international, post-Modernist phenomenon. (Think of Borges, of Calvino, of Barth.) The narrative may thus be both self-reflexive and omniscient: "These are [moralistic] details we could dispense with," somebody says, "but there are others of greater relevance, such as the rains and storms which have intensified during the last two days, wreaking havoc on the ragged Shrove Tuesday procession, but to speak of them is as tiring for the narrator as for the reader" (143–44). No, they are not at all tiring, we may protest; nor are they relevant.

The Year of the Death of Ricardo Reis is in no functional sense metafictional: its subject is not the creation of the work of art which we are reading but rather the disintegration of a man's psyche. That the man happens to be an artist at once blurs and compounds the issue, however, for as the novel's sole point of view, he is capable of erecting narrative as well as psychic defenses. His playing at omniscience and metafiction, the one extensive, the other brief, is a more elaborate form of the defenses which he has built around himself,[11] of the distance which he maintains even from himself, designed somehow to stave off his disintegration (more accurately perhaps, to stave off his acknowledgement of disintegration): serious play, indeed.

But for Saramago, his creator, the playing with omniscience may be more, well, playful, his pleasure at manipulating the narrative tools both of an generation earlier than his, the Victorians, and of a later one, the presumed post-Modernists, albeit always to a purpose that we may identify as essentially Modernist. That is, while we sense the novelist's delight in these seeming narrative excesses—as well as in confusing their source—we are driven to inquire: Are they the produce of Saramago or of Ricardo Reis? The attentive reader recognizes as well their quite serious thematic purpose. The omniscient tropes and the hints of metafiction alike function as ploys of the self-aware author/protagonist to protect his threatened psyche. That Ricardo Reis never adequately explains the reasons for his return to Lisbon; that he need not rationalize (to himself or anyone else) the frequent appearances before him of a man who died before that return; that he makes no effort to explain his reactions once in his homeland (to events or to people): these narrative gaps are signs of his state of mind. The balancing excesses—seeming authorial intrusions from without and reminders of the protagonist functioning within as potential author of his own narrative—serve ironically the identical, destabilizing function. They do not balance the gaps but, rather, accentuate them; they cannot serve to save Ricardo Reis from himself but work to condemn him. Hiding behind his creator, the protagonist/author strives desperately not to find or to save himself. His narrative concludes, then, with his ambiguous success, his final spectacle:

And the book, what do you want that for. Despite the time granted me, I never managed to finish it, You won't have time, I will have all the time I could possibly want. You are deceiving yourself, reading is the first faculty one loses, remember. Ricardo Reis opened the book, saw meaningless marks, black scribbles, a page of blotches. The faculty has already left me, he said, but no matter, I'll take the book with me just the same. But why. I relieve the world of one enigma. As they left the apartment, Fernando Pessoa told him, You forgot your hat. You know better than I do that hats aren't worn where we're going. On the sidewalk opposite the park, they watched the pale lights flicker on the river, the ominous shadows of the mountains. Let's go then, said Fernando Pessoa. Let's go, agreed Ricardo Reis. (357–58)

And so at last he finds relief, or so at least it seems, although neither he nor his reader ever quite learns from what.

＊

Ricardo Reis, like Leopold Bloom an alien in the city of his birth, strives like Bloom to be both honest and defensive about his life, to acknowledge his predicament as far as he is able but at the same time to shield himself from it. He serves both as center of the narrative world in which he works and, at least at times, as creator of that world. But as an author, his defenses may be far more elaborate than Bloom's. Where Bloom is arguably the creator of some small part of the narrative of Bloomsday, Reis is the sole creator within his.[12] All of the tropes of omniscience, along with the occasional metafictional suggestions, prove to be his own narrative ploys, his own misleading hints that some other, more confident hand than his is at work ensuring his continuity. For Saramago, the seeming omniscience of his novel is a sign of his playfulness; for Ricardo Reis, his protagonist, a man with little humor or sense of play, it is a mark of his failure, deadly serious in its effects.

The Year of the Death of Ricardo Reis is rich in narrative play. But to a Portuguese audience, there is still further play that is likely to go unnoticed by the uninitiate. For the name "Pessoa" means both *person* and persona in Portuguese, and "Ricardo Reis" is one of the several *personae* under which Fernando Pessoa wrote most of his works. (Another is "Bernardo Soares," to whom the second of the novel's three epigraphs is attributed.) No wonder the character Pessoa knows so intimately the poetry of Ricardo Reis; no wonder the latter is from the first unable to create and finally feels compelled to join his mentor in the cemetery at Prazeres.[13] If their novel's involved narrative structure is arguably the product entirely of the protagonist—including the omniscience which we might otherwise assign to José Saramago—then the unique nexus of the three writers (or is it four?) may profitably be seen as a new use for and way out of omniscience: as a metafiction in which not a work but its author is created; as a late Modernist creation which only pretends to be anti-Modernist; as a warning that our world is so rife with ambiguities that even omniscience cannot save us from their effect, so that even omniscience in a novel today may be made to contribute to the inevitable uncertainty. To this worthy end, Saramago might almost be said in this novel to have turned himself into another of Pessoa's *personas*.

The Rhetoric of Modernist Fiction

At Play in the Fields of Omniscience (II): Carol Shields

The Stone Diaries (1993), Carol Shields' quietly moving and challenging account of a woman's life, spans most of the twentieth century, whose volatile events serve largely as background for her own undramatic yet somehow volatile life. Its point of view, similarly quiet yet challenging as it too cuts across the century, brilliantly illustrates the spectrum of possibilities available to the novelist of a generation after the Modernists. It moves from seeming omniscience to conventional first-person narration to an unannounced speaker whose presence is barely hinted at yet is central; from an epistolary interlude, to an amateur historian's gathering of documents, photographs and oral accounts, to an imaginative reconstruction of characters and events which may glance at Proust and Simon but whose model is older by far: From its quiet, shocking opening episode—the unexpected birth of the evident narrator of the account— *The Stone Diaries* is rooted deeply in Laurence Sterne's *Tristram Shandy.*

True, one might convincingly argue that *Tristram Shandy* (1759–1767) is the source of all Modernist innovation in point of view. Although this claim has never adequately been examined in depth, it seems somehow so self-evident that it hardly requires detailed analysis. Sterne's idiosyncratic vision and techniques—so deeply at odds with the conflicting streams of narrative technique (and accompanying worldviews) established by his contemporaries Richardson and Fielding—appear to mesh perfectly with the Modernist novelists' readings of their challenging world, as well as their technical solutions to its accurate depiction in fiction. I do not claim that Joyce, for example, learned any specific technique from Sterne, and yet, in a sense, he learned everything from him: *Tristram Shandy,* at least as much as Freud, made it possible for Joyce to explore human consciousness and enabled him to search for and develop forms appropriate to depicting it (in its many variations) on the page. And Sterne confirmed for Joyce—if he needed assurance—that it was possible to be at once deeply serious and extremely playful in creating a text and a legacy. Sterne is not so much specific source, then, but inspiration: an influence to be respected and, if possible, made use of, but not one to be at all anxious about. In much the same impressionistic sense, it seems to me, Shields too learns from and attempts to build upon Sterne: the narrator's account of her own birth is explicit notice to the reader of her lineage.

There can be no doubt that the "I" who opens the narrative of *The Stone Diaries* is the protagonist, Daisy Goodwill Flett, or so, at least, it would seem. There is no question, in any event, that it is intended to represent her voice: "My mother's name was Mercy Stone Goodwill," she begins. The narrative center quickly shifts to the mother ("It shames her how little the man [her husband] eats"), with occasional references back to the daughter-narrator ("Well, it was a different story for her, for my mother. . . . In our day, we have a name for a passion as disordered as hers," 1–2).[14] We cannot tell at this point of the narrative just how well the daughter knows her mother, what she may have been told, what she may be guessing. But we have no reason to doubt her reliability. From the start, then, even when the narrative shifts to a character whose responses Daisy cannot possibly know (or so it would seem: "the old Jew" peddler, for instance, whose intervention saves the life of the baby but cannot save the mother), it would appear that it is Daisy, reconstructing these events (from yet unknown sources), who serves as sole point of view. And she speaks, it would seem, in varied voices, even one with strong echoes of omniscience: on the death of her first husband on the first day of their honeymoon in Europe, "You might like to believe that Daisy has no gaiety left in her, but this is not true, since she lives outside her story as well as inside" (123). We note the direct comment to the reader and the seeming authorial certainty—albeit probably not omniscience, since this is the voice of a character-as-narrator which we hear and not that of Carol Shields. We note also what would appear to be Daisy's surprising ability (she is a woman of the early part of the cernury, after all) to view herself objectively.

But there are problems with this reading, problems created by the narrator herself as she comments on narration:

> Well, a childhood is what anyone wants to remember of it. It leaves behind no fossils [one of the novel's principal metaphors], except perhaps in fiction. Which is why you want to take Daisy's representation of events with a grain of salt, a bushel of salt.
>
> She is not always reliable when it comes to the details of her life; much of what she has to say is speculative, exaggerated, wildly unlikely. (148)
>
> The narrative maze opens and permits her to pass through.... [S]he possesses ... the startling ability to draft alternate versions. (190)

This narrative is not simply self-reflexive, however—a surprising trope in itself for a non-literary woman of Daisy's generation; it serves also, as does *Tristram Shandy*, as a commentary on the novel form itself: "(Biography, even autobiography, is full of systemic error, of holes that connect like a tangle of underground streams)" (196), a parenthetical voice advises us.

Whose voice is this? we may wonder. Is Daisy, even though she did go to college, capable of such judgments, of such sophisticated, willing distance from her own life? Is she capable of the artfulness with which her narrative prepares us gradually for the fact of her mother's monumental girth and then foreshadows her own unexpected birth? When she delves inside the minds of her parents (she has never known her mother, after all, since Mercy Goodwill dies giving birth to Daisy, and she does not even meet her father until she is eleven), is she extrapolating from what she may have been told (perhaps by the neighbor who is present at that birth and then raises the child until the moment of her

The Rhetoric of Modernist Fiction

own death), or is she inventing? Does Daisy, like Tristram, her model, reconstruct characters and events based upon her own future knowledge, or is this merely the hope of a reader (one with an agenda of his own) that this is not just another post-Modernist reversion to Victorian omniscience?[15] Is all of this merely an elaborate scheme to enable Shields to function omnisciently while not seeming to? How else could she have access to so many sources and speak in so many voices? (She is even present at the solitary death of Daisy's father, Cuyler, privy to his sensations and thoughts, as she had earlier known intimately the details of Daisy's birth. And her narrative continues, albeit in a more objective vein, after Daisy's death, with a catalogue of her personal effects, an account of conversations about her by unnamed people who were close to her—probably her three children—and a final dipping into her consciousness in her final moments of life: what can this be but omniscience?)

Describing Daisy's depression at the age of fifty-nine, the seeming narrator speaks of her in the third person—"She knows how memory gets smoothed down with time" (262)—and of herself in the first—"I feel a part of her wanting to go back to the things she used to like" (263)—and we suddenly realize what we may have intermittently begun to suspect: that this "I" is different (in tone, in confidence) from the earlier one, that the speaker now is neither Daisy, the protagonist, nor Shields, her creator; that the novelist has been playing all along with omniscience, playing with us, using the Modernist rejection of omniscience as a means of first hiding, and then supporting, an unnamed but actual narrator—not Daisy herself, to be sure, telling of her life and reconstructing her mother's, but her daughter telling of, reconstructing them both.

Although never announced—not even at the narrative's end—the sole point of view of *The Stone Diaries*, it seems to me, is Daisy's daughter Alice, an academic in England, with a strong scholarly interest in Chekhov and herself a failed novelist. She alone has the required interest, the knowledge, the experience, the sensibility to be both intimate with Daisy and somewhat distant from her. The sense of wonder that sometimes punctuates Daisy's account (what we have assumed to be her account, that is) may well be the modern daughter's surprise at and admiration for her mother, not a modern woman to be sure, but one who adapts astonishingly well to modern life: not exactly a role model perhaps—at least, not an obvious one—for a woman of our time, yet a person of substance, worthy of respect and affection and, even more, of interest: especially of her own daughter's interest. (The recreation of the dying moments of Cuyler Goodwill suggests that the narrator holds a comparable respect and affection for her grandfather,[16] a businessman out of Sinclair Lewis' Midwest yet capable still of surprises—note his second marriage, to a sensuous, younger Italian woman who barely speaks English: perhaps he is also out of Thomas Mann.) When the narrator, then, reconstructs the moment of Daisy's birth, it is not Daisy who is doing so, but Alice, her daughter, another generation removed, reconstituting her mother as if she were in the act of reconstituting her own birth. It is Alice similarly who penetrates Daisy's consciousness on her deathbed—to the point of including her dreams about Alice. Even Proust, with his imaginative interconnecting of sources, stories and parallel narrations, of reconstructive accounts and eras, never undertakes quite so daring a narrative discourse as this.

The artfulness of the narrative, then—the foreshadowing of images and events and the sense of a sophisticated controlling intelligence, the development of the metaphors of plants (the mother's métier) and of stone (the grandfather's), the gathering of sources and source materials, the narrative inclusions that the mother, Daisy, cannot logically uncover (or perhaps even imagine: of the grandson of the peddler who witnesses Daisy's birth, for example [257–61])—these are not the acts of an amateur but of a skilled critic and creator. And if Alice's first novel was indeed a failure, as we are told, then she seems to have learned well from that failure. Perhaps it is that failure which leads her to omit her name from this narrative.

This leaves one question unanswered: What is gained, playfulness aside, from so elaborate a narrative scheme? This world is not Proust's, after all, and hardly seems to demand such depth, such cleverness, such covertness. The answer lies, I think, again in Sterne and in what he has taught such followers as Joyce and, potentially, those influenced by him. Tristram's voice is both unique in its time and aware of its uniqueness (and serves as the principal sign of his identity); it sets out to tell of his life but, inevitably, tells us mostly of others (he is, after all, only a child at his narrative's end); his narrative is, from the very start, a strange mixture of confidence and uncertainty, of seriousness and humor, yet one which manages, miraculously it would seem, to seem unified. His theory of "the animal spirits ... transfused from father to son" is surely a joke, yet one which he takes seriously and which his narrative constantly illustrates (beginning with the unfortunate timing of his mother's question, " *Pray, my dear, ... have you not forgot to wind up the clock?* " and the resulting dispersal of those necessary "animal spirits").[17] Lacking first-hand knowledge of the facts surrounding his conception, Tristram is, of course, dependent for them on others—"To my uncle Mr. *Toby Shandy* do I stand indebted for the preceding anecdote," he tells us, adding that his father "had oft, and heavily, complain'd of the injury."[18] It is Uncle Toby who alerts Tristram to the direful significance for him of these facts.

There is, to be sure, no Uncle Toby in *The Stone Diaries,* nor could there be: no reasonable author would even attempt to emulate him. But the vigorous lovemaking scenes envisioned by Shields's narrator between (diminutive) Cuyler and (gigantic but passive) Mercy Goodwill may well echo this one with Tristram's parents (as, in a sense, does the scene with Molly and Leopold Bloom at the window); the resultant births, in each case, are at once emblematic and tragic (Rudy Bloom's fatal birth defect, Mercy's death in childbirth and Tristram's feared impotence). These births may also provide their narra-

The Rhetoric of Modernist Fiction

tives' dominant image, setting the scene for every event to follow, the image most likely to be remembered by readers.

Only in the Goodwill-Flett family, however, is future generation assured, a passing on of values as of genes (if not of family names): reason enough for Alice Goodwill, adopting the maiden name of her mother, to attempt to memorialize her. She does so as both historian and novelist, imaginatively recreating that life which she once knew only from the outside (with but one of many possible outside views at that), the interior of which she discovers by the simple act of imagining herself there. (Daisy's childhood friend, Fraidy Hoyt, is convinced that Alice is incapable of knowing her mother truly: "You don't expect [her] to believe in her mother's real existence, do you?" [240].) The daughter cannot become her mother, to be sure, but narrating her mother's story as if she were is the key to understanding her—as well as, perhaps, to understanding herself. To all of this, point of view is central. We are interested in the life of Daisy not for its events but because her daughter convinces us by her indirect yet involved presentation (involved in large part, paradoxically, because it is so indirect, because it lures us into the narrative by its play at omniscience, its effort to reconstruct a life from fragments both witnessed and imagined, the mystery of its hidden narrator). We are interested in Alice herself not for her life or her character, but for her narrative technique. Playing with omniscience in the manner of the three-generation Victorian novel, but using it to her own, modern ends, Shields revivifies the old form. Unlike the English New Victorians, who turned to omniscience as an overt means of rejecting Modernism—a symbolic act that led to the century's deadliest fiction—Shields toys with the Victorians' own favorite point of view, adapts it in a distinctly Modernist way (but one rooted in the novel's earliest days) and thus, very practically, points a way to the future.

CHAPTER 10

The Subjective Uses of Narrative Objectivity

Of the many terms employed in studies of point of view, perhaps the most troublesome and misleading is the obvious one, "objective"—unless, of course, it is that other seemingly simple one, "subjective." Everyone knows the meaning of these terms, but their application in discussions of point of view may prove surprisingly uncertain. For while "objective" surely indicates a view coming from outside a character, it may also describe the objective sense perceptions of a character; in may refer, that is, alike to a perspective which presents a character entirely from the outside, as if seen by some undefined source that draws no conclusions, and, alternatively, to one that presents the world entirely as the character perceives it sensuously. This latter objectivity may prove in practice quite subjective, even if it carefully avoids delving into the character's mind. Is it objective or subjective if we view everything through a character's senses and he or she is blind in one eye or suffers a severe hearing loss?

Less blurred perhaps is another meaning of "subjective," one associated usually with omniscience: the drawing of conclusions, the making and offering of personal judgments—what Wayne Booth calls "commentary." Yet even here we must note the distinction between an author's judgments and those which derive directly from a character: An omniscient author's judgment of the world is subject to no limitations, while a character's judgment is inherently limited by the knowledge, experience, sensibility provided for him or her by the author. It is true that in the end both will reflect the novelist's worldview, but there is a considerable difference in the ways in which that worldview is communicated—and in its effects—most notably in the role and responsibilities reserved for the reader. The modern reader is unlikely to accept an authorial injunction about the truth with the same readiness as a possibility of truth discovered on one's own through a character. Distance, for example— and especially the irony that distance sometimes provides—is impossible in omniscience but may be central to our judgment of a character's judgments (as when we are drawn, for example, to reject a character's view of himself: think of Dowell in Ford's *The Good Soldier*). Where Dickens' reader was content as a rule to sit back and await his instructions, the reader raised on Joyce—even the early Joyce of *Dubliners*—has been weaned on the need to participate.

Modernist Objectivity

In the Modernist novel, it is not only the author's subjectivity (his or her explicit judgments) that must be avoided, but also his or her objectivity. It is the modifier that matters, that is—"the author's"—and not the substantive noun, whether "subjectivity" or "objectivity." Authorial presence alone is the villain, deemed universally as an intrusion from an earlier narrative world and as unrealistic in ours—the single most egregious violation of realism in our world from which God may have fled (or if not God, at least certainty). The only universally accepted truth in the world of the Modernist novel is that there are no truths acceptable to all, neither in individual matters of fact nor in worldview; true believers aside, there can in the twentieth and early twenty-first centuries be no certainty. Indeed, the paradoxical truth may be that the existence of so many true believers in our time, with their desperate need to know truth—their certainty that theirs is the only possible truth—is itself certain proof that there is no certainty. Even the hint of an authorial presence, however unobtrusive, thus violates our most basic reality.

And so we must be wary of even those simplest of terms, "objective" and "subjective," wary of using them without qualification, of using them judgmentally, as if, out of context, they actually told us something significant about a novel's point of view. This is a too common problem; at times, it is Wayne Booth's problem, too.

Booth, Joyce and "Authorial Objectivity"

For Booth, a key to understanding Modernist point of view is its presumably characteristic "authorial objectivity or impersonality" (16), whose corollary is the absence of "commentary" (64).[1] "Objectivity" has many synonyms for Booth, including "impersonality, detachment, disinterestedness, neutrality," among which "we can distinguish at least three separate qualities: neutrality, impartiality, and *impassibilité*" (67). (The last of these is Flaubert's term, which Booth defines as "an unmoved or unimpassioned feeling toward the characters and events of one's own story" [81]). When Booth condemns Robbe-Grillet and Céline, it is in large part for their near-perfect, unmoved objectivity. As for Joyce—the Joyce of *A Portrait of the Artist as a Young Man*—Booth tends to tar him with the same label, since his "explorations came just at the time when the traditional devices for the control of distance were being repudiated, when doctrines of objectivity were in the air, and when people were taking seriously the idea that to evoke 'reality' was a sufficient aim in art" (331). This judgment at once underestimates Joyce's originality, misses the degree to which *A Portrait* is a traditional Edwardian *künstlerroman,* and overstates the case against (or for) objectivity—which, by the way, is not at all Joyce's aim: There is nothing neutral or unmoved (or unmoving) about the effects of point of view in any of his fictions; Booth is again confusing Joyce with Stephen Dedalus' conception of the "artist, [who] like the God of the creation, remains within or behind or beyond or above his handiwork, invisible, refined out of existence, indifferent, paring his fingernails."[2]

If anything, it seems to me, Joyce may at times be too sentimentally attached to his characters—although, even then, he manages to maintain an often ironic distance from them. Think not just of Stephen but of Leopold Bloom and of their later, expanded manifestations, Shem the Penman and Shaun the Post, of *Finnegans Wake.* While Joyce often presents them from within, through one or more forms of interior monologue, he also allows them to present themselves objectively, through their own sense perceptions. We note how seamlessly the internal and external views—the subjective and objective—merge: as when Bloom walks home from the butcher shop in the morning, or Stephen walks along Sandymount Strand in the afternoon, or Bloom and Stephen consult late at night in "Ithaca."

It would thus be more accurate to say, I believe, that Joyce makes use of what appears to be narrative objectivity in order to create a more intense subjectivity, that he distances us from his characters (as they are sometimes distanced from themselves) in order to draw us more intimately to them (noting Bloom's weakness, for instance, is likely to remind us of his humanity and so bind us even closer to him). Still, there is much that we can never know about them; we can never penetrate with objective certainty any of their significant secrets. (There are times when they obscure these truths even from themselves.) What we can do—what Joyce's presumed objectivity induces us to do—is to draw as near as we can to these characters, while retaining a certain distance of our own from them. Events in *A Portrait,* by and large (for Joyce's technique is not yet perfected in that early novel), are viewed through Stephen's senses and within his consciousness, and although he strives for the indifference of his own narrative theory, he never does quite achieve it. As callow as he is emotionally, as biased to the intellectual, he nonetheless registers his fears and desires and leads us to mark them as well. He scorns our understanding and at the same time evokes it. What his attempted objectivity most clearly reveals—and it is his failed attempt at objectivity that matters and not Joyce's—is his inevitable subjectivity. But he reveals this on his own, for his reader to discover it (the novel closes on Stephen's thoughts, both those within his consciousness and those written in his diary); there are few signs here of his author, and none—as I read it—in *Ulysses.*

None of this means, however, that the terms "objective" and "subjective" are in themselves critically useless and that no meaningful judgments can follow from them. For even if the objective sense perceptions of a character prove inevitably subjective—because of a physical disability perhaps, or even a disabling environment in which to view events (think of the blurred light in Conrad's *The Secret Agent* and of the blurred reasoning of its protagonists)—there remain differences between this sort of subjectivity and the sort which locates us within the consciousness of a character. Not all Modernist novelists, however anxious they may be to avoid omniscience, are interested in taking us into the minds of their characters, to discern their workings and to participate along with them as they progress (or regress) toward some sort of conclusion. The creation of a consciousness on the page is not easy work, and not every Modernist novelist is drawn to do it or finds it a necessary means to communicate his or her vision.

A point of view may be Modernist in method and may serve a Modernist worldview even though it does not immerse us within an individual consciousness. It need merely avoid the authorial. Conversely, even when a novel does attempt to explore human consciousness, it may do so in a way that reminds us constantly of the author and thus deny one of the most basic Modernist concerns. D. H. Lawrence is to my view not a Modernist, despite his desire to expose his characters' profoundest thoughts, because he does so in a manner that reminds us constantly of his own presence: it is his hand, eye, voice which do the exposing, leaving little for his readers to discover on their own. Lawrence's protagonists are at least as much his puppets as are Thackeray's. Who can possibly follow Kate Leslie on her tortuous path through *The Plumed Serpent* without being aware that it is Lawrence's hand which leads her—and us; his eye which foresees her way; his voice which we hear constantly defining her choices, whether in describing the surface perceptions of her senses or her deepest fears and desires; his voice which constantly judges. The reminder, inevitably, is of an old fashioned omniscience, no matter how modern Lawrence's subjects may be. It is a novel's point of view that both makes possible and defines its worldview.

Paradoxically—and so many judgments about Modernist narrative technique do go against the grain of what we might otherwise expect—the Modernist novelists whose handling of point of view is most difficult to describe are not those with the most innovative and elaborate techniques. Joyce is a much easier study in this regard than is Kafka, for there seems at first glance so little to say about point of view in Kafka, and while there is so much to say about Joyce, it is all of a developing piece: from his re-working of his first published story, "The Sisters," so as to avoid an authorial presence and to limit our knowledge to what his protagonist is able and willing to tell us; to the varied sources of and approaches to point of view in *Ulysses;* to the complex, multiform, yet unified (in universal dream) perspective of *Finnegans Wake,* Joyce's purpose and technique in point of view are consistent. There is more and more to describe as we follow his progression, but the general goal is always the same: to inform, but indirectly; thereby to involve the reader in the lives and mysteries of the characters; to show us life as it is in our time in the most realistic ways possible; and, increasingly, to delight. The method grows richer, more complex, and we may argue about its workings and effects in individual stories in *Dubliners,* or in chapters in *Ulysses* or the *Wake,* but the goal remains unchanged from those first manuscript revisions in "The Sisters."

But with Kafka, it is difficult to know where even to begin. Those stories of his told in the first person seem reasonably straightforward: the speakers are not always reliable; we may be distanced from them even as we sympathize with their condition; the possibilities for distance and irony are everywhere. The technique is wonderfully efficient and subtle, never calling attention to itself, but once we have noted, say, the scholarly evasions of the speaker in "Investigations of a Dog," or the dreamlike meanderings of "A Country Doctor," or the paranoid if justified fears of "The Giant Mole" (also called "The Burrow"), there is not very much more to say about point of view *per se* in these tales.

Those Kafka stories told in the third person, however, for all their seeming simplicity, are a different matter indeed. To call them merely "objective" is entirely to miss the point: theirs is not only a highly subjective mode of objectivity, but much that is most intensely subjective in Kafka's tales arises directly from, is even caused by, the presumably objective technique. The very form that seems to distance the reader from these strange, all too human protagonists and their wrenching predicaments—from the private tragedy of "The Judgment," to the public career of "The Hunger Artist," to the universality of *The Metamorphosis*—works, in the end, to entrap us.

Where "A Country Doctor" begins, "I was in great perplexity" and continues to describe a state of affairs that we only gradually come to recognize as dreamlike (we recognize it so slowly because it is described so realistically), *The Metamorphosis* opens, "As Gregor Samsa awoke one morning from uneasy sleep" only to discover that he has become an enormous insect (a beetle, he says, but I like to think of him as a cockroach, probably of the large, German variety). "What has happened to me? he thought," in one of the novella's rare digressions into the first person (67)—albeit, of course, it is viewed through the third.[3] As he observes the physical changes which have taken place in him overnight, as he interacts with his family and contemplates the many changes in his status ("It was clear to Gregor that his father had taken the worst interpretation of [his sister] Grete's all too brief statement and was assuming that Gregor had been guilty of some violent act," 107), as "from his nostrils came the last faint

The Rhetoric of Modernist Fiction

flicker of his breath" (127) and his corpse is swept away with the trash, even as the story continues without him, we are aware both of how personal this little adventure has been and of how impersonally it has been described.

Presenting events from outside Gregor's immediate purview allows Kafka to continue the story after his death; it also enables us to note how, in a sense, outside himself Gregor has been from the start, accepting his changed status (if only as a means to evade his onerous responsibilities) yet continuing to think of himself as the man that he was. We are similarly caught somewhere between the two. The situation, as in the first-person "Country Doctor," seems dream-like, and we experience, even as we strive to distance ourselves from the characters, the same intensity, the same immediacy, the same reluctant involvement. But where the personal narrative of "A Country Doctor" seems to warn us that we are expected to be involved, the outward, objective form of *The Metamorphosis* would appear to promise distance—as does the wonderfully absurdist premise; and so the shock may be greater when we cannot quite attain it and find ourselves committed.

Similar narrative and emotional developments take place in "The Judgment," as Georg Bendemann leaps to his death, "like the distinguished gymnast he had once been in his youth, to his parents' pride" (63), and we experience intensely both the foolishness of his gesture and its necessity, its mix of comic and tragic, as we both identify with and remain aloof from the protagonist and his point of view. The events of the story are revealed, as it were, as the character experiences them; the objective point of view, which at first seems designed to distance us from Georg, acts instead to entangle us in his fate. His presumed objectivity involves us as intimately as does the country doctor's subjectivity: more so perhaps, since it promises a distance that we never quite manage to achieve. For while his relationship with his father may indeed be absurd—it surely is as a reason for his suicide—we cannot help but be aware of a comparable potential with our own fathers and sons. It may be dangerous for us to judge Kafka's characters, made so especially by his involving use of a seemingly objective point of view.

In "A Hunger Artist," the point of view seems at the start more firmly distant, almost as if this were some historian offering a bit of local lore. ("During these last decades the interest in professional fasting has markedly diminished," he begins, 243). He moves ever closer to his subject as he proceeds, both physically and historically ("only the artist himself could know that," 246), perhaps even identifying with the overseer, who bends over to hear the artist's final words, in what is surely one of the funniest—and most harrowing—moments in all of Modernist fiction:

"I always wanted you to admire my fasting," said the hunger artist. "We do admire it," said the overseer, affably. "But you shouldn't admire it," said the hunger artist. "Well then we don't admire it," said the overseer, "but why shouldn't we admire it?" "Because I have to fast, I can't help it," said the hunger artist. "What a fellow you are," said the overseer, "and why can't you help it?" "Because," said the hunger artist, lifting his head a little and speaking, with his lips pursed, as if for a kiss, right into the overseer's ear, so that no syllable might be lost, "because I couldn't find the food I liked. If I had found it, believe me, I should have made no fuss and stuffed myself like you or anyone else." (255)

The broad general "you" of the hunger artist's final declamation indicates surely that we, his public, are included in his audience, even to the end. And while we may ridicule his choices, we cannot help but feel implicated somehow in his fate. Why else might he want to kiss his listener? This is the pattern in many of Kafka's presumably objective narratives, as we both witness and experience the characters' fates, judge them and yet empathize with them, perhaps even see a bit of ourselves in them, or of them in us. While not the spectacularly innovative technique that critics, both admiring and hostile, have seen as the basis of Modernist narrative, this model of Kafka's is very likely the most enduring and representative of Modernist survivals at the end of their century and the beginning of the next.

Modernist Narrative Survivals and Adaptations: From Kazantzakis to Bellow, Allegra Goodman, Don DeLillo

For those Modernist novelists not interested in exploring the various modes of internal monologue—stream of consciousness most prominent among them—or even the more readily available first-person narrative, objectivity serves as the solution: an objectivity, of course, that pointedly (if quietly) omits an authorial presence and that may prove on close reading to be highly subjective.

Among the most daring and ambitious of the Modernist novelists is Nikos Kazantzakis, whose long epic poem *Odysseia* (1938, brilliantly translated into English, by Kimon Friar, as *The Odyssey: A Modern Sequel*), dares to challenge Homer directly and—although some readers are shocked to be told this—in many ways succeeds in surpassing its model. In its grasp of both the Bronze Age and modern worlds, in its effort to blend a variety of sources (literary, historical, archaeological, political, philosophical, mythic, linguistic) with a complex plot and rich characterization, it can be matched only by Joyce's *Finnegans Wake* in its reach. Kazantzakis' novels are similarly daring, *The Last Temptation of Christ*, in particular, willing to challenge our most sacred icons. As one of my students once commented, "This is a dangerous book because it makes me want to challenge my faith," only to be answered by a classmate, "I think it's a dangerous book because it makes me want to have faith." Yet Kazantzakis' novels seem very conservative in their narrative choices.[4]

Indeed, the only evident example of Modernist innovation in Kazantzakis' novels occurs in *The Last Temptation,* as Jesus confronts his rather disreputable follower Matthew and asks to read what he has been writing.

> "Matthew," said Jesus, "bring your notebook here. What do you write?"
> Matthew got up and handed Jesus his writings. He was very happy.
> "Rabbi," he said, "here I recount your life and works, for men of the future."
> Jesus knelt under the lamp and began to read. At the very first words, he gave a start. He violently turned the pages and read with great haste, his face becoming red and angry. Seeing him, Matthew huddled fearfully in a corner and waited. Jesus skimmed through the notebook and then, unable to control himself any longer, stood up straight and indignantly threw Matthew's Gospel down on the ground.
> "What is this?" he screamed. "Lies! Lies! Lies! The Messiah doesn't need miracles. He is the miracle—no other is necessary! I was born in Nazareth, not in Bethlehem; I've never even set foot in Bethlehem, and I don't remember any Magi. I never in my life went to Egypt; and what you write about the dove saying 'This is my beloved son' to me as I was being baptized—who revealed that to you? I myself didn't hear clearly. How did you find out, you, who weren't even there?"
> "The angel revealed it to me," Matthew answered, trembling.
> "The angel? What angel?"
> "The one who comes each night I take up my pen. He leans over my ear and dictates what I write."
> "An angel?" Jesus said, disturbed. "An angel dictates, and you write?"
> Matthew gathered courage. "Yes, an angel. Sometimes I even see him, and I always hear him: his lips touch my right ear. I sense his wings wrapping themselves around me. Swaddled in the angel's wings like an infant, I write; no, I don't write—I copy what he tells me. What did you think? Could I have written all those miracles by myself?"
> "An angel?" Jesus murmured again, and he plunged into meditation. Bethlehem, Magi, Egypt, and "you are my beloved son": if all these were the truest truth . . . If this was the highest level of truth, inhabited only by God . . . If what we called truth, God called lies . . .
> He did not speak. Bending down, he carefully gathered together the writings he had thrown on the ground and gave them to Matthew, who rewrapped them in the embroidered kerchief and hid them under his shirt, next to his skin.
> "Write whatever the angel dictates," Jesus said. "It is too late for me to . . ." But he left his sentence unfinished.[5]

Only in this single moment during his long career does Kazantzakis demonstrate an interest in the narrative revolution being conducted by his contemporaries, and even this interest is driven by the particular demands of his theme: It is the reliability of the Gospels that matters here—the various aspects of reliability—and not that of a narrator or character. As my students together recognized in their comments, Kazantzakis in *The Last Temptation of Christ* affirms the example of the historical Jesus while opening to question the institutions and beliefs that have been built up around him. But note how neatly he raises the most fundamentally subjective of all Modernist questions—the ambiguity of his theme, the reliability of its source—and that he does so by means of a point of view that is itself objective, with no sense of an authorial presence, no narrator within the story, hardly a glimpse of the characters' thoughts and none at all of the workings of their minds. In this scene, too, point of view remains largely outside the characters. It is the subject of the scene that raises the question of reliability and not its technique.

The key narrative concern for Kazantzakis is meticulously to avoid anything resembling omniscience in his presentation of his characters and their contexts—even when that context may require explanation (as in the religious and political background of first-century C.E. Judea and Galilee, or the exodus of the Anatolian Greeks after World War I in *The Greek Passion* [1948], or the post-World War II Greek Civil War in *The Fratricides* [1954]). He limits what we are shown to what his characters can perceive through their senses and what they may think or recall about events. For late Modernist and current (the terms at times overlap, still) novelists who have decided, as Kazantzakis has, that they are uninterested in or incapable of constructing elaborate, inventive interior points of view but who recognize the inappropriateness of Victorian technique in the late twentieth century, this has become the characteristic approach.

In every other moment in every one of Kazantzakis' novels, point of view is rigidly objective: with every action viewed through the sense perceptions of the characters and with an absence of editorial comment, either from the author or from any other potential source. Only the fact that he sometimes moves from the sense perceptions and surface thoughts of the protagonist to those of another character—although even then judiciously, briefly, when it seems natural and inevitable to do so—begins to hint at the author's possible presence within his story. If we apply Levitt's Law here, however, and suspend disbelief when to do otherwise would distort the narrative and our understanding (for we know who wrote these words, and we understand that he does not intend to call our attention to his presence), we may recognize in Kazantzakis' practice the fullest, most disciplined development of Henry James's central intelligence—from which James himself was never quite able to eliminate his own presence.

The technique is hardly revolutionary—not at all what either Modernism's admirers or detractors seem programmed to expect—but it may well be the most characteristic of Modernist techniques, more prevalent even than the various, often spectacular forms of internal monologue. (We tend to associate Joyce, for example, with stream of consciousness, the most daring of those forms. But even Joyce's stream of consciousness is combined with objective points of view closely resembling Kazantzakis'.) Many of the second-, third- and fourth-generation Modernist novelists employ a similar technique. Serious and popular fictions alike, at the end of the century, are apt to develop through such a form.[6]

We find a variant, for example, in *Kaaterskill Falls* (1998), Allegra Goodman's absorbing account of Orthodox Jewish life in late twentieth-century (urban and rural) New York. Its action—mostly internalized—is revealed as perceived by a dozen or more different but inter-connected characters; indeed, it is the differences in their perceptions which provide much of the action. Subtly and acutely, Goodman probes the consciousnesses of her creations, revealing their thoughts about the closed world in which they live, their perceptions about their loved ones and neighbors and, ultimately, about themselves, their developing sensibilities and characters. While religiously interior, little or none of this should be thought of as internal monologue: while much of it is personal, even intimate, the technique which reveals it—both actions and thoughts—develops directly out of the objective points of view of such Modernists as Kafka and Kazantzakis.

I was attracted originally to *Kaaterskill Falls* by several reviewers' comments that it made creative and original use of a variety of points of view. But what do we mean when we speak of a novelist's employing a variety of points of view? Are we referring to the number of characters through whose perspectives we are led to view the action? Or are we speaking instead of the different techniques through which these perspectives are realized? So much have these terms' meanings been blurred: Everyone uses them, it would seem, but many do not recognize that "point of view" and "objective" offer as many possibilities as do the concepts they are meant to describe. *Kaaterskill Falls* affords an opportunity to sort them out a bit further.

The novel explores (intelligently, if not very deeply) the consciousnesses of various characters—of different backgrounds, ages, religious beliefs—but its technique in doing so is essentially unvaried. Defined largely by the community of which they are a part (or against which they react), these very different individuals are revealed to the reader through a unitary, undifferentiated point of view: Whether it is thought or action which is being presented, it is—dialogue aside—offered in the third person, close to the characters yet somewhat removed, at once intimate and a bit distant, and in an unchanging language. I cannot help but conclude that a greater variation—even if limited to vocabulary, syntax and sentence rhythms—might have made available to us a greater variation of personality and consciousness, and thus a richer novel.

More limiting still, the unitary technique may make us question—by the time we reach the final chapters—the single, authorial hand which appears to control all of this. Goodman works hard to avoid omniscience and is almost entirely successful. But even so, she cannot at times escape its effects. And since her theme is the variation possible even within Orthodoxy—the potential for ambiguity underlying what may seem to outsiders to be monolithic certainty—it would be better served, I believe, by a more varied technique, one which does not make us think of the author and thereby hints at even the possibility of certainty. Still, this is Goodman's first novel, and it is reasonable to assume that she will soon enough come to master fully that union of technique and theme which characterizes the Modernist novel.

I am suggesting, that is, that Goodman may come to follow a route comparable to that of Don DeLillo, among the most adventurous of contemporary American novelists. From such early novels as *Ratner's Star* in 1976 and *Running Dog* in 1978, he has limited his readers to the consciousnesses and sense perceptions of his characters, offering generalizations and judgments only through the characters. If there are moments when we may be inclined to suspect that a judgment is really that of the author, masquerading as a character's, it is always possible to attribute it as well to the character: and so, even here, we suspend disbelief and give the novelist the benefit of the doubt. DeLillo's technique is totally consistent even in these early novels. Yet we may sense beneath the objective technique a perception, language and even sensibility that are largely invariable, both within individual novels and among them: not just a novelist's vision (of American history and culture) that remains consistent but a presence and a style that may be so unvarying that, despite ourselves—and the novelist's evident intentions—we may become aware of his hand in the midst of his creation: nothing Dickensian, to be sure, but also not quite the distance that the carefully controlled technique seems to promise and is capable of delivering.

In his later, still more ambitious works, however, DeLillo has learned to vary the details of individual consciousnesses and scenes, of both perception and expression, so that we are no longer suspicious of his authorial presence. This helps to account, I believe, for much of the success of his most daring and challenging work to date, the novel *Underworld* (1997), in which even the most objective, seemingly authorial introductions may be read as personal observations by a character. Halfway through the 827-page novel, a character named Matt Shay, who previously has been seen only briefly and only through the eyes of his distant older brother, now appears in his own right, as seen through his own point of view, however objective the presentation:

> The poets of the old nations of the basin told stories about the wind.
> Matt Shay sat in his cubbyhole in a concrete space about the size of a basket-ball court, somewhere under the gypsum hills of southern New Mexico.
> This operation was called the Pocket.
> There were people here who weren't sure whether they were doing weapons work. They were involved in exploratory research and didn't know exactly what

happened to their findings, their simulations, the results they discovered or pre-
dicted. This is one of the underlying themes of the systems business, where all
the work connects at levels and geographic points far removed from the desk toil
and lab projects of the researchers. . . .

   The Pocket was one of those nice tight societies that replaces the world. It was
the world made personal and consistently interesting because it was what you
did, and others like you, and it was self-enclosed and self-referring and you did it
all together in a place and a language that were inaccessible to others. . . .

   It was part of the reason he'd come here in the first place. For the questions
and challenges. For the self-knowledge he might find in a sterner life, in the fix-
ing of willful limits.[7]

Whether in the second person or the third—there is no "I" here, except occasionally in dialogue—the description is clearly subjective, the world as viewed
from within, although the form may appear on the surface to be objective.
Moreover, Matt Shay's world is clearly different from that of, say, Cotter Martin, the adolescent boy from Harlem who captures the prize baseball from the
most famous of all baseball games. Where the objective approach remains
essentially the same as for the older, more sophisticated scientist, we can sense
the different rhythms, vocabulary, syntax:

   Next thing Cotter knows he is sidling into the aisle. The area is congested
   and intense and he has to pry his way row by row using elbows and shoulders.
   Nobody much seems to notice. The ball is back there in a mighty pileup of shirts
   and jackets. The game is way behind him. The crowd can have the game. He's
   after the baseball now and there's no time to ask himself why. They hit it in the
   stands, you go and get it.[8]

Unlike pure stream of consciousness, or even first-person narration by an eyewitness or protagonist, there is no effort here to provide only the words that a
Negro boy would use in New York in 1951. Cotter is not the narrator of this pivotal scene; indeed, there is no narrator here. Nor do we find ourselves deep within
his consciousness, privy to (and subject to) the workings of his mind. Descriptions
and words here seem totally objective, yet we cannot mistake the boy's presence,
the fact that it is his point of view through which this action is visualized. It is not
so much that we can recognize this as his language and sensibility; it is through
the language and sensibility that we begin to learn who he is, especially when we
contrast his point of view with others'. (Note, for example, the way in which his
nearest contemporary in the novel, a contemplative sixteen-year-old Puerto Rican
subway graffiti artist, regards his own thought processes: "He sat on the Broad-
way train listening to the way his mind was reasoning," 436). DeLillo's narrative
technique—and although he may manage it better than most, he is not unique
among contemporary novelists in developing the objective/subjective approach

to point of view—has clearly been chosen generally as the method best suited to an era post- (or, perhaps, very late) Modernism. The most intensely inward use of that technique, however, is by a novelist who is not only our contemporary.

Saul Bellow is both a late Modernist (second-, or perhaps third-generation, most accurately) and a current force in the novel, noted for both the intensity of his vision and the intensity of his language. The two forces fuse in his unique point of view, a version of the objective approach which does delve more deeply into consciousness. Bellow develops the technique rather early in his career, but not always seamlessly: objective and subjective are not always fused perfectly; some of the narrative keys and transitions are overly evident. Thus, in the superb story "The Old System" (1969), a famed Jewish scientist contemplates the death of the last of his older relatives:

> Mankind was in a confusing, uncomfortable, disagreeable stage in the evolution of its consciousness. Dr Braun (Samuel) did not like it. It made him sad to feel that the thought, art, belief of great traditions should be so misemployed. . . .
>
> He opened a fresh can of coffee, much enjoyed the fragrance from the punctured can. Only an instant, but not to be missed. Next he sliced bread for the toaster, got out the butter, chewed an orange . . . when he discovered that a sentiment was approaching. It was said of him, occasionally, that he did not love anyone. This was not true. He did not love anyone steadily. But unsteadily he loved, he guessed, at an average rate.
>
> . . . Braun now discovered that he and Cousin Isaac had loved each other. (46)[9]

But that technique would develop, become seamless, sense perceptions and thoughts now part of a unified whole. Bellow's mature technique—as seen, for instance, in *The Dean's December* (1982)—seems to me a direct outgrowth of Leopold Bloom's point of view as he walks to and from the butcher shop, early on the morning of 16 June 1904, in the "Calypso" episode of *Ulysses*. We can recognize here the similarity with DeLillo's technique and, at the same time, Bellow's uniqueness.

Bellow's use of point of view in *The Dean's December* is at once seemingly conservative and an apotheosis of late Modernist narrative technique. There is not a hint of omniscience here—so perfectly under control is the technique— and, at the same time, no evident indication that anything "experimental" is going on. The language is totally objective, and so seems the tone; yet, as we look closely, we learn how subjective are both tone and language. Although there are only a few moments when the novel's point of view is evidently that of Albert Corde, everything, in fact, is seen from his perspective, and nothing is removed and objective. Whatever the language—and it varies somewhat— whatever the apparent tone, every single event, conversation, memory, judgment is presented as Corde views, remembers, judges it. What seems objective and removed is thus intensely subjective. As Corde contemplates the relationships among his nephew, his sister and himself, for example, the point of view starts out in the third person, but the intensity of the prose and of the perceptions notifies us almost immediately how very personal this is:

His nephew, as Corde saw him, was at an uncomfortable stage of development. Uncomfortable? Bright, light, he was also bristling, writhing. The young racket wasn't doing him a bit of good. Well, the field was very crowded; he was one of global millions. . . . Corde looked down on these crowded fields packed with contenders; he was prepared to admit that. He was prepared to admit quite a lot about himself. For instance, you would not need to press hard to get him to concede that his patient air was only assumed, a pis aller and a burden. But it would have been a terrible mistake to try to discuss things with Mason frankly, or (still worse) on a theoretical level: youth, age, mass tendencies, self-presentation, demagogy. Corde had observed to [his sister] to Minna not long ago that although people talked to themselves all the time, never stopped communing with themselves, nobody had a good connection or knew what racket he was in—his *real* racket. Did Corde actually know? For most of his life he had had a bad connection himself. There was just a chance, however, that he might, at last, be headed in the right direction. Just a chance. (35–36)[10]

Corde is a man whose appearance to the outer world is of a man under control—at least so it seemed before his return to his native Chicago and his involvement in some highly controversial public events—yet we come to recognize that he internalizes everything, runs every incident and person through his personal screening process. And how intensely self-aware and revealing that process is.

Where such Modernists as Kazantzakis and Kafka were not especially interested in narrative innovation and were content with a kind of Jamesian central intelligence but without the Jamesian voice—with all of the action developing around the protagonist and no omniscient intrusions of any sort—Bellow takes the process a step—a significant step—further: for his practice in this novel avoids even the small distance from the narrator's consciousness that we find in the earlier usage. There is no distance here whatsoever. Without the flashiness of a Joyce or Faulkner, with no narrator *per se* as in Proust, avoiding the potential confusion that will lead some critics to find a "narrator" in Woolf, what Bellow manages in *The Dean's December* is actually an advance on Modernist technique and not a conservative consolidation. He does not merely avoid omniscience; he finds a way to turn a technique that is designed to provide some objectivity into the purest subjectivity.

The appearance of objectivity yet with intense subjectivity: the point of view seems perfectly designed for Bellow's protagonist, who is carefully portrayed as a non-Jew but has the same combination of practicality-idealism-emotion-rationality-universality-humanism that we find in Bellow's Jewish protagonists. Bellow's implicit claim would seem to be that the Jew is indeed the universal man in the modern world (a claim built, of course, on the example of Leopold Bloom). The point of view thus serves the essential Bellow themes—those universal Modernist themes—of human emotions, involvement, idealism in the face of a complex, often hostile world. The technique, as with Joyce, albeit differently, makes significant demands on the reader, but offers powerful rewards (in intellectual and emotional involvement, especially) for our efforts.

What these American novelists collectively have shown is that the Modernist narrative example need not be intimidating; that it is both foolish and self-defeating to follow the path of the English novel after World War II in rejecting Modernism so completely—and particularly Modernist narrative technique; that the potential inherent in Modernist point of view is far from exhausted and much remains for contemporary novelists to build on. The very technique which Leavis and Snow and their followers saw as inherently anti-human proves, in practice, to provide continued, perhaps even richer access to humanity.

CHAPTER 11

Metafiction as Narration

*I*n his well known list of the characteristics of the Modernist novel—among the first and still one of the most often cited of the many such lists—Maurice Beebe includes reflexivism and comments, "Much Modernist literature is about itself."[1] Known also (redundantly) as self-reflexivism, (gracelessly) as self-referentiality and (more fancifully) as metafiction, the practice of writing books whose subject is their own composition has also been cited by many as among the most important characteristics of post-Modernist fiction. (This overlap may lead one to suspect that there is less of a distinction between the two modes of fiction than various interested parties have been able to acknowledge.) Whether Modernist or/and post-Modernist, the so-called metafiction is an outgrowth of the Romantic poet's obsesssion with himself and with his art (inspired, if hard-earned). It is no great leap from Rousseau's *Confessions* or Wordsworth's *Prelude* to John Barth's *Lost in the Funhouse*—with waystations at those landmark texts whose heroes determine at their end to write the books which we have just read: Proust's *A la recherche du temps perdu* and (implicitly) Joyce's *Ulysses*.

Comic Strips and Movies

Lest we be carried away by metafiction's distinguished, if surprising, history, however, we should note that its modern origins are less notable venues: in vaudeville comedy (comics constantly referring to the routines in which they are performing as they perform them), as well as in a now-defunct but once widely read comic strip whose jokes were stolen from vaudeville routines, "Mutt and Jeff." It is likely no accident that contemporary comic strips, from "Fred Bassett," "Overboard," and "Beetle Bailey" to "Ziggy" ("sometimes I feel like I'm just a figment of someone's imagination," Ziggy says to his psychiatrist as a huge hand is seen drawing them both); "Doonesbury" (the cartoonist Gary Trudeau is called back by his publishers, in a strip titled "The

Putsch of the Supporting Characters," after their attempt to take over the strip self-destructs: "We're even losing our color intensity," one of the characters laments as they fade to pastels); and my own favorite, "Broom Hilda" (in which the characters complain in the opening panel that the cartoonist gets all the credit and glory while they do all the work—so that the next panel goes black—and so they must draw themselves—although they can do no better than stick figure representations of themselves—they acknowledge their dependence on their creator—and he graciously consents to draw them anew—although, in the final panel, he transposes their heads). No one would call this high art, but it is hardly different—in conception, cleverness or execution—from what some critics have in recent years considered current fiction's outstanding attribute.[2]

✳

Self-reflexive forms have also been prevalent of late in another popular, but more highly regarded medium, the movies. Films filled with references to moviemaking have become a commonplace, as directors—none more artfully than Robert Altman—turn their knowledge of their craft into their subject matter. The first of the form which I remember noting will still serve to mark its boundaries, assets and limitations. In François Truffaut's *Day for Night* (1973), for example, a crew of actors and technicians, led by the director François Truffaut (played by the sometime actor François Truffaut), make a film by day while they enact at night the same roles outside their formal roles. The technical term of the title, in which a scene shot during the daytime passes as a nighttime scene, serves very neatly as a metaphor both for the film's action and for its characters and casting.

Similarly, in Alain Robbe-Grillet's *Trans-Europ-Express* (1966, in his second career, as a film director), two French filmmakers (one of them played by Robbe-Grillet) discuss on a long train journey a film which they are planning to make, while in alternating (but simultaneous) sequences, actors (one of them playing a Robbe-Grillet *persona*) act out the scenes which they are discussing. When the filmmakers arrive at their destination, they are passed in the station, unrecognized, by the characters whom they have been creating, who seem somehow to have acquired a life of their own, independent of and unknown to their creators.

Perhaps the best of the early self-reflexive films is Paul Mazursky's *Alex in Wonderland* (1970), made soon after his surprising success with *Bob and Carol and Ted and Alice*. The film's subject is a director who has had a surprising success with his first film and who is being pursued by producers to make his next film for them, but who cannot decide what that next project will be. Paul Mazursky plays a part in the film (as a would-be seducer producer), and so do various members of his family. In the film's wonderful final scene, the indecisive director (the character of the indecisive director, that is) travels to Rome to watch his idol, Federico Fellini (played, of course, by Federico Fellini), make his own film about filmmaking, *8 1/2.*

Detective Novels

There is a certain charm in these early self-reflexive films and comic strips that the later, still more self-conscious versions may lack. For all the form's intellectualizing and turning inward—and for all the theorizing about it by critics—the audience might easily suspect that the real purpose and justification of the form is its fun. Much the same may be said for metafictional novels: among the most clever, delightful, tantalizing of these works is Italo Calvino's *If on a Winter's Night a Traveler* (1979), which turns the reading of mystery novels on its metaphorical head. The detective novel for some time now—going back to Robbe-Grillet's *The Erasers* (1953) and Butor's *Passing Time* (1956)—has served as a device for undercutting certainty: no form more surely promises certainty; but what if the search leads nowhere? Could there be a more devastating attack on certainty than the search which promises definition but delivers only confusion? In *The Erasers,* the detective/protagonist turns out to be the killer, with the crime taking place only after he has begun to investigate it; apparent references to *Oedipus the King* complicate the matter still further (or else, perhaps, compromise the confusion by suggesting a different certainty: offering to the reader the possibility of a Freudian resolution to the mystery). The victim, after all, may well be the killer's long-lost father.

Turning constantly in on itself, offering glimpses of possibility after possibility of resolution, each one undercutting the one before, *If on a Winter's Night a Traveler* tantalizes the reader (the activist Modernist reader, that is, and not the passive Victorian reader), warning us that our own role in the creation of the text has become suspect, in as much danger of passing from the scene of creation as the role of the heroic Modernist novelist may be.

John Barth

The novelist John Barth for a time protested his label as a post-Modernist and then came to accept it, enthusiastically, it would appear. The labels which artists accept for themselves are probably no more meaningful than those that critics assign them; what makes this case potentially useful is my sense that Barth's almost career-long involvement with metafiction is, in fact, a continuation of old forms and interests and not their repudiation. I suspect that Barth would agree, for he has never been reluctant in his work (his earlier work especially) to note his ties to his predecessors and to use them as a key to our understanding of the fictional process as practiced by John Barth. In his later fictions, Barth himself—

first as a writer of fiction and then as a character within his fictions who happens also to be a writer of fiction—takes precedence over, say, James Joyce.

But this may also be a little misleading, for Joyce is vital to the *künstlerroman Lost in the Funhouse* principally in the sense that he provides a model of the artistic life for the protagonist, as well as a model of form for the author. But it is young Ambrose, who is presumably based on the young Barth (at least as the older Barth would come to see him/himself), whose development is central. I call *Lost in the Funhouse* a *künstlerroman* even though it is not, technically, a novel, for its separate stories surely chart the development of the artist and his artistry: its joint models are *Dubliners* (as a body of integrated, developing stories) and *A Portrait of the Artist as a Young Man*. Each of the stories of *Lost in the Funhouse* may be seen as a stage in Ambrose's development, as an individual and as a storyteller: from the marvelous opening tale "Night-Sea Journey," which charts the artist's birth in first-person narrative and archetypal myth; to the title story, in which the adolescent Ambrose endeavors to stand outside himself and turn the traumas of youth into a form of narrative art; to the stunning closing narrative, "Anonymiad," the kind of story that a more mature Ambrose might some day come to write. In later years, Barth would abandon his surrogate and enter more directly into his fictions, but his concern for the nuances and effects of narrative art would never diminish.[3]

Barth's entire career as a writer of fiction, now some forty years long and long distinguished, has been devoted to the cause of narration—not simply in the sense of telling a good and compelling story, but as an advocate for the cause, a philosopher, as it were, of the possibilities of narration as they are developed within the framework of a narrative. He is, without doubt, a devoté of the metafictional. I had the good fortune to attend Barth's first public reading, when we were both members of the English Department at Penn State (he beginning to make a national reputation, I at the start of my career). The story was that he had had to be coerced by the department chair, Henry Sams, to read from his current work, *Giles Goat-Boy*, and I had the sense that his extraordinary success that night encouraged him not only as a public reader of his work but in his dedication to his overweening theme.

There was a time, however, when it seemed that Barth had painted himself into a kind of artistic corner with his seeming obsession with this one theme (a theme utterly indistinguishable from the technique used to display it—I know of no better example of the union of function and form in the contemporary novel). He cannot possibly find yet another way to tell the story of storytelling, yet other implications for the storyteller and his audience, I thought for a time. Yet by and large he has. Perhaps he would have had left a more lasting heritage had he turned his very considerable skills to other, larger purposes. For in an American age of fine storytellers and stylists, Barth is surely one of the very best. What he has left us, though, is a pretty much definitive statement about that aspect of point of view that has come to be called metafiction, within the general category of narration.

In "Dunyazadiad," one of the three novellas in *Chimera* (1973), the eponymous heroine is the kid sister of Scheherezade, the necessary audience for the teller of tales: it is because she keeps falling asleep that Sherry is still alive the next morning(s) to complete her tale(s). She is Barth's tribute to the power of the active and imaginative reader (Henry James's ideal, the need of all novelists, but the creation in particular of the Modernist novelists: if Modernism seems to some an elitist enterprise, it is because she has too often been absent). As Scheherezade and her Genie (who looks and sounds suspiciously like Barth) agree,

> Narrative was a love-relation, not a rape: its success depended upon the reader's consent and cooperation, which she could withhold or at any moment withdraw; also upon her own combination of experience and talent for enterprise, and the author's ability to arouse, sustain, and satisfy her interest—an ability on which his figurative life hung as surely as Scheherezade's literal. (34)[4]

The statement is original, if its subject is as ancient as storytelling itself. When metafiction is more than just fun and gamesmanship, it offers a new way to emphasize narration's traditional concerns. But it is vital that we recognize that what is new here is merely the form and the emphasis; metafiction is merely a new way—often charming, sometimes provocative, too often derivative and bland—for novelists to make their own critical statements about their enterprise. Looking back, say, at Coleridge's "Kubla Khan," however, we recognize that the creative and intellectual leap seems almost inevitable in retrospect.

Philip Roth

Literary *personae* following Chaucer function essentially as masks behind which the author can hide what matters most—disguise his own personality, disguise (and perhaps in the process of disguising, to realize) his theme. For Stendhal, for example, with his seemingly compulsive need for pseudonyms, a *persona* appears to provide a personal mask, playing little if any part in the work itself; for Swift, as in "A Modest Proposal" (1729), his *persona* provides both a mask (since his political subject was potentially explosive) and the central strategy for realizing his theme. Were "A Modest Proposal" presented in Swift's own voice, we would recognize it as an obvious fiction and easily dismiss it as an exaggerated account of the Irish predicament under English colonial rule. But the extravagant proposals made by the naïve economist behind whom Swift hides—to turn starving Irish babies into food and other products for their English rulers—precisely because of this matter-of-fact presentation, are profoundly shocking. The irony around which Swift's theme develops is thus the direct product of his *persona*.[5]

In more modern times, the most exquisite use of the literary *persona* is by the Argentine writer Jorge Luis Borges, probably the most influential modern writer of fiction after the apogee of Modernism. His *persona* in the early story, "Tlön, Uqbar, Orbis Tertius" (1944), for instance, is named Borges and is clearly based—all the more clearly if we know even a little about the writer's life—on the character and life of Borges. As with Chaucer, it is the *persona*'s ultimate denseness—his unwillingness to accept and live in a world of which he so evidently disapproves (note the story's date)—which makes possible the story's ironic theme. And as with Swift, it is the reversal effected by our recognition of his denseness which makes that theme so powerful: This is not a world to be escaped so easily by a retreat into literature.

This is the literary background to Philip Roth's development of his recurring and overlapping *personae*. The personal background is a matter of public record, going back to the furor caused by some of Roth's earliest works, especially the collection of stories called *Goodbye, Columbus* (1960) and the novel *Portnoy's Complaint* (1969). Both were widely assumed to be autobiographical and were widely criticized for that reason: Everyone seemed to know the original of the girl jilted by the scoundrel protagonist of the title story of *Goodbye, Columbus* and condemned Roth for writing about her, and everyone—especially every Jewish mother in New York City and every critic who had such a mother—decried the way that Alexander Portnoy treated his mother (assuming that Roth did much the same to his mother). Eventually, because so many readers assumed that Roth's work was autobiographical (whatever that simplistic term might mean in this context), he evidently set out to challenge that perception head-on.

Roth has devised a battery of strategies to represent himself (better yet, to appear to represent himself) as he confronts his art, his subject matter, his public. It is a brave and surprisingly effective approach, which may perhaps have started out as something of a narrative game but which has become a means of expanding the boundaries of both the traditional theme of the *künstlerroman*, the so-called development of the artist as a young man novel, and Roth's own understanding of the relationship among the writer, his life, his narrative art, his predecessors, his audience, his Jewishness. More charged even than the practice of John Barth, which explores and develops most of these same motifs,[6] Roth's metafictions take off from a life that is widely known to the public and that remains controversial; none of his *personae*, however, has yet explored the possibility that he keeps at least part of his life before the public—and controversial—so that he can then explore its potential for fiction.

Among Roth's recurring *personae* are David Kepesh, the novelist and public figure whose career seems more or less the conventional one for a *künstlerroman*; Nathan Zuckerman, whose fictional life as an American Jewish novelist often gives the impression of reprising that of Philip Roth, including his relationships to Bernard Malamud and Saul Bellow; as well as a series of "Philip Roths," from the writer of the presumably autobiographical texts, *Patrimony*, subtitled "A True Story" (1991), and *The Facts*, subtitled "A Novelist's Autobiography" (1988); to the story (which appears to be an essay) "I Always Wanted You to Admire My Fasting; or, Looking at Kafka" (1973), in which the adolescent Philip Roth is the student of the old man Franz Kafka, who escaped from the Nazis to the United States only to become a Hebrew school teacher to such unresponsive students as young Philip Roth; to the novelist Philip in the novel *Deception* (1990).

Are the "facts" of *The Facts* more factual than those of, say, *The Anatomy Lesson* (1983) or *Zuckerman Unbound* (1981)? Why should we assume that *Patrimony* is any more "autobiographical" than *The Counterlife* (1986)? In *Operation Shylock*, subtitled "A Confession" (1993), the character Philip Roth encounters an impostor, and, in Israel, hears a newspaper account, in Hebrew, accompanied by a photograph supposedly of himself, of a meeting that he has supposedly had with Lech Walesa in Poland: ""Philip Roth Meets Solidarity Leader." In smaller letters, "Poland Needs Jews," Walesa Tells Author in Gdansk,"" an Israeli friend translates.

""Poland Needs Jews,"" I repeated. "'My grandparents should only be alive to hear that one.'" And his friend responds, "'Philip, I feel that I'm reading to you out of a story you wrote.'" To which Philip Roth responds, "'I wish you were'" (31–31).[7] Roth, the novelist within the novel, then concludes,

> Although the idea probably originated in Aharon's remark that he felt that he was reading to me out of a story I'd written, it was nonetheless another ridiculously subjective attempt to convert into a mental event of the kind I was professionally all too familiar with what had once again been established as all too objectively real. It's Zuckerman, I thought whimsically, stupidly, escapistly, it's Kepesh, it's Tarnopol and Portnoy—it's all of them in one, broken free of print and mockingly reconstituted as a single satirical facsimile of me. In other words, if it's not Halcion and it's no dream, then it's got to be literature—as though there cannot be a life-without ten thousand times more unimaginable than the life-within. (34)

When life and art meet, when the life within art and the life without become indistinguishable, the result may be trying for the man who is also an artist. But for the artist who is also a man and who makes a living writing about their various interpenetrations, the possibilities for the fiction are as rich and vital as they may be threatening to the man who is also an artist. However his various *personae* may have impacted on the private life of Philip Roth (assuming that he still has one), they have never been a mask behind which he can hide. Whatever the object lesson that we may see here for subsequent novelists, for

Roth himself (?) it has clearly been a brave and perilous and, one suspects, not yet complete journey. Should we label it metafiction or metalife? Should we think of it only as a narrative game, with a limited lifespan, or does it offer to novelists of the future a form of point of view that is especially viable for twenty-first century realities?

CHAPTER 12

Time as a Function of Point of View

From Victorian Chronology to the Time of the Mind

Sometimes listed independently as one of the principal characteristics of the Modernist novel, one of the ways in which novelists for three generations—from Joyce, Proust, Mann and Woolf to Faulkner to Claude Simon and Carlos Fuentes—have distinguished themselves from their predecessors, time functions more accurately not as a separate technique but as an aspect of point of view. This is easy enough to demonstrate, in Modernist as in Victorian fiction.

Few Victorian novelists even needed to think about the phenomenon of time as an aspect of narrative art; with rare exceptions—only *Great Expectations* and *Wuthering Heights* come readily to mind—Victorian novels follow the obvious chronological pattern: They begin at the beginning, continue through the middle of their events and end at the end. If Dickens' novels do go on beyond their end—in a chapter tacked on after the story's completion, so that readers might know what happened in later years to the characters whom they had come so deeply to care about—this merely proves the absolute mastery over time of the Victorian novelist. Thus, even though *Great Expectations* begins *in medias res* and only then turns to the past, it soon enough goes on to the present and future in order to complete and round out its story chronologically. This control of time is but one more, inevitable aspect of the omniscient author's absolute control of his narrative and of his characters' lives. (Dickens, who loved to raise mysteries, never leaves any of them unresolved; his rare attempt to break out of the omniscient mold, in the limited, even subjective point of view of the opening chapter of *The Mystery of Edwin Drood*, quickly reverts to Victorian form, either because he cannot sustain the more demanding limited form, or because he is unwilling to test his readers too far. Time, too, in this unfinished novel—but for which he left voluminous notes—only starts out as subjective and soon becomes part of the objective, plot- and time-driven mystery to be resolved.)

Wuthering Heights (1847) remains the only Victorian novel to attempt to link a partly subjective point of view—Nelly Dean's tale, as revealed to the character/narrator within the story—and a not fully chronological time scheme and to maintain them throughout the novel. But Emily Brontë's work is so idiosyncratic that it had no real influence and could simply be dismissed or ignored.

Chronological time—the time of the clock, time as an evidently objective phenomenon—goes hand in hand with, is an indispensable aspect of, the Victorian novelist's familiar and comfortable omniscience. Not surprisingly, when English novelists after World War II agressively chose to return to omniscience (as if the Modernist novel had not intervened between the days of Bennett, Galsworthy and Wells and their own era), they also reverted to stories defined chronologically. It is surely easier to write such a novel than to construct one based on the seemingly erratic, idiosyncratic workings of the mind, including the time of the mind. After Freud and Einstein, however, it was no longer realistic to write chronological narratives: knowing that our lives—not to speak of the universe—are not a straightforward development of past, present and future, in that inevitable and unyielding order, the novelist who continues chronologically must ignore a basic and vital fact of modern life. Realism demands at least the possibility of a break from the chronological mold.

Time for Mann/Biblical Time

Thomas Mann, in the "Prelude" to his tetralogy *Joseph and His Brothers,* advises that our conceptions of time are subject to forces beyond our control, forces both within us and without, forces of our individual memories and of our memories as a tribe, a nation, a people, the human race, going back to our most ancient records and memories of our past, memories which remain alive within us today. In tracing the progression(s) of time within the Hebrew Bible, Mann dramatizes the shared history which, at the time of his writing—just before and during the Second World War—he might reasonably have despaired would even have a future. In this early Biblical world, Mann's *persona* writes in the "Prelude,"

> Time has uneven measure, despite all the objectivity of the Chaldean chronology. Six hundred years at that time and under that sky did not mean what they mean in our western history. They were a more level, silent, speechless reach; time was less effective, her power to bring about change was both weaker and more restricted in its range—though certainly in those twenty generations she had produced changes and revolutions of a considerable kind: natural revolutions, even

changes in the earth's surface in Joseph's immediate circle, as we know and as he knew too. . . .

. . . Memory, resting on oral tradition from generation to generation, was more direct and confiding, it flowed freer, time was a more unified and thus a briefer vista; young Joseph cannot be blamed for vaguely foreshortening it, for sometimes, in a dreamy mood, perhaps by night and moonlight, taking the man from Ur for his father's grandfather—or even worse.[1]

Mann's narrative, following its Biblical model, proceeds in an essentially chronological order. But we are aware throughout *Joseph and His Brothers* that this is both less and more than a history—in a sense, humanity's first history—that we are reading. It is also the story of the development of a way of looking at and responding to and telling the story of the world as it is defined through time: The story of a people—the people who may be said to have invented history—it is also the story of an individual mind, perhaps the first Western mind: the most subjective of stories, by self-definition.

Joycean Time

When Leopold Bloom, in the "Circe" episode of *Ulysses,* responds to the whore Zoe's injunction to "Go on. Make a stump speech out of it. . . . Talk away till you're black in the face" (390–407), and imagines himself as the new Irish leader, rising and falling as Parnell had done, he is illustrating subtly Joyce's understanding of the newly revealed time of the mind. For the many years and eighteen pages of Bloom's imaginative construction take place in the instant between Zoe's two sentences. Yet the action of *Ulysses* as a whole takes place more or less chronologically, from 8:00 in the morning of 16 June 1904 to 2:00 the next morning, with Joyce carefully providing the physical clues (the ringing of church bells, for example) for our delineation of his time scheme. Not every hour of Bloomsday is accounted for, but we can determine fairly accurately the time of each of its episodes. Joyce—not for the first or only time—thus has it both ways, reinforcing chronology at the same time that he immerses us in the shifting, unpredictable (yet always logical) clock of the mind.

In *Finnegans Wake,* similarly, the dream which constitutes the novel would appear to progress throughout the night, presumably from some time after falling asleep to time spent lying in bed partially awake in the morning, with the radio on in the background. No one, to my knowledge, has yet noted all of the clues to isolate clock time as the dreamers and their dream progress throughout the night, but I am reasonably confident that they are nonetheless present. This is but one more area of the novel that has not yet been fully explored. The larger time scheme of the *Wake,* of course, is that of human history as the members of the Earwicker household conjure up the images of their universal dream: they develop, for example, through a disorderly sequence of battle scenes evoked by the dream, or through an even more disorderly sort of literary history.[2]

The logic of time in *Finnegans Wake*—the realism underpinning its circular progression (perhaps even as a series of expanding circles)—is, naturally enough, the logic of the mind in its freest, most creative, most vulnerable state, the dream state. The ability of the dream of the *Wake* to encompass all ages and aspects of time is a necessary concomitant of a point of view that transports us directly into dream. In *Finnegans Wake*, the ultimate Modernist text, point of view and time are irretrievably linked, even though there are comparatively few explicit references to either.

Proustian Time

Proust, in *A la recherche du temps perdu*, follows a time scheme at once chronological and subjective, both within the novel as an entity and within each of its volumes. That is, we move from memories of childhood through adolescence through youth through middle age, more or less chronologically, as volume follows volume of a search through a presumably lost past. At the same time, Marcel, the protagonist/observer/narrator, is recalled within each volume to the memory of his past—to a particular and representative moment of his past, which is then filled in and developed—until he reaches the present. The method of recall, in each volume, is an unplanned, involuntary, sensory image: most famously, the lime blossom tea and madeleine of his illness in middle age, which recalls Marcel sensuously to a childhood illness whose significance he can only now recognize. Each such image serves simultaneously as an aspect of narration and of time. The novel's very title, of course, warns us that the two will be virtually interchangeable throughout.

And then the dual and simultaneous scheme becomes amplified, almost exponentially, as we realize that Marcel has all along been writing—perhaps has already written—the memoir which he determines that he must write only when he reaches the end of his search, in the vast novel's final chapter (which was written, to be sure, immediately after Proust had completed the first chapter). To frame it a bit differently, the time scheme of *A la recherche* acts simultaneously on several levels, as a function of the several levels of Proust's point of view: For the narrator, Marcel, there is more than one present, and so more than a single, expired past, as well as more than one future yet to be encountered. There is the present moment in which he recalls the past; the present tense in which these memories are relived and related in his mind; and the present in which he writes down his separate memories and makes of them a continuous narrative. (This last we never actually experience within his narrative, but we know from internal evidence that it occurs, must already have occurred.)

The Rhetoric of Modernist Fiction

For the reader, too, there is a dual present here, as we discover on re-reading *A la recherche* that Marcel has already written the narrative which he determines at the end of our first reading to write. His fiction—perhaps, more completely, his metafiction—is at once, then, prospective and retrospective, as we realize that his discoveries about his life and his art have already been deployed in the narrative—Marcel's, as well as Proust's—that we are now (once again) reading. The seemingly simple point of view and more or less straightforward time scheme of the novel—which seem on first reading to be but a minor (if rather complex) advance over the traditional forms—are thus far richer, more complex, more revealing than we might have imagined: not a Modernist gesture made for its own sake, because the novelist has the power to make it, but a profound and powerful means of enhancing the reading experience and our comprehension of the interpenetration not just of present and future and past, or even of time and narration, but of literature and life in the most complex and challenging century that humanity has known.

✻

The realistic concern of the Modernist Masters is in every respect consistent with that of their predecessors: to find and make use of the forms which will most accurately depict life as men and women experience it in their time. The new forms may alter our perceptions of our reality, but they do not alter reality itself. The great novelists may enable us to recognize and to articulate changes which have taken place in our reality, but they do not create those changes. We are mistaken when we assign them either blame or credit for doing so. The responsibility, as always, is our own. The new task assigned to us by the Modernist novelists—of becoming active participants in the novel's development—brings with it moral responsibilities as well.

Time Passes: Faulkner, Simon, Woolf

Time, in Joyce, passes incrementally, in forms—whether totally subjective or seemingly objective—that are measurable by one or another recognizable standard. The time of the clock and that of the mind pass more or less in unison in *Ulysses* and, I suspect, even if their progress is more difficult to measure, in *Finnegans Wake* as well. Much the same may be said of time in Proust: We may not recognize all at once the various and simultaneous time sequences of *A la recherche du temps perdu*, but it is no great task in retrospect to sort them out. The time of society, the time of the social historian, the time of the novelist are at once distinct and inseparable, definable both by objective and subjective standards. No one would ever mistake Joycean or Proustian time for that of the Victorian novelist; yet once we accept the fact of the subjective origins and determinations for time as Leopold and Molly Bloom, HCE and Anna Livia and Marcel experience it, we should have little difficulty in recognizing those constituents of time which remain familiar: as an historical process, denoting the rise and fall of nations and of their heroes; as an everyday measure, recording the daily (and nightly) activities of many individuals; as an inescapable force in the lives of both individuals and nations.

When Marcel sets out to record the events of his own life and to pass before it, as if in review, the social and political life of late nineteenth- and early twentieth-century France, he is doing no more or less than Balzac and Zola, for instance, had already done. When we enter the consciousnesses of those young Joycean artists, Stephen Dedalus and Shem the Penman, and follow with them—at once intimately and at an artist's remove—the events of a representative day and/or night, we are seeking much the same goal (if by a somewhat different path) that Dickens had sought. (Remember that Dostoevsky called Dickens his master.) I have little doubt that Edwin Drood's consciousness was one of the models for HCE's.

I do not mean by this to diminish the originality and accomplishment of Proust and Joyce, those masters. I want only to emphasize the degree to which they were—and to which they thought of themselves as—working within a tradition. If their Victorian predecessors gave little thought to time when elaborating their points of view, it is because there was simply no need or reason to in their seemingly so-stable world. If Proust and Joyce had to incorporate time into their already elaborate and demanding points of view, it is because Freud, Einstein and the political and military leaders of Europe, will-they, nill-they, compelled them to. Again, reality had changed, and with it realism.

The immediate follower of both Proust and Joyce, both in his development of point of view and in his conception of time, is William Faulkner. No Modernist novelist disguises his sources as thoroughly as Faulkner does, however. In his pose as a non-intellectual, in his frequently misleading comments about his own art, Faulkner manages to blur very effectively his particular place within the tradition of the novel. I have long thought that the key to Faulkner's sudden, surprising success as a novelist lay within his reading of *Ulysses*. An interesting, possibly promising, young regional novelist, who had written little of note in his career, suddenly turns into a master, and in a four-year period (1929–1931) produces perhaps the most extraordinary body of work ever produced by a novelist in so brief a time:[3] This may be a miracle, indeed, or merely a sudden creative explosion that had been building up for some time (although his work before this hardly seems to justify such a conclusion), or it may be the result of Faulkner's reading *Ulysses*, which we know he had a copy of, and learning from it to create the various forms of internal monologue appropriate to his various characters. The Compson siblings in *The Sound and the Fury* owe nothing to Joyce's *Dubliners*, except, I am certain (but without definitive archival or textual proof), their means of expressing themselves to themselves. I also have the sense reading Faulkner—both the very early and the mature work—that he found in Joyce's ability to harness style to the needs of his individual chapters (as in "Sirens," "Cyclops" and "Penelope") the way to discipline his own propensity to stylistic excess. I find no other way to understand the difference between *Soldier's Pay* (1926) and *Mosquitoes* (1927), on the one, ineffectual hand, and the marvelous *The Sound and the Fury* (1930) and *Light in August* (1932), on the other.

But if Faulkner owes to his reading of Joyce his ability to integrate point of view and prose style, it is from Proust that he learns to incorporate a powerful narrative voice within an ongoing historical frame. Quentin Compson's narration in *Absalom, Absalom!* does not sound like Marcel's—the tone is more heightened, the progression less leisurely, the sense of control (the speaker's, that is, and not his creator's) far less certain. But reading Faulkner alongside Proust makes it unmistakably clear that Yoknapatawapha's reconstructed historical chronicle—in which history is viewed as the product, as well as the cause, of human idiosyncracy, in which emotional excess determines the lives of a region as well as of its people—begins in the narration of *A la recherche du temps perdu*. By inventing the character of Shreve McCannon to listen to and participate in Quentin's narrative, Faulkner may be said to improve on his model—better yet, to make it more appropriate for his region and subject. The reconstruction of history which takes place in that Harvard dormitory room is among the most telling manipulations of time in all of Modernist fiction.

While there may be no definitive archival proof of Faulkner's indebtedness to Joyce and to Proust, all the evidence we need, I suspect, is found in the work of Faulkner's greatest immediate successor, Claude Simon. Indeed, Simon's joint and proclaimed obligations to Faulkner (*The Flanders Road* as a World War II French version of *Absalom, Absalom!*); to Joyce (the character of Blum in *The Flanders Road* and of the Bloom-like Montès in *The Wind*); and to Proust (characters who read *A la recherche* and who emulate its characters in *The Battle of Pharsalus*) offer, almost uniquely, a sign of literary continuity along three generations of novelists: a road map, as it were, of continuity. Simon's concern throughout his oeuvre is not so much with the time of the individual mind as with the impact of history upon individuals, an impact which is magnified exponentially by the narrative process of *réconstitution,* a term found as frequently in his work as in Proust's.[4]

Virginia Woolf's reaction against what she thought of as Joyce's extravagances is well known. From the start, at a time when she was still labelling their joint enterprise "Georgian," she understood that bold, dramatic stylistic displays were not her forte. Yet there are ways in which Woolf's solutions to the narrative dilemmas faced by all of the Modernists—particularly as they relate to the passage and power of time—are considerably more radical than Joyce's. For where Joycean time never fully foregoes the chronological—never entirely abandons the conventional ways of measuring time's passage (of hours, of years)—and continues to use humans as the measure of time's power, Woolf posits Nature, an indefinable, almost abstract force, in their place. In most of *Ulysses* and throughout *Finnegans Wake,* Joyce devises brilliant and varied means of displaying the time of the mind as a function of internal monologue, or of stream of consciousness, or even of straightforward narration. Some of these forms are more daring, more dramatic, more effective than others; none manages not to call attention to itself. It is easy to understand both why Woolf would find fault with such displays as, say, "Circe" or "Wandering Rocks" and why she might feel compelled to best Joyce.

I suspect that Woolf feared that Joyce might be more effective than she was in fashioning on the pages of his fictions the new reality post-Freud, post-Versailles. I have no doubt that she saw Joyce as her rival. Her seeming reticence of form should not be taken as a sign that she was acknowledging Joyce's primacy. She knew very well, I believe, just how radical her own work could be, especially when she was working with time. The conclusion of *The Waves* may be her most radical statement about time, as an aspect of what may be her most adventurous use of point of view. Her most successful, most representative passage on time, however, is the "Time Passes" section of *To the Lighthouse* (1927).

Section III of "Time Passes" begins with an unidentified voice, typically, of course, called "the narrator" by critics, but I think a voice that is at once more precise than that name would suggest (in the sense that Woolf was not simply reverting, because they were easier, to Victorian forms) and less specific (for it can be traced to no specific, named source, neither Woolf herself nor one or more of her characters). I am inclined to think of this as the voice, as it were, of the process which it is describing: of the natural process to which we are all subject, very nearly the voice of Nature itself. This is not some sort of mystic pantheism on either Woolf's part or my own. The subject of "Time Passes" is natural process, and Woolf endeavors, as I read the episode, to get as close to her subject as she can, to describe it, as it were, from within. "But what after all is one night?" the voice begins, describing the empty Ramsay family house and its setting, as the seasons begin to change.

> The nights now are full of wind and destruction; the trees plunge and bend and their leaves fly helter skelter until the lawn is plastered with them. ... Also the sea tosses itself and breaks itself, and should any sleeper fancying that he might find on the beach an answer to his doubts, a sharer of his solitude, throw off his

The Rhetoric of Modernist Fiction

bedclothes and go down by himself to walk on the sand, no image with semblance of serving and divine promptitude comes readily to hand bringing the night to order, and making the world reflect the compass of his soul. (192–93)[5]

The "sleeper" of this passage may perhaps be Mr. Carmichael, who is seen at the end of Section II of "Time Passes," reading Virgil and blowing out his candle at midnight; or he may be Mr. Ramsay, who appears next, in one of the most moving passages in modern literature, "stumbling along a passage one dark morning, stretch[ing] his arms out, but Mrs. Ramsay having died rather suddenly the night before, his arms, though stretched out, remained empty" (194). The passage moves us not only by the shock of its news, but because—beyond the shifting, seemingly objective, third-person account—we have been implicated in the lives of these people, and especially of Mrs. Ramsay. She has served until now, more or less consistently, as the fulcrum (James's central intelligence) around whom all activity flows, and she must somehow now be replaced. The fact that both Mr. Carmichael and Mr. Ramsay have just been described in brackets would seem to indicate that they are but momentary replacements, not even quite parenthetical.

But the description of nature continues, even without them. It is no more dependent on them than on Mrs. Ramsay—on any human presence—merely to record it. Clearly, no one now is present, yet time continues its inexorable passage, as if in images reflected on the wall of Plato's cave:

Only the shadows of the trees, flourishing in the wind, made obeisance on the wall, and for a moment darkened the pool in which light reflected itself; or birds, flying, made a soft spot flutter slowly across the bedroom floor. . . . Then again peace descended; and the shadow wavered; light bent to its own image in adoration on the bedroom wall. (194–96)

Light reflects itself, bends to its own image, creates its own shadows. No human need manipulate it, need even, ideally, observe it. Point of view and time, too, may function independently of humans.

What human presence remains is provided by the housekeeper, Mrs. McNab, who by her presence, her labor, silently, "tear[s] the veil of silence with hands that had stood in the wash-tub" (196). News from the world outside continues to enter the house, however, although always in brackets: Prue Ramsay marries in the spring and, during the summer of the following year, dies in childbirth; Andrew Ramsay is blown to death in the war in France—"mercifully," his death "was instantaneous" (201); Mr. Carmichael publishes a book of poems that is surprisingly well received—"The war, people said, had revived their interest in poetry" (202). Albeit in brackets, news and opinion from the outside world do penetrate the empty house; we can assume that the judgment "mercifully" is not the omniscient author's but public opinion's.

For days, seasons, years, the empty Ramsay house remains the measure of times' slow, swift, inevitable movement, "Night after night, summer and winter, ... (for night and day, month and year ran shapelessly together)" (202–03)—"shapelessly" because there is no human there to give it form. If there is a point of view for this shifting if predictable scene—and technically, of course, we assume that there must always be a point of view—it is surely no human's: the house's perhaps? the seasons'? the voice of time itself?

Mrs. McNab returns to thoughts of the house in section VIII, and the point of view is now unquestionably hers, quietly internal, as she picks her flowers. "She was fond of flowers. It was a pity to let them waste" (203). She does not think at this point of Mrs. Ramsay, who planted and tended these flowers, but we are likely to, even if no one is present to direct our thoughts. "The house was left; the house was deserted. ... The long night seemed to have set in; ... What power could now prevent the fertility, the insensibility of nature?" (206–207), as the empty house itself seems to have become part of nature. And then, in the amorphous section IX, "one of the young ladies wrote: would she get this done; would she get that done; all in a hurry. They might be coming for the summer" (209). The letter is received by Mrs. McNab, and it is she, with the aid of Mrs. Bast, who "stayed the corruption and the rot; rescued [the house] from the pool of Time that was fast closing over them" (209).

With Lily Briscoe's arrival at the house, point of view shifts generally to her, as Mrs. Ramsay's protege and surrogate, but not entirely (as it was never entirely derived from Mrs. Ramsay herself during her lifetime). "Then indeed peace had come. Messages of peace breathed from the sea to the shore. ... Through the open window the voice of the beauty of the world came murmuring, too softly to hear exactly what it said—but what mattered if the meaning were plain?" (213). Note how subtly Woolf omits the subject from this last sentence: no one is awake to hear the message, which needs no audience. "[T]he voice of the beauty of the world"—the phrase is extraordinary; no one else, to my knowledge, has ever described a novel's point of view in such terms: and made us believe it.

Even if no one in the house is awake, even the next morning, "gently then without complaint, or argument, the voice would sing its song. Gently the waves would break. ... why not accept this, be content with this, acquiesce and resign?" (214). There is, of course, no choice. Whether we accept it or not, we are subject—as "Time Passes" makes absolutely clear—to the message that the voice within the waves would communicate, whether we even hear it or not.

We can describe Woolf's narrative accomplishment here in the conventional terms: Time as a force of the natural process, to which every human being is prisoner, functions in the "Time Passes" section of *To the Lighthouse* as an aspect of point of view, which centers around and shifts among humans when they are present, but which continues even in their absence. A similar technique appears in Woolf's *The Waves* (1931) and *Between the Acts* (1941), embodying a similar theme of permanent changeability, the awful, beautiful, comforting destructive power of Nature. However we may choose to identify this continuing point of view (which I am inclined to think of as the voice of Nature), we need somehow to acknowledge that voice and its message of the passage and power of time. "[T]he voice of the beauty of the world," and a large part of its beauty, Woolf tells us through the voice, is our transience.

Time's Calendar: Carlos Fuentes

No novelist since Faulkner makes more intimate and powerful use of the juncture of time and point of view than does Carlos Fuentes in *The Death of Artemio Cruz* (1964). His rendering of both point of view and time and of their union is at once complex yet manageable, as we follow the shifts and alterations within both, but always with road signs provided carefully by the author. For those novelists (and critics) reluctant to turn to Faulkner, or to Proust, or to Joyce or even Woolf as exemplars for the handling of time as technique and as theme, Fuentes provides here—much more manageably than in his later, still more ambitious work, *Terra Nostra* (1975)—a potential model for an approach that remains meaningful even in the twenty-first century, even if this were indeed a post-Modernist age.

Shifting among first-, second- and third-person perspectives—each of them a manifestation (inconstant) of the eponymous hero—turning at once distant and intimate, the point of view leads us, almost despite ourselves, into involvement with, even empathy for, a character whom we would otherwise scorn. Alternating among several past times, at least two different presents, as well as a possible future, time emerges as a force in the life of Artemio Cruz and of the nation which he, sometimes proudly, sometimes distressingly, represents. On the simplest level, time is denoted in the novel by the calendar of the dates provided for each chapter; on a deeper level, due to its almost perfect blending of function and form, time becomes the novel's principal theme. Historical time as experienced in Mexico (or, at least, in those novels by Fuentes which attempt to recapture the history of Mexico and its effects on the present) is not linear but circular, so that a certain, seeming repetitiveness is not only permissible but inevitable. As Fuentes put it a few years after the publication of *Artemio Cruz:*

> In retrospect, one can now see it wrapped in the shadows of history, nurturing the promises of a local culture, knowing that its time (I employ the crucial distinction made by Octavio Paz) was not the linear, positivistic measure of the West, but rather the circular, cosmogonic, re-volution understood by the aboriginal mind. ... A time symbolized by the self-devouring deity [of the Aztecs] that witnessed the murder of Jarmillo [a contemporary peasant leader.][6]

Each chapter of the novel is headed by a date (provided, of course, by the author, but also perhaps by his protagonist/point of view), beginning with 9 April 1959, the present, the day on which Artemio Cruz will die, and ending with 9 April 1889, the day of his birth. Each event is seen through his point of view, although, of course, he cannot logically (physiologically) remember and relive his birth or describe and live beyond his death.[7] Other key events in his life are presented not chronologically but in a kind of psychological order, as they might appear to a dying old man on an operating room table. Thus, the sixth of July 1941, just before his daughter's wedding, is followed by the twenty-sixth of May 1919, when he first meets his wife; by events after the Revolution as he becomes powerful in provincial Puebla and then, later, in Mexico City; then 22 October 1915, when the young captain Cruz is captured by the enemy Villistas but manages to survive. Ever resourceful, he replaces his idealistic concern for Mexico with concern for himself, his own power. He comes to represent the betrayal of the Revolution for which he once fought. Even for those readers who do not understand the terribly complicated, often tragic details of the Mexican Revolution, this remains a powerful statement of the meaning of those events for the people of Mexico. *The Death of Artemio Cruz* is the best political novel that I know. Its greatest success, though, is its melding of the political and personal.

A large part of the novel's power derives from its ability to connect us to this man whose business, political and amatory career we are likely to despise. Yet we are moved, often despite ourselves, by Artemio Cruz's losses and by the way that he deals with them, especially with the death of his son, Lorenzo, while fighting for the Loyalist cause in the Spanish Civil War. Knowing only his father's youthful idealism and not his cynical maturity, Lorenzo is moved to repeat his father's career as a fighter for a cause. Artemio, through whose imagination his son is presented, accepts the irony. The novel's key scene is of Lorenzo's death, the details of which Artemio reconstructs largely on the basis of his own earlier experience in war (and partly from a letter that may have been written by his son before his death). The resulting identification—of father and son, of point of view and reader—is very nearly complete. "I have a son," Artemio on his deathbed remembers, "I sired him: because now I remember that face: where shall I put it, where, so that it won't escape me, where, for God's sake, where, please, where" (215).

A similar identification continues until the instant of Artemio's death, at which point he envisions his birth and starting out on his own as a boy: identifying now with the youth who will become Artemio and be merged in his imagination with Lorenzo: "You will be there on the first crest of the mountain," he thinks to himself, envisioning himself as he was, "Freed from the destiny of birth and birthplace, bound now to a new fate" (299). "You will not know," referring now to himself as a terminal patient: "you will not know your open heart tonight, your open heart, Scalpel, they say, scalpel. I hear it, I who continue knowing when you no longer know and before you know" (305). As times, characters and voices merge, Artemio Cruz discovers at last what all humans must, even if not many do:

> I don't know . . . don't know . . . I am he or if . . . you were he . . . or if I am the three . . . You . . . I carry you inside me and you will die with me . . . God . . . He . . . I carry him inside me and he will die with me . . . the three . . . who spoke . . . I . . . I will carry him within me and he will die with me . . . alone . . . (305)

For an instant, it seems, the voice manages to go on even after Artemio's death, as if somehow separated from his body, perhaps even representing Time itself. By this time, the identification with Artemio Cruz has become so complete that the reader is virtually compelled to join in, even though it is hardly comfortable for us to unite with a man whose public and private lives are in so many ways hateful. Fuentes' brilliant success in *The Death of Artemio Cruz* derives substantially from his ability to induce us to feel for this man, as for his people.

No one has suggested that empathy *per se* is a necessary concomitant of Modernist narrative technique. The Modernist novelists were at one time criticized for not being sufficiently humanistic, more recently for being overly so. It happens to be a quality that I admire, and so I applaud that element of technique which facilitates our involvement with those characters in fiction whose lives cut across time and reach out to us, who implicate the reader in ways and lives that even the great Dickens could never have imagined. The datelines of the chapters of this novel may seem at first to suggest a history lesson, and to a certain extent, that is what they provide, possibly even for Mexican readers, surely for *Norteamericanos*. In another, more meaningful sense, however, *The Death of Artemio Cruz* provides an object lesson, for critics and novelists alike, in the development of time as a function of point of view, in the union of technique and theme, in the power of these subjects and tools in the hands of a Modernist Master. For Fuentes continues and builds on one of the principal discoveries of the Modernist narrative tradition: As Proust, Joyce, Mann, Faulkner, Woolf and Simon have similarly shown us, what may from a distance seem the most technical modern advance—time's union with point of view—may be a new way to manifest the novel's most ancient force.

Notes

1. The Art of Point of View (pages 1–6)

1. All references are to Wayne Booth, *The Rhetoric of Fiction* (Chicago: University of Chicago Press, 1961).

2. See my book, *Modernist Survivors: The Contemporary Novel in England, the United States, France and Latin America* (Columbus: Ohio State University Press, 1987) for a sustained argument that there is no post-Modernism in the novel that will survive, that whatever remains vital in the novel today can be best understood as Modernist.

3. All references are to Alain Robbe-Grillet, *For a New Novel: Essays on Fiction,* trans. Richard Howard (New York: Grove Press, 1965).

4. Robbe-Grillet does not mind if his novels seem at times to refute his theories. Why should more consistency be demanded of him than of any other novelist?

That there is no more than a loose parallelism between the three novels I have published up to now and my theoretical views on a possible novel of the future is certainly obvious enough. Moreover, it will be regarded as only natural that a book of two or three hundred pages should be more complex than an article of ten; and also, that it is easier to indicate a new direction than to follow it, without failure—partial or even complete—being a decisive, definitive proof of the error committed at the outset" (50–51).

5. I prefer the original spelling of the term "Modernism," as opposed to the more popular current form "modernism," because the former is in line with traditional practice, that is, we continue to name the poets of the previous age the "Romantics" and not the "romantics." Moreover, the assumption that we should eliminate the capital in "Modernism" may not be entirely innocent: If a critic thought of himself or herself as a "postmodernist" and assumed both that the predecessor age had already passed and that it was overly "heroic" to begin with—a status much too large for our own avowedly lesser time—how better to make that point than to bring "Modernism" down to its own level. When I use the spellings "Modernism" and "post-Modernism" I do not pretend to critical innocence. See my *Modernist Survivors.*

6. This is not the same as saying that the text is autonomous and that no outside sources can possibly matter, as some of the early New Critical theoreticians appeared to claim. No one has ever actually practiced that puristic, theoretical New Criticism. Almost from the start, we made use of what Malcolm Cowley termed an eclectic New Criticism, in which all other sources—historical, biographical, psychological, mythic, philosophical, what have you—were potentially of use, so long as their presence in the analysis respected the primacy of the text.

7. All references are to Gérard Genette, *Narrative Discourse: An Essay in Method,* trans. Jane E. Lewin (Ithaca, N.Y.: Cornell University Press, 1980). See also Genette's sequel, *Narrative Discourse Revisited,* trans. Jane E. Lewin (Ithaca, N.Y.: Cornell University Press, 1988).

2. Booth, Joyce and Modernist Points of View (pages 7–16)

1. For a delightful personal overview of the making of Booth's career, see his article, "Where Have I Been, and Where Are 'We' Now, in this Profession?" in *PMLA,* CIX (October 1994), 941–50.

2. Maurice Beebe, "*Ulysses* and the Age of Modernism," *James Joyce Quarterly,* X, 1 (Fall 1972), 172–88. Rpt. Thomas F. Staley, ed., *ULYSSES: FIFTY YEARS* (Bloomington: Indiana University Press, 1974).

3. Critical neutrality also means that we must not impose ourselves on our readings: I typically tell my students that the best subjectivity is objectivity, that young critics are most likely to convince their own readers when they do not call attention to themselves.

4. The first use of "Modernism" as a literary term occurred in 1961, in Harry Levin's essay, "What Was Modernism?" But it did not begin to become popular until 1965, when the essay was reprinted in Levin's *Refractions: Essays in Comparative Literature* (New York: Oxford University Press, 1966). In graduate school and as a young instructor in the early 1960s, I never heard the term "Modernism"; we spoke only of "modern" and "contemporary" as (inadequate) means of defining the novel. I first used the term "Modernism" in 1971, when I organized a conference at Temple University called "The Death of Modernism," the title of which was suggested by Maurice Beebe. Prior to this time, "Modernism" was used sometimes to refer to the visual arts and, more generally, to architecture, in which it served as a synonym for "International School."

5. James's observation derives from a review in *The Atlantic Monthly* for October 1866, p. 485.

6. Booth quotes William Empson as saying that *Ulysses* "'not only refuses to tell you the end of the story, it also refuses to tell you what the author thinks would have been a good end to the story'" (326). "The Theme of *Ulysses,*" *Kenyon Review,* XVIII (Winter 1956), 36. Not explicitly a complaint about Joyce, this comment nevertheless echoes Booth's complaint about Robbe-Grillet.

7. Booth is certainly wrong when he seems to accept "the open assumption that [Joyce's] later works, *Ulysses* and *Finnegans Wake,* cannot be read; they can only be studied" (325). My own teaching experience, at levels from freshman to adult evening to graduate courses, disproves that assumption, and there are thousands of teachers throughout the world with comparable experience—not to speak of all those who have undertaken the (admittedly demanding) task on their own.

3. A Brief History of Point of View in the Brief History of the Novel (pages 17–46)

1. Homer, *The Odyssey,* trans. Robert Fitzgerald (Garden City, N.Y.: Doubleday, 1963), 328.

2. Ian Watt, *The Rise of the Novel* (Berkeley: University of California Press, 1957), 257.

3. Watt, 274.

4. All references are to Henry Fielding, *Tom Jones* (New York: Random House, 1950).

5. Watt, 175.

6. All references are to William Makepeace Thackeray, *Vanity Fair* (New York: New American Library, 1962).

7. Anthony Trollope, *Barchester Towers* (New York: Random House, 1950), 342–43.

8. All references to Nathaniel Hawthorne's work are to *Selected Tales and Sketches* (New York: Holt, Rinehart and Winston, 1960), 13–33 and 108–22, respectively. All references are to Anton Chekhov, *Stories,* trans. Richard Pevear and Larissa Volokhonsky (New York: Bantam, 2000).

9. In this preface, dated 1851, Hawthorne distinguishes between the objective reality of the novel ("presumed to aim at a very minute fidelity, not merely to the possible, but to the probable and ordinary course of man's experience") and what we would today call the psychological reality of the romance (which "sins unpardonably so far as it may swerve aside from the truth of the human heart"). Hawthorne speaks here neither of "realism" nor of "psychology," and when he mentions "point of view" he expects it to mean "intention" or "attitude" and not to relate to "narrative." Yet his statement, half a century and a world away from Freud, has served over the years as an enabling means for novelists who are intent on reaching within for the realities of their characters. Nathaniel Hawthorne, *The Complete Novels and Selected Tales* (New York: Modern Library, 1937), 243–44. It is interesting that in his book on Hawthorne (1879), James has almost nothing to say about his predecessor's use of point of view.

10. Henry James, *The Art of the Novel,* ed. R. P. Blackmur (New York: Charles Scribner's Sons, 1937), 63; Preface to *The Princess Casamassima,* volume V in the New York Edition.

11. James, *The Art of the Novel,* Preface to *The Ambassadors,* 324, volume XXI in the New York Edition.

12. James, *The Art of the Novel,* Preface to *The Golden Bowl,* 328, volume XXIII in the New York Edition.

13. This is only seemingly a paradox: We cannot arbitrarily remake the world to suit our own moral needs, however we might wish to do so. We must live both in the world and up to our own moral standards. We cannot reject ambiguity's presence—as in, say, a Robbe-Grillet fiction—simply because we deplore it. To reject ambiguity *per se,* or to reject *per se* those who would present ambiguity as a normal state of modern affairs, is not only unwise and perhaps unrealistic, but also may prove, in certain circumstances, itself amoral. I think, for instance, of the so-called Comforters of Job.

14. All references are to Henry James, *The American* (New York: Dell, The Laurel Henry James, 1960).

15. Henry James, *The Spoils of Poynton* and *The Aspern Papers* (New York: Dell, The Laurel Henry James, 1959).

16. James, *The Art of the Novel,* 123, 126. Volume X in the New York Edition, containing *The Spoils of Poynton,* "A London Life," and "The Chaperone."

17. There is also the question of Mr. Verver's responsibility for his wife's moral development, for in keeping his knowledge of events from her, he may be depriving Charlotte—alone of the principals—of the opportunity for moral growth.

18. All references are to Henry James, *The Golden Bowl* (New York: Grove Press, 1962).

19. James, *The Art of the Novel*, Preface to *The Golden Bowl*, 327.

20. James, *The Art of the Novel*, Preface to *The Golden Bowl*, 327. If, in practice, James is not quite able to turn away completely from an authorial presence within his fictions, he surely does so in principle. Hence his idea of the center of consciousness: As he writes in the preface to *The Wings of the Dove*, "From the moment we proceed by 'centres'—and I have never, I confess, embraced the logic of any superior process—they must *be*, each, as a basis, selected and fixed; after which it is that, in the high interest of economy of treatment, they determine and rule." As for multiple centers within a narrative, "I understand no breaking-up of the register, no sacrifice of the recording consistency, that doesn't rather scatter and weaken." Volume XIX, 300.

21. "It's not that the muffled majesty of authorship doesn't here *ostensibly* reign; but I catch myself again shaking it off and disavowing the pretence of it while I get down into the arena and do my best to live and breathe and rub shoulders and converse with the persons engaged in the struggle." Henry James, Preface to *The Golden Bowl*, 328.

22. "Edgar of Ravenswood for instance, visited by the tragic tempest of 'The Bride of Lammermoor,' has a black cloak and hat and feathers more than he has a mind." Henry James, Preface to *The Princess Casamassima*, 68.

23. "He tells us all he knows, all he suspects, and if these things take no account of the moral nature of man, it is because he has no window looking in that direction, and not because artistic scruples have compelled him to close it up. The very compact mansion in which he dwells presents on that side a perfectly dead wall." Henry James, "Guy de Maupassant," *The Future of the Novel*, ed. Leon Edel (New York: Vintage Books, 1956), 205.

24. "There are two kinds of taste in the appreciation of imaginative literature: the taste for emotions of surprise, and the taste for emotions of recognition. It is the latter that Trollope gratifies, and he gratifies it the more that the medium of his own mind, through which we see what he shows us, gives a confident direction to our sympathy. His natural rightness and purity are so real that the good things he projects must be real." Henry James, "Anthony Trollope," *The Future of the Novel*, 259–60.

25. James, *The Art of the Novel*, Preface to *The Ambassadors*, vol. XXI in the New York Edition, 320.

26. Henry James, *The Art of the Novel*, Preface to *The Princess Casamassima*, 62.

27. Henry James, *The Future of the Novel*, 24.

28. James, *The Art of the Novel*, Preface to *The Princess Casamassima*, 65.

29. All references are to Stendhal, *Scarlet and Black*, trans. Margaret R. B. Shaw (Baltimore: Penguin, 1964). Stendhal's desire to realize at least some scenes through the consciousness of an individual character—anticipating Henry James's idea of the central consciousness or intelligence—reaches its peak in *The Charterhouse of Parma* (1838), in the famous scene of the Battle of Waterloo as viewed by a terrified participant. Harry Levin has said that "Here a substantial case can be made for Stendhal as the technical innovator who abdicated the narrator's omniscience and attached himself to the protagonist's consciousness" (*The Gates of Horn* [New York: Oxford University Press, 1966], 93).

30. All references are to Gustave Flaubert, *Madame Bovary: Patterns of Provincial Life*, trans. Francis Steegmuller (New York: Random House, 1957).

31. When, a century afterward, the English novelist William Cooper would condemn the inherent immorality of French art, it is obvious that he did not consider the French condemnation of *Madame Bovary*. By the mid-twentieth century, however, the French had managed to grow beyond such superficial responses.

32. "Simony," with its implication of the selling of indulgences (the job of Chaucer's Pardoner and a principal cause of Martin Luther's crusade), appears to suggest the possibility of some a- or immoral relationship between the boy and the priest of "The Sisters" and perhaps also of other, similar relationships in *Dubliners;* "gnomon," among other meanings a geometrical figure in which a part stands for the whole, suggests the metaphorical relationships which function throughout these stories; and "paralysis," of course, is the figurative and sometimes literal condition of these Dubliners, as Joyce views them.

33. As for the (fortuitously) ubiquitous Hemingway: shortly after I wrote these lines, on the bus from Trieste to Rijeka, near the head of the Adriatic littoral in the Croatian resort town of Opatija, I saw out the window a passing sign advertising the "Café Bar Hemingway." Not everyone who sees the sign, obviously, appreciates the reference, but many—locals and foreigners alike—evidently do. More recently, I came across another "Hemingway Bar" in the Portuguese Algarve.

34. All short story references are to *The Short Stories of Ernest Hemingway* (New York: Charles Scribner's Sons, 1938).

35. All references are to Ernest Hemingway, *A Farewell to Arms* (New York: Charles Scribner's Sons, 1957).

36. James Joyce, *Dubliners,* 29.

4. To Narrate, Narration, Narrator, Narratology (pages 47–67)

1. More elaborately, Browning effects much the same union of a theme dealing with knowledge of human nature and a point of view which abjures omniscience in the long narrative poem *The Ring and the Book* (1868–1869). The shifting, partial points of view of the poem's separate sections (eleven in all, ranging from the gossip of the Roman community about a sensational murder case, to the adversarial attorneys in the case, to its principals, to the Pope) come together, theoretically, in the twelfth, concluding section, which seems to offer the poet's resolution of all issues. But even here we may come to a conclusion different from his; seen from a Modernist perspective, Browning may well have wrought even better than he knew.

2. In Walter E. Houghton and G. Robert Stange, eds., *Victorian Poetry and Poetics,* 2nd ed. (Boston: Houghton Mifflin Company, 1968), 575–80.

3. In the Victorian pornographic memoir, Walter X's *My Secret Life,* the narrator tells us that there was one young prostitute to whom he did reveal his private troubles. But this Victorian gentleman is less fiercely proud, less closed to others than Rossetti's character. Still, the reader is tempted to link the two and to wonder whether Walter's intended audience—if, in fact, he has one in mind as he writes—is somehow the same as that of Rossetti's speaker. Is it to some future self, that is, that each of them speaks? In *The Other Victorians* (New York: Basic Books, 1966), Steven Marcus discusses the

anonymous memoirist's inconsistent efforts to mask his identity and the connections of his work to the Victorian novel.

The critic Austin Briggs tells the story of a time when George Bernard Shaw was scheduled to deliver a political speech at Hyde Park Corner only to discover that the only person present was a sleeping drunkard. Shaw promptly awakened the man and began his speech, continuing even as the man again fell asleep. The drunkard would awaken periodically, however, calling out, in evident approval, "'Ere! 'Ere!" Is he perhaps our ideal audience?

4. Feodor Dostoevsky, *The Best Short Stories of Dostoevsky,* trans. David Magarshack (New York: The Modern Library, n.d.).

5. Albert Camus, *The Fall,* trans. Justin O'Brien (New York: Vintage Books, 1956).

6. All references are to Joseph Conrad, *The Nigger of the "Narcissus" (New York: Dell, 1960).*

7. All references are to Joseph Conrad, *Heart of Darkness* (New York: Dell, 1964).

8. All references are to Joseph Conrad, *Lord Jim* (Boston: Houghton Mifflin, 1958).

9. Claude Simon, *The Flanders Road,* trans. Richard Howard (London: Jonathan Cape, 1962).

10. All references are to William Faulkner, *Absalom, Absalom!* (New York: The Modern Library, 1951).

11. One of my younger colleagues might say that the traditional historian "privileges" fact over invention, implying by that term a strongly negative value judgment; it would likely not occur to that colleague that doing so thus "privileges" (my own negative judgment may be inferred here) the unknown, the uncertain, the invented over knowledge—or, at least, what has passed for knowledge from the beginnings of historiography. For critics of literature, the rough parallel is the widespread post-Modernist belief that the true creator—the only heroic figure that contemporary culture has managed to throw up—is the critic himself, especially the critic/theoretician. The New Criticism taught us that the critic did indeed have a creative role to play in the comprehension and dissemination of demanding Modernist novels and poems. But it did not encourage its adherents to confuse their roles with those of the true creators of art and culture.

12. This last comment, at first glance, might well seem omniscient, or simply a flaw—an inconsistency—in Faulkner's handling of point of view. It might also, of course, be Quentin's reading of Shreve's current predicament as narrator. Under the principle that we are obliged to give the author credence for all specifics about point of view when his general plan and pattern are apparent, we are obliged, as I read it, to regard the point of view here as anything but omniscient.

13. Faulkner's Genealogy at the end of *Absalom, Absalom!* informs us that Shrevlin McCannon graduated from Harvard in 1914, served as a captain in the Medical Corps of the Canadian Expeditionary Forces in World War I from 1914 to 1918, and now practices as a surgeon in his hometown, Edmonton, Alberta. We appreciate Faulkner's bringing us up to date on the details of Shreve's life and wonder what he may have been thinking, all these years, about the death of his roommate and of his own role in that suicide. The genealogical note reminds me of the past life which Hemingway created for Robert Jordan in *For Whom the Bell Tolls* (1940), events which he never intended to publish in his novel but which he needed in order to visualize how the mature Jordan

would act in the last weeks of his life. Both authors, however, chose to leave ambiguous for their readers these key facts in their characters' lives.

14. The incest in *Absalom, Absalom!* is both between half-brother and sister (Judith Sutpen and Charles Bon, if only envisioned and never actually realized) and between father and daughter (Thomas Sutpen and Milly Jones—see the similar situation in *Go Down, Moses* [1942]). As if to make the matter explicitly mythic, Thomas Sutpen names his half-Negro daughter Clytemnestra. But we would recognize the mythic resonances and possibilities of Faulkner's fiction even without the reminder of the *Oresteia* and its tales of relationships among brothers and sisters and parents and children.

5. *(Good Old Fashioned) Reliability and Its Modernist Face, (Potential) Unreliability (pages 68–78)*

1. John Fowles, *Daniel Martin* (New York: New American Library, 1977).

2. The more we read, in fact, the more likely we are to conclude that the adult Daniel Martin is indeed the narrator of this scene involving the young Daniel Martin, as of all the others. That is, he speaks as the novelist who has made himself a character (the presumably autobiographical, omniscient creator of characters) in this narrative. His narration is in both the first person and third person, the forms as he uses them more or less equally subjective, and one of the characters whom he creates is the boy that he was, the adolescent that the mature novelist imagines (or re-imagines) himself to have been. Implicitly, then, there is an interesting metafictional mix of characters, voices and times when, in the final paragraph of this opening scene, we read,

I feel in his pocket and bring out a clasp-knife; plunge the blade in the red earth to clean it of the filth from the two rabbits liver, intestines, stench. He stands and turns and begins to carve his initials on the beech-tree. Deep incisions in the bark, peeling the gray skin away to the sappy green of the living stem. Adieu, my boyhood and my dream. (10)

Unfortunately, as the somewhat clumsy metaphor of the incised beech tree may already suggest, the author is not able to sustain the magic of the scene in the self-involved narrative which follows. While the self-involvement is definitely that of Daniel Martin the novelist and only possibly that of John Fowles, the failure is one which they share.

3. Gide appears to have been influenced in his use of a reliable spokesman by Aldous Huxley, in almost all of whose novels, beginning with *Crome Yellow* in 1921, there is one character whose sole function is to serve as the authoritative voice of the author, especially on matters of culture and morals. While Huxley is a noted ironist, he never does turn on his reliable spokesmen in quite the ironic way that Gide does here. All references are to André Gide, *The Counterfeiters*, trans. Dorothy Bussy; the *Journal*, trans. Justin O'Brien (New York: Modern Library, 1955).

4. Ford Madox Ford, *The Good Soldier* (New York: Vintage Books, 1955).

5. The range of critics' reactions to Dowell is unusually broad, from Elliott B. Gose, Jr.'s, "he is an essentially honest if not very passionate person whose attitude toward the characters and events with which he deals is in constant evolution as the novel progresses. Although we certainly cannot take all his prejudices as being Ford's, I believe

we will find that the two make essentially the same evaluation of life" ("The Strange Irregular Rhythm," *PMLA*, LXII (June 1957), 495), to Mark Schorer's contention, "How can we believe *him*? His must be exactly the *wrong* view." (Introduction to the Vintage edition, vii.)

6. See, for example, Alan Wilde's *Horizons of Assent: Modernism, Postmodernism, and the Ironic Imagination* (Baltimore: Johns Hopkins University Press, 1981). While Wilde does not always find irony where I do in *The Good Soldier* (largely because he is less concerned than I am with point of view and with those moments when it intersects with irony), he does see Dowell as the representative Modernist ironic hero (31). Also intriguing is the fact that Wayne Booth followed *The Rhetoric of Fiction* with *A Rhetoric of Irony* (1974), in which, not surprisingly, most of his examples come from literature before the Modernist period.

7. Herman Melville, *Selected Tales and Poems,* ed. Richard Chase (New York: Rinehart & Company, 1960), 303. Among James's earliest books is his study of Hawthorne, the first book-length study of any American author and among the first declarations by an American author that he was working within a tradition that is particularly American (alongside, of course, the more general English tradition). Interestingly, James has nothing to say directly of Hawthorne's use of point of view; many of his comments, however, deal with the polarities of Realism on the one hand ("I am not sure that he had ever heard of Realism, this remarkable compound having [although it was invented sometime earlier] come into general use only since his death") and, on the other hand, "imagination" or "fancy." But there may be early hints here of what James would eventually come to recognize as aspects of point of view; thus, "The fine thing in Hawthorne is that he cared for the deeper psychology, and that in his way, he tried to become familiar with it" (3, 51). The "deeper psychology," of course, was key also to James's foremost concern, and it was through his fine tuning of point of view, principally, that he too "tried to become familiar with it."

8. *Pierre* is to my mind the worst novel ever written by a great novelist, and it was widely regarded in its own time as the work of a madman—but, then again, so was *Moby Dick.*

9. Herman Melville, *The Confidence Man* (New York: Grove Press, 1955), 18. All references are to this edition.

10. As editor of the *Journal of Modern Literature* since 1986, I have seen dozens of submissions which posit one or another novelist as the first of the post-Modernists, going back as far as E. M. Forster, who wrote his last novel, *A Passage to India,* in 1924, a full generation before the term *Modernism* was applied to literature. I cannot but be mistrustful of such backward glances at history, especially when those who make them typically demonstrate how little of literary history they actually know.

6. Narration within Narration (pages 79–90)

1. As an example of Marcel's using Swann's affair with Odette as a key to comprehending his own affair with Albertine, we note the unexplained mystery of Swann's equanimity regarding his wife's unfaithfulness, as if the jealousy which had driven him so neurotically to pursue her has been subsumed by their marriage and the birth of

their daughter. Contrast this with Marcel's enduring, even growing, obsession with Albertine after her death. Using his own affair to help reconstruct Swann's—how else to understand such raging jealousy than to experience it oneself?—Marcel may hope through Swann (through the act of telling/creating about Swann) to achieve his own equanimity.

2. Mme. de Villaparisis' memoirs have not yet been published when Marcel first refers to them. What this proves, however, is not that either Proust or Marcel is omniscient, but rather that the narrator Marcel, having already lived through the events which he now recounts, is distinct from his character Marcel, who is only now living them. The reference to these memoirs, then, is not only not an inconsistency, but serves as one further proof of the narrative possibilities offered by the dual points of view and dual time schemes of *A la recherche*.

3. It is the narration to Papa Totone which appears to inspire Marie Sophie to write down her father's life in her notebook.

4. All references are to Patrick Chamoiseau, *Texaco*, trans. Rose-Myriam Réjouis and Val Vinokurov (New York: Vintage, 1998).

5. In *Solibo Magnificent,* the title character is a famous storyteller who dies in the midst of a performance. The police assume that he has been murdered. "The writer with the curious bird name was the first suspect to be interrogated. . . . No, not writer: *word scratcher,* it makes a huge difference. . . . [T]he writer is from another world, he ruminates, elaborates, or canvasses, the word scratcher refuses the agony of oraliture, he collects and transmits." Trans. Rose-Myriam Réjouis and Val Vinokurov (New York: Vintage, 1997), p. 115.

6. See the chapter "'The Fortunate Explosion': Contemporary Fictions in Latin America," in my *Modernist Survivors,* 181–245.

7. In his effort to provide a more literary context to Marie-Sophie's oral narrative, Ti-Cirique reads to her many writers outside her tradition, among them Faulkner, "to show me the dark disorders in the head-depths of men," and Kafka, "to throw the world off balance" (366). Faulkner and Kafka, of course, are also among the major influences on the novelists of the Boom. "[T]he Caribbean," says Ti-Cirique, "calls for a Cervantes who has read Joyce" (327).

8. The occasional academic footnote provided by the novelist-as-character, along with the frequent library references (e.g., "Notebook No. 11 of Marie-Sophie Laborieux. 1965. Schoelcher Library, or "The Urban Planner's Notes to the Word-Scratcher. File No. 6. Sheet XVIII. 1987." Schoelcher Library," 192, 148), emphasize the formal French aspect of his version of her narrative. It may thus give to Marie-Sophie's *mémoire* something of the character of Proust's *Recherche*. In terms of recent Latin American fiction, however, a better comparison might be to José Lezama Lima's *Paradiso* (1968), a Cuban rendition of Proust which often seems more formal than the original.

9. In one of the most famous images of Magic Realism, when the senile, old patriarch of the Buendía clan is tied to a tree so that he will not wander off, in Gabriel García Márquez's *One Hundred Years of Solitude* (1967), he becomes part of the tree. It makes little difference if Chamoiseau intended the homage; the image has become part of late modern culture.

10. While technically, then, a metafiction, *Texaco* makes little play of the reflexive possibilities found in that form. Even learning at the end that Texaco also provides

Marie-Sophie's secret name (382) does not add much either to her story or to the telling(s) of her story.

11. Yet to write, Marie-Sophie knows, is "to die a little" (321), especially when one writes of her own life. "Writing does well at the end of an edge of oneself. . . . Oiseau de Cham, are you a writer?" (359–60). Chamoiseau has himself been actively involved in a campaign for the oral tradition, which he links with virtually all other aspects of local culture and names *créolité*. See, for example, his interview with James Ferguson, "Return of the Creole," 2 July 2001, http://www.patrickchamoiseau.cwc.net/interview.htm.

7. Narrative Invention (pages 91–101)

1. All references are to James Joyce, *Ulysses,* ed. Hans Walter Gabler (New York: Vintage Books, 1986), citing page and line numbers.

2. Stephen's famous dictum, "The artist, like the God of the creation, remains within or behind or beyond or above his handiwork, invisible, refined out of existence, indifferent, paring his fingernails" (*A Portrait of the Artist as a Young Man* [New York: Viking Press, 1960], 215), is an obvious rejoinder to the omniscient, omnipotent Victorian author, but it is not an accurate description of Joyce's own practice, even in *A Portrait.* Despite the narrative fireworks of *Ulysses* and *Finnegans Wake,* which seem to some to call attention to Joyce's presence within his fictions, his entire career seems to me to be designed to eliminating that presence. Nonetheless, he is never "indifferent," never simply neutral to the lives of his characters and to their wider, human implications. He is also so busy devising narrative strategies to suit the different episodes of his later novels that he can hardly find time to tend to his manicure. If I had to reformulate today Stephen's famous comment (which served as epigraph to my dissertation, a long-ago first draft for this book), I would suggest that Joyce's invisibility within his novels does not deny his very real moral, humanistic presence: that his varied points of view are designed not merely to showcase his own rare skills but also to involve the reader as an active presence in determining the outcomes and significance of these lives.

3. In one infamous comment, Woolf questions Joyce's taste and his intelligence, noting that *Ulysses,* in its "emphasis . . . upon indecency," "fails because of the comparative poverty of the writer's mind." Virginia Woolf, "Modern Fiction," *The Common Reader,* First Series, ed. Andrew McNeillie (New York: Harcourt Brace Jovanovich, 1984; 1925), 151. Woolf's relationship with Joyce is fraught with possibility, if with very little certainty. We know that she turned down the manuscript of *Ulysses* for publication by the Hogarth Press, and we may regret the possibility lost. Leonard and Virginia Woolf's daring and innovative press (which, of course, published her novels and profited doing so) would have been the ideal venue for that daring and innovative book. But this is not one of those potentially metaphoric events which may delimit the boundaries of Modernism. My sense is that her rejection represents no more than a minor lapse in confidence on the part of Woolf, that she understood intuitively the similarity of her goals and Joyce's and that somehow she feared that he might be accomplishing them more capably and imaginatively than she was. None of this is susceptible of proof, however, and, in the end, it does not really matter very much. What does matter is the point, made over and over again in her critical essays and manifested consistently in her novels, that the nature of the modern world had changed and that it was the obligation of the modern novelist to reflect (and at

times to abet) that change in her/his art: to devise, that is, points of view which are appropriate to realities whose provenance now lies within the individual.

4. Virginia Woolf, "Modern Fiction," *The Common Reader*, First Series (New York: Harcourt Brace Jovanovich, 1984), 150.

5. John Bayley, *Tolstoy and the Novel* (New York: Viking, 1966), 59.

6. Malcolm Bradbury, *Possibilities: Essays on the State of the Novel* (London: Oxford University Press, 1973), 130. While few English readers of Woolf today are likely to be quite so outspoken—so aggressively foolish—as Bayley and Bradbury were a generation ago (secure as they were in the knowledge that everyone who mattered shared their view of Woolf), an American admirer of her work is still likely in England to detect a certain distrust, an unease with Woolf far greater than any persisting with Joyce or Beckett.

7. Virginia Woolf, "Mr. Bennett and Mrs. Brown," in *Approaches to the Novel*, ed. Robert Scholes (San Francisco: Chandler, 1961), 224–25.

8. Although Woolf frequently has been accused of vagueness—a kind of romantic, poetic, feminine vagueness at that—I find it difficult to envision a more explicit statement of a novelist's needs and expectations from her literary tradition than her comment about Realistic points of view in "Mr. Bennett and Mrs. Brown": "That is what I mean by saying that the Edwardian tools are the wrong ones for us to use. They have laid an enormous stress upon the fabric of things. They have given us a house in the hope that we may be able to deduce the human beings who live there. To give them their due, they have made that house much better, worth living in. But if you hold that novels are in the first place about people, and only in the second about the houses they live in, that is the wrong way to set about it" (224–25).

9. All references are to Virginia Woolf, *The Waves* (Harmondsworth, Middlesex: Penguin Books, 1966).

10. Cited in Brenda R. Silver, "'Anon' and 'The Reader': Virginia Woolf's Last Essays," *Twentieth Century Literature*, 25 (1979), 356.

11. Virginia Woolf, "Anon," in *Collected Essays*, I, 56, cited in Silver, 380. Or, again, "It was they who made the playwright capable of his great strides, of vast audacities beyond the reach of the solitary" (395). I was taught as a graduate student that the first true insight into the rare quality of the Elizabethan playgoer was Alfred Harbage's in *Shakespeare's Audience*, but it seems that Woolf may have preceded him—as well as going further than he does in evaluating that audience. I am indebted to Diane McManus for bringing "Anon" and its possibilities to my attention.

12. "Anon," 383. Even Chaucer, in Woolf's conception, is more folk poet than court poet, part of the oral tradition rather than the bookish. That begins with Spenser, but even he did not close out the literature of the people: "Had the poet remained in the great room, preferring his book to the little group of readers, English poetry might have remained book poetry, read aloud" (391–92).

13. "The voice that broke the silence of the forest was the voice of Anon. . . . The audience was itself the singer" ("Anon," 382).

14. "Anon," 424. Among Woolf's preliminary notes for the essay are the phrases:
1. Anon.
2. [*The audience*] The ear & the eye.
3. The individual. 3. The audience.
4. Words?

   . . .

The chorus.

   . . .

The writer—what is his mark? That he enjoys dispassionately: has a split in his consciousness?" (376–78)

Taken together, they serve very well to characterize Woolf's development of point of view in *The Waves*.

For my awareness of the essay and character "Anon," I am indebted to Diane McManus and her 1989 dissertation, *Resurrecting Shakespeare's Sister: The Evolution of Virginia Woolf's Narrative Voice from the Common Reader to Anon.*

15. *The Waves* begins and ends and is punctuated throughout by nature passages whose point of view cannot possibly be that of the characters, whether individually or collectively. In my book *The Modernist Masters* (Lewiston, N.Y.: Mellen Press, 2003, 92–95), I suggest that this may be the voice of Nature itself—not in any literal sense, to be sure, but from somewhere within, even beyond, the collective human consciousness.

8. The Creation of Consciousness on the Page (pages 102–123)

1. O'Connor's full formulation reads, "Jewish literature is the literature of townsmen, and the greatest Jew of all was James Joyce. Never once in all his work, so far as I know it, do we get a hint of what life was like in Ireland outside of Dublin." Frank O'Connor, *A Short History of Irish Literature: A Backward Look* (New York: Capricorn Books, 1968), 198. To the extent that Modernism is also a Jewish phenomenon—and I believe that the extent is significant—O'Connor's full comment reinforces my use of it in this context.

2. All references are to Virginia Woolf, *Mrs. Dalloway* (New York: Harcourt, Brace and Company, 1925).

3. Woolf, of course, had read the manuscript of *Ulysses,* had been appalled somewhat by it and had rejected it for the Hogarth Press. It is not impossible, however, that she also learned something from it, perhaps even the aptness of the city—with its contrast between the gross, unknowing outer world and the almost unknowable inner world—as setting for the sort of novel of discovery which she wanted to write—perhaps even beginning with a pedestrian on the streets of the city. While I am convinced that Woolf came to fear that Joyce might be accomplishing her goal more successfully than she was, the city, obviously, was available to them equally. But how interestingly different are their points of view, yet how much they do share in common. In her wonderfully personal essay, "Street Haunting: A London Adventure," Woolf finds in the winter streets of the city a metaphor for the possibilities of knowing its walkers: "It is at once revealed and obscured." And she continues, using the imagery of the flowing stream, "But, after all, we are only gliding smoothly on the surface. The eye is not a miner, not a diver, not a seeker after buried treasure. It floats us smoothly down a stream; resting, pausing, the brain sleeps perhaps as it looks.

" . . . But here we must stop peremptorily. We are in danger of digging deeper than the eye approves; we are impeding our passage down the smooth stream by catching at some branch or root." *The Death of the Moth and Other Essays* (Harmondsworth: Penguin Books, 1965), 24–25. In acknowledging the dangers of delving beneath the surface—perhaps the most recurrent metaphor in her art and life—Woolf is not say-ing, as I read her, that we must not attempt to do so; such a voyage, though, is not the province of the eye alone, and dangers may be entailed when we undertake it.

4. Woolf, we know, disapproved of the overly indelicate imagery and tone of *Ulysses*. Yet she too could appreciate, if only at a distance, "the carnal splendour of the butchers' shops with their yellow flanks and purple steaks" ("Street Haunting," 25).

5. Woolf clearly believed that she could enter only so far and for so long into the minds of her characters. As she says in "Street Haunting," "Into each of these lives [per-ceived on city streets] one could penetrate a little way, far enough to give oneself the illusion that one is not tethered to a single mind, but can put on briefly for a few min-utes the bodies and minds of others" (35). The evidence of *Ulysses*, however, and espe-cially of *Finnegans Wake*, would seem to suggest that Joyce accepted no such limits.

6. For Freud, of course, free association was the starting point of his exploratory technique. It was his "'obscure intuition,'" as Freud put it, that at the end of the trail of such trivial details—themselves part of a patient's "resistance"—the truth of his illness might well be found. As Freud's first biographer comments, "It could not have been very difficult to surmise that the roundabout meanderings were an expression of this resis-tance, an attempt to postpone the emergence of the significant memory, and yet they followed a route ultimately connected with it. This would justify his patience in follow-ing the trains of thought with the closest attention and in the greatest detail." Ernest Jones, *The Life and Work of Sigmund Freud* (Garden City, N.Y.: Doubleday, 1963), 156. Variants of free association, such as automatic writing, were important also to the early Surrealists. The result of free association—as practiced by Freud, or even perhaps by André Breton—might indeed be epiphanic; but in our individual daily lives, the realiza-tion that we have been associating freely will rarely lead us to do more than identify the trail which we have been following: a very minor truth at best.

7. Nathaniel Hawthorne, "Preface" to *The House of the Seven Gables: A Romance*, in *The Complete Novels and Selected Tales of Nathaniel Hawthorne* (New York: Mod-ern Library, 1937), 243; Henry James, in his "Preface to *Roderick Hudson*," in *The Art of the Novel* (New York: Charles Scribner's Sons, 1937), 16. "The fine thing in Haw-thorne," wrote James, who seems also to be speaking of himself and to anticipate Joyce and Woolf, "is that he cared for the deeper psychology, and that, in his way, he tried to become familiar with it." Henry James, *Hawthorne* (Ithaca, N.Y.: Cornell University Press, 1956; originally written 1879), 51.

8. The ability to interject such terms into dialogue, without the disruptive effect of multiple quotation marks, is the reason that Joyce chose to use the initial dash in place of the customary, surrounding marks.

9. In making dream available to artists, both as subject matter and as technique, Freud was, as he said about the unconscious in general, simply providing a means for analyzing a state which the artists themselves had long since discovered. This is not to say, of course, that Freud's predecessors had available to them the same breadth and depth of possibilities as did those artists who followed Freud—even if they had not read him. I think, for example, of the rather crude sense of the dream state in French Symbolist paintings of the late nineteenth century—crude not in their execution but in their concept of the constituents of dream. In Paul Gauguin's "The Little Dreamer" (1881), for example, the figures flying above the head of the sleeping child (Gauguin's

daughter) are not entirely distinct, and the doll-like jester figure on the floor below her bed appears to be a self-portrait of her father. In "Tahitian Woman" (1898), the grass is red, the trees partly blue, and the figures are massive, yet flattened, as if seen through some strangely distorting lens. And in "Adam and Eve" (1902), the scene seems primal not just in its subject but also in its feeling. All of this is suggestive, rather than illustrative, of dream—precisely what one would expect from artists before Freud had provided them a vocabulary.

10. For proof that Joyce had indeed read at least some Freud, note the sequence in "Cyclops" in which Bloom envisions himself as the new Parnell. "Go on," says Zoe the whore. "Make a stump speech out of it," and Bloom does, rising and falling as Parnell had done; and then, one instant and eighteen pages afterwards, "Talk away till you're black in the face" (469–88), she concludes. Joyce is reflecting here Freud's belief—since disproven by the phenomenon of REM sleep—that our dreams take place in the instant before we awake and last for only a few moments.

11. For an enlightening discussion of these Surrealist plays, see Annette Shandler Levitt, "Artaud, Vitrac, and the Cruelty of Theatre," in *The Genres and Genders of Surrealism* (New York: St. Martin's Press, 2000), 27–41.

12. For more on Jung's rejection of *Ulysses* and the parallels between Joyce's mythopoesis and Jung's, see my essay "A Hero for Our Time: Leopold Bloom and the Myth of *Ulysses*," in *James Joyce and Modernism: Beyond Dublin*. I am inclined to think that Tom Stoppard made a mistake in his play, *Travesties,* in not including Jung along with those others then resident in Zurich—Joyce, Lenin, and Tristan Tzara, the Dadaist—as staging points for his developing dialectic. Jung would have made a much more viable antithesis to Joyce than does his declared enemy Henry Carr (see "Circe" for Joyce's own revenge).

13. Jacques Mercanton, "The Hours of James Joyce," trans. Lloyd C. Parks, in Willard Potts, ed., *Portraits of the Artist in Exile: Recollections of James Joyce by Europeans* (Seattle: University of Washington Press, 1979), 207; cited in John Bishop, *Joyce's Book of the Dark: Finnegans Wake* (Madison: University of Wisconsin Press, 1986), 8. Bishop's is one of the very best books on the *Wake,* but it is not intended as an introduction for a hopeful, beginning reader. Perhaps the best of them remains one of the earliest, Bernard Benstock's *Joyce-again's Wake: An Analysis of Finnegans Wake* (1965), which is, naturally, somewhat outdated; but I also like John Gordon's *Finnegans Wake: A Plot Summary* (1987), which does more than its subtitle promises, and the section on the *Wake* in A. Nicholas Fargnoli and Michael P. Gillespie, *James Joyce A to Z: The Essential Reference to the Life and Work* (1995). As every reader of the *Wake* knows, however, the best way to approach the novel is in a reading group, some of which today can even be found on the Web.

14. With a single possible exception, this shifting dream in its shifting scenes is all that there is in the *Wake.* The exception: I suspect that as HCE lies in bed in the morning, in Book IV, with the radio playing in the background, this is more preconscious than dream. But since Joyce may not have known of Freud's term "the preconscious" (he surely did not know about REM sleep), it may be quibbling to attempt to make the distinction.

15. James Joyce, *Finnegans Wake* (New York: Viking Press, 1958), 3: 4–6, citing page and line numbers.

16. Various writers have been put forward as making use of and learning from the *Wake,* but, on examination, that typically proves to mean that they have tried to play

with language much as Joyce does. Thus, the works of Christine Brooke-Rose and Philippe Sollers are, at best, pale shadows of Joyce's, even though we may applaud their efforts. We will have to wait for a full translation of Arno Schmidt's *Zettel's Traum* before we can judge that work fully.

17. "Modern Fiction," in *The Common Reader: First Series,* ed. Andrew McNeillie (New York: Harcourt Brace Jovanovich, 1984; orig. pub. 1925), 147, 150.

18. In an almost symbolic note putting an end to this foolishness, the contemporary English novelist Pat Barker has written a superb, historically based trilogy dealing directly with the problem of shellshock—the literal disintegration of consciousness—during and after World War I: *Regeneration* (1991), *The Eye in the Door* (1993) and *The Ghost Road* (1995).

19. William Cooper, "Reflections on Some Aspects of the Experimental Novel," *International Literary Annual,* ed. John Wain (New York, 1967), pp. 40–41.

20. Even Robbe-Grillet is incapable always of shutting off emotion entirely, so that in *La Maison de rendez-vous* (1965), for example, we are likely to be moved—as the narrator/protagonist is—by the death of an old woman in a nursing home (it may even be that his narration has been an effort to divert her during her final days). But Robbe-Grillet has advised us, hasn't he, that he should not be expected as novelist to follow all of his strictures as theoretician. Yet there can be no doubt that, in such novels as *Le Voyeur* and *La Jalousie,* Robbe-Grillet uses point of view to evidence and even enhance the disintegration of the individual consciousness—and that he does so with no evident hint of emotion; but he sees this process as an attack on Modernist and not on pre-Modernist goals, as the English enemies of the Nouveau Roman blithely assumed. We need also to be wary of the term "Nouveau Roman" and the implication that all of its practitioners are interchangeable. There are very few connections among Butor, Robbe-Grillet, Marguerite Duras, Robert Pinget, Nathalie Sarraute and the profoundly humanistic Claude Simon beyond the fact that their early novels were published by Gallimard.

21. All references are to *Passing Time,* trans. Jean Stewart (New York: Simon and Schuster, 1960); *Degrees,* trans. Richard Howard (New York: Simon and Schuster, 1961); and *A Change of Heart,* trans. Jean Stewart (New York: Simon and Schuster, 1959).

9. Omniscience (pages 124–139)

1. C. P. Snow, *London Sunday Times* (27 December 1953), as cited in David Lodge, *The Novelist at the Crossroads* (Ithaca, N.Y.: Cornell University Press, 1971), 18. As the lead reviewer for the *Sunday Times* through much of this period, Snow exerted considerable influence both on what was being read and what was written. Although publicly at odds with Leavis over the issue of the so-called "Two Cultures," he was Leavis' major ally in the fight against what they equally derided as "experimentation." As Rubin Rabinovitz has written, "Snow's critical formula is too predictable: any warm, human, readable novel which displays no experimental tendencies is approved of. Using this formula Snow praised many mediocre books and rejected many that were worthwhile; nevertheless Snow's theories were, on the whole, approved of in England" ("C. P. Snow vs. The Experimental Novel," *the Columbia University Forum,* X [1967], 40–41).

2. William Cooper, "Reflections of Some Aspects of the Experimental Novel," *International Literary Annual*, ed. John Wain (New York, 1967), 29.

3. Amis is reasonably forthright in commenting on point of view as a particular problem for these anti-Modernist, presumably post-Modernist novelists. "The idea about experiment being the life-blood of the English novel is one that dies hard. 'Experiment,' in this context, boils down pretty regularly to 'obtruded oddity,' whether in construction—multiple viewpoints and such—or in style," *The Spectator* (2 May 1955), 565, cited in Rubin Rabinovitz, *The Reaction against Experiment in the English Novel, 1950–1960* (New York: Columbia University Press, 1967), 40–41.

4. See my *Modernist Survivors*, "Honored Past? Fearsome Present?" 73–123.

5. All references are to Margaret Drabble, *The Realms of Gold* (New York: Alfred A. Knopf, 1975).

6. For the reader who might wonder if *The Realms of Gold* is an anomaly in Drabble's canon, we find much the same usage in *The Waterfall* (1969), in which the omniscient voice purports to be that of the protagonist, supposedly writing the story of her own life. We soon recognize, however, that the subject matter, the view of (a woman's) life, even the tone are virtually identical to those in *The Realms of Gold*, indeed, to those of virtually all of Drabble's novels: this is indisputably her voice that we hear. And as she has turned from novels to literary history, it seems no coincidence that Drabble has chosen to write the biography of Arnold Bennett, Virginia Woolf's particular pre-Modernist *bête noire*.

7. See the discussion of point of view in *The Last Temptation of Christ* in Chapter 10. Kazantzakis is generally disinterested in the technical innovations of his Modernist contemporaries, but when he requires ambiguity, even divine ambiguity, he evidently knows well how to provide it. His novels normally need no more than an avoidance of omniscience, however, and so his characteristic point of view is simply straightforward, objective presentation of events seen through the senses and thoughts of his characters: there is nothing inherently Modernist about this, except for the careful avoidance of a certain and definitive narrative center.

8. The streetcar named "Prazeres" is one of the most exciting urban transport rides in the world.

9. All references are to Jose Saramago, *The Year of the Death of Richard Ricardo Reis*, trans. Giovanni Pontiero (New York: Harcourt Brace, 1991).

10. Of the many signs of Stephen's and Bloom's linked sensibilities, the most compelling relate to point of view: to images remembered by one that only the other had experienced (e.g., Bloom's hearing in "Circe" [p. 440] the auctioneer's handbell that is associated in "Wandering Rocks" [p. 186] with the Dedalus family's poverty); and to knowledge demonstrated by one that only the other can possibly possess (e.g., Stephen's thinking of his father immediately after Leopold has visualized Rudolph ["Circe," p. 412]). The most dramatic of their shared images are the face of Shakespeare which each sees in his mirror [p. 463] and the jointly remembered line, Stephen (in "Scylla and Charybdis," p. 166): "In a rosery of Fetter Lane of Gerard, herbalist, he walks, greyedauburn. . . . One life is all. One body. Do. But do.") and Bloom (in "Sirens," p. 230): "In Gerard's rosery of Fetter lane he walks, greyedauburn. One life is all. One body. Do. But do." All references to James Joyce's *Ulysses* are to the so-called Gabler edition, Hans Walter Gabler, *et al*, eds. (New York: Random House, 1986).

11. In this regard, Ricardo Reis almost certainly holds political views—likely, more or less liberal ones—but in his desperate effort to maintain self-control, he must put them aside. To acknowledge Franco's successes in Spain, for example, might put a further strain on his psyche. That he understands the nature of psychogenic illness is apparent in his early discussions with Marcenda, the lovely middle-class girl with the crippled hand and a domineering father. Although Doctor Reis raises the issue with her, he fails to pursue it, as if to do so might endanger his own psychic security. (He does make a hurried journey to Lourdes, however, without acknowledging whether it is on her behalf or his own.)

12. It is possible, I believe, to argue that Bloom is not only the point of view of the second half of the "Nausicaa" episode of *Ulysses,* but also that he is the source of Gerty McDowell's narrative in the first half of the chapter. If true, this would be a delightful play on Joyce's presumed use of Samuel Butler's theory that the writer of the *Odyssey* was a woman, perhaps the Princess Nausicaa herself. But Bloom, as we will discover in "Circe," is himself powerfully androgynous.

13. Ricardo Reis is that *persona* of Pessoa who has been categorized as "coldly classical," as "the morose, coldly Augustan member of the team." Roy Campbell, *Fernando Pessoa,* in George Monteiro, *The Presence of Pessoa: English, American, and Southern African Literary Responses* (Lexington: University Press of Kentucky, 1998), 110. Saramago obviously plays on this quality, along with those of some of the characters created in his poetry by the *persona.* For instance, Reis's lover Lídia has nothing to say in the poems presumably inspired by her, and it even seems that they are never truly lovers. But the chambermaid Lydia does indeed sleep with the hotel guest Dr. Ricardo Reis, becomes pregnant with his child (if not precisely heir) and has a good deal to say at times, especially about the political situation on which Reis himself makes no comment.

14. All references are to Carol Shields, *The Stone Diaries* (New York: Penguin Books, 1995).

15. Neither the word "reconstruct" nor the concept appears in *Tristram Shandy,* yet surely this is what Tristram must be doing: how else account for his apparent intimate knowledge of events not only before his birth, but before even his conception? "I wish either my father or my mother, or indeed both of them," he begins, "as they were in duty equally bound to it, had minded what they were about when they begot me" (Laurence Sterne, *Tristram Shandy* [New York: The Odyssey Press, 1940], p. 4). He refers, of course, to the infamous winding of the clock at the time of his conception; but so much more may be inferred from his comment. Tristram's concern with time, incidentally, calls forth a comparable concern in Shields's narrator.

16. Such incidents, in another context, might well seem omniscient. But by this point in *The Stone Diaries,* that possibility no longer even occurs to the reader.

17. Sterne, 4. For another tale indebted to this theory and voice, see John Barth's "Night-Sea Journey" in *Lost in the Funhouse.*

18. Sterne, 6.

10. The Subjective Use of Narrative Objectivity (pages 140–154)

1. All references are to Wayne Booth, *The Rhetoric of Fiction* (Chicago: University of Chicago Press, 1961).

2. James Joyce, *A Portrait of the Artist as a Young Man* (New York: The Viking Press, 1960), 215.

3.References to all Kafka stories are to Franz Kafka, *The Penal Colony: Stories and Short Pieces,* trans. Willa and Edwin Muir (New York: Schocken Books, 1977). There are no significant differences, in the stories cited here, between this old translation and the acclaimed newer one by Joachim Neugroschel, *The Metamorphosis, In the Penal Colony, and other Stories* (New York: Simon & Schuster, 1995).

4. See my book *The Cretan Glance: The World and Art of Nikos Kazantzakis* (Columbus: Ohio State University Press, 1980).

5. Nikos Kazantzakis, *The Last Temptation of Christ,* trans. P.A. Bien (New York: Simon and Schuster, 1966), 391–92.

6. What might be called the objective/subjective point of view appears today even in popular fiction, even in detective and spy novels, which would seem so much easier to write if the author simply manipulated his characters and moved point of view among them as he wishes, or if he spoke in his own voice to provide needed information or to foreshadow events. I think, for example, of the British novelist Lionel Davidson's complex thriller, *Kolymsky Heights* (1994), which meticulously presents all scenes involving the protagonist, Dr. Johnny Porter, from his carefully controlled perspective and does similarly with scenes from which Porter is absent, such as those involving his antagonist, the major general of the Russian security sevices who very nearly catches him, or those others, often minor figures, who assist him. Davidson moves around as he needs to, covering vast distances from the Black Sea to Siberia, even leaping back and forth in time, especially when arranging the final details of the plot, after his protagonist has presumably been killed. But there is no sense of omniscient manipulation here.

Only rarely does Davidson succumb to the temptation to speak in his own, all-knowing voice: "But there had been an attachment," we are told, just after one CIA agent has said to another, "'He had no real attachments, you know'" (New York: St. Martin's Press, 359). The scene then returns to Siberia and the Russian medical officer who has aided Porter and become his lover: the comment is not so much omniscient as structural, a trivial trope that the novelist cannot resist. Other seemingly omniscient comments may turn out to be ironic, or even misleading. Thus, when the general questions the medical officer and is given some misinformation by her, we are told, "And this general, a persistent man, was not going to let it go. Where it would lead, in the end, was to the right conclusion; but that was not yet" (296). At least, the general believes that in the end he has reached the right conclusion; but by then, we know that he has not, that he, like the reader has been misled—very definitely not the appropriate Victorian use for omniscient-seeming information.

7. Don DeLillo, *Underworld* (New York: Scribner, 1997), 401, 412, 413.

8. DeLillo, *Underworld,* 45.

9. Saul Bellow, *Mosby's Memoirs and Other Stories* (Harmondsworth: Penguin Books, 1971).

10. Saul Bellow, *The Dean's December* (New York: Pocket Books, 1983).

11. Metafiction as Narration (pages 155–162)

1. Maurice Beebe, "*Ulysses* and the Age of Modernism," *James Joyce Quarterly,* X, 1 (Fall 1972), 185. Beebe's other characteristics of Modernism are "formalism. It insists

on the importance of structure and design"; "an attitude of detachment and non-commitment which I would put under the general heading of 'irony'"; and "myth . . . as an arbitrary means of ordering art" (175). I suspect that if the eminent editor and literary historian Beebe were alive today, he would want to alter his list and definitions somewhat. The term "metafiction" appears to have been coined by the American novelist William Gass (see his *Fiction and the Figures of Life* [New York: Knopf, 1970]).

2. Cf. George Orwell's essay on postcard art, "The Art of Donald McGill," in *A Collection of Essays* (Garden City, N.Y.: Doubleday, 1954), 111–22. The comic strip process is ongoing and adaptive to popular attitudes: a "Doonesbury" cartoon published in late July 2002 is dedicated to "Denny Klatz," who, we are told, has purchased "name placement" in the strip; "He was scheduled for an actual likeness, but he couldn't afford it." The final panel shows a shirt and tie without an occupant, but with the toast, "To Denny!" May he get it together!" These are not the first such usages. Morris Beja reminds me of the earlier Looney Tunes cartoons and Buster Keaton's *Sherlock, Jr.,* and David Hayman adds the mid-nineteenth-century Swiss Topffer and his brilliant M. Pincel.

3. The most presumably autobiographical of Barth's fictions is *Once Upon a Time* (1994), which appears to provide at least some of the facts on which his art is based and to explain various references in his earlier work. The novel ends suddenly, however, its third act—of his present marriage—never written, for his wife protests the intrusion into their lives. She—her character in the novel—is thus presumably left, somewhere in the reeds of the lower Chesapeake Bay, waiting for her sailing husband to return to their boat, for he has abandoned the fictional premise of his search through his life. Barth's playfulness has in no way been hindered by the metafictional form.

4. John Barth, *Chimera* (Greenwich, Conn.: Fawcett, 1973).

5. On the other hand, when Swift became too closely identified with one of his characters, the results—for understanding his work, for his critical reputation—could be disastrous. Identifying Swift with Gulliver, as when the disillusioned traveler, at the close of Book IV of *Gulliver's Travels,* retreats to his stable to live with his horses, early readers assumed that the author was advocating a similar withdrawal from the world. They were thus able to dismiss one of the most powerful satiric studies in literature and to dismiss Swift as well, as a presumably insane man.

6. Barth, a non-Jew, has borrowed even the Jewish theme in his reflexive fictions—married into it, more accurately. In *Once Upon a Time* (1994), he indicates his admiration for his wife's (that is, his *persona's* wife's) heritage as the ideal one for a writer. *Cf.* also John Updike's Bech novels, which treat the life of the Jewish American writer, as it were, from a little further outside.

7. All references are to Philip Roth, *Operation Shylock: A Confession* (New York: Vintage, 1994).

12. Time as a Function of Point of View (pages 163–176)

1. Thomas Mann, *The Tales of Jacob,* trans. H. T. Lowe-Porter (New York: Alfred A. Knopf, 1963), 7–8.

2. Where Joyce provides a virtual catalogue of his sources in the "Oxen of the Sun" episode of *Ulysses*—which progresses from the earliest modes of English to the prose writers at the end of the nineteenth century—along with many individual literary refer-

ences elsewhere in the novel, the literary history which he offers in *Finnegans Wake* is both less chronological and far more difficult to follow in any recognizable order. Like every other form of reference in the *Wake,* literature is made subject to the prevailing, but hardly chronological, logic of the dream.

3. Between 1929 and 1932, Faulkner published *Sartoris, The Sound and the Fury, As I lay Dying, Sanctuary* and *Light in August,* as well as a collection of stories.

4. It is surely no coincidence that when Simon, in the early 1970s (beginning with *Conducting Bodies* [1971])—possibly under the influence of the newly ascendant literary theory, broke away from his accustomed explorations of the individual consciousness searching through the detritus of the past in an effort to understand history and one's own place within it—as in *The Flanders Road* (1960), *The Palace* (1962), and *Histoire* (1967)—his characters became flatter, his plots less complex and more chronological and his prose style infinitely less challenging and rich. The change may have helped Simon to win the Nobel Prize in 1985, but the Nobel citation does specify the profound humanistic concerns of these earlier works, concerns made manifest through the rich agglomeration of style, point of view, time, theme and reader involvement—or, to put it a bit differently, of Faulkner, Joyce and Proust—in his best and most characteristic work. Simon's latest fictions, not coincidentally, I suspect, make an effort to return to the earlier forms, albeit with less complexity and, unfortunately, less success.

5. All references are to Virginia Woolf, *To the Lighthouse* (New York: Harcourt, Brace & World, 1955).

6. Carlos Fuentes, "Viva Zapata" [a review of John Womack's *Zapata and the Mexican Revolution*], *The New York Review of Books* (13 March 1969), p. 6.

7. Nonetheless, we have this account, which we are free either to dismiss as illogical or to accept as a forceful, involving narrative; should we need them, rationalizations of such accounts—beyond Fuentes' theory of the circularity of Mexican history—are always possible. Thus, for example, the "I" who closes out the narrative—"I carry you inside and with you I die. The three, we . . . will die. You . . . die, have died . . . I will die" (306)—can be seen not as Artemio but as some form of life force, his own and/or Mexico's, just as the vivid and immediate scene of his birth can be attributed to his intense desire/need to keep his own dead son alive in his imagination.

Index

DeLillo, Don, 146, 150–152; *Underworld,* 150–152
Dickens, Charles, 13, 14, 20, 22, 23, 35, 56, 68, 140, 163, 168, 175; *Great Expectations,* 163; *The Mystery of Edwin Drood,* 22, 68, 163; *The Old Curiosity Shop,* 20
Distance in the Modernist novel, 11, 13, 14, 54, 71, 82, 83, 95, 101, 140, 141
Doctorow, E. L., 39, 126
Dostoevsky, Feodor, 48, 49, 168; *Notes from Underground,* 49–50
Drabble, Margaret, 7, 126–127, 192n6; *The Realms of Gold,* 126–127, 192n6
Dujardin, Édouard, 107–108
Duras, Marguerite, 190n20

Einstein, Albert, 39, 164
Eliot, George, 19
Eliot, T. S., 23
Empson, William, 23

Faulkner, William, 5, 7, 19, 30, 36, 57, 79, 115, 125, 153, 163, 167, 168, 169, 175, 182n12, 182n13, 182n14, 185n7, 196n3, 196n4; *Absalom, Absalom!,* 36, 57, 58, 60–67, 79, 182n14; *The Sound and the Fury, 115, 169*
Fielding, Henry, 13, 18, 19
Flaubert, Gustave, 29, 31, 32, 100, 119, 141; *Madame Bovary,* 31
Ford, Ford Madox, 68, 72–74, 77, 140, 183n5; *The Good Soldier,* 72–74, 77, 140, 183n5
Forster, E. M., 39
Fowles, John, 68, 69, 182n2; *Daniel Martin,* 69–70, 182n2
Frazer, Sir James G., 5, 39
Freud, Sigmund, 5, 39, 99, 108, 114, 115, 117, 119, 135, 164, 189n6, 189n9, 190n10
Fuentes, Carlos, 36, 57, 163, 173–175, 196n6; *The Death of Artemio Cruz,* 36, 173–175, 196n6

Galsworthy, John, 164
García, Márquez, Gabriel, 185n9
Gauguin, Paul, 189n9
Genette, Gérard, 28
Gide, André, 68–72, 76, 77, 183n3; *The Counterfeiters,* 69–72, 76, 77

Gilbert, William S., and Sir Arthur Sullivan, 111
Golding, William, 125, 126
Goodman, Allegra, 146, 149–150
Greene, Graham, 125, 126

Hawthorne, Nathaniel, 19, 22, 23, 33, 108, 115, 119, 179n9, 184n7, 189n7
Hemingway, Ernest, 7, 30, 40–46, 98, 125, 181n33, 182n13, *A Farewell to Arms,* 41, 44–46; "On the Quai at Smyrna," 41–42; "Soldier's Home," 41–44
Homer, 17
Humanism in the Modernist novel, 1, 2, 8, 10, 40, 60, 143, 175, 186n2, 191n20
Huxley, Aldous, 183n3

James, Henry, 2, 3, 11, 12, 23, 24, 28, 29, 32, 35, 43, 52, 56, 148, 159, 171, 179n17, 180n20, 184n7, 189n7; *The Ambassadors,* 12; *The American,* 24; *The Golden Bowl,* 23, 24, 26–27, 28, 179n17; *The Princess Casamassima,* 29; *The Spoils of Poynton,* 25; *The Turn of the Screw,* 12
Johnson, B. S., 125
Joyce, James, 5, 6, 7, 8, 9, 11, 12, 13, 14, 16, 27, 30, 35, 37–40, 43, 44, 45, 47, 58, 74, 79, 91, 92–95, 97, 99, 124, 125, 131, 135, 141, 142, 143, 144, 146, 153, 155, 158, 165–166, 167, 168, 169, 170, 175, 178n7, 180n24, 181n32, 186n2, 186n6, 189n8, 190n10, 195n2, 196n4; *Dubliners,* 6, 13, 37–40, 41, 44, 45, 76, 126, 141, 144, 158, 169, 181n32; "The Sisters," 143; *Finnegans Wake,* 11, 13, 14, 15, 31, 36, 38, 39, 40, 44, 79, 83, 112, 114, 116–118, 123, 142, 144, 146, 165, 166, 167, 170, 178n7, 186n2, 189n5, 190n13, 190n14, 190n15, 195n2; *A Portrait of the Artist as a Young Man,* 13, 14, 15, 40, 109, 141, 142, 158, 186n2; *Ulysses,* 13, 14, 15, 16, 27, 35, 36, 39, 44, 79, 83, 92–95, 98, 102–106, 107, 109–116, 118, 131, 142, 144, 155, 165, 167, 168, 170, 178n7, 186n2, 188n4, 189n5, 190n12, 192n10, 193n12, 195n2; "Circe," 113–114, 165; "Cyclops," 190n10; Ithaca," 112; "Oxen of the Sun," 27, 195n2; "Penelope," 112; "Proteus," 110–112; "Telemachus," 109–110

Richardson, Dorothy, 107–108, 124

Richardson, Samuel, 18, 19; *Clarissa*, 19

Richardson, Tony, 19

Robbe-Grillet, Alain, 1, 2, 3, 4, 9, 10, 12, 24, 25, 30, 39, 120, 122, 141, 157, 177n4, 191n20; *The Erasers*, 157; *For a New Novel*, 3, 4; *Trans-Europ-Express*, 156; *The Voyeur*, 1, 3, 10

Robbins, Harold, 36

Romanticism, 8

Rossetti, Dante Gabriel, 48–49, 181n3

Roth, Philip, 159–162; "I Always Wanted You to Admire My Fasting; or, Looking at Kafka," 161; *Operation Shylock*, 161

Rousseau, Jean-Jacques, 121, 155

Sams, Henry, 158

Saramago, José, 127–134, 192n11; *The Year of the Death of Ricardo Reis*, 127–134, 192n11

Sarraute, Nathalie, 191n20

Schmidt, Arno, 190n16

Shaw, George Bernard, 181n3

Shields, Carol, 127, 136–139, 193n15; *The Stone Diaries*, 136–139

Simon, Claude, 19, 36, 57, 58, 59, 87, 123, 135, 163, 169, 175, 191n20, 196n4; *The Battle of Pharsalus*, 169; *The Flanders Road*, 36, 57, 58, 67, 169; *The Wind*, 169

Snow, C. P., 22, 69, 118, 119, 120, 124–125, 154, 191n1

Sollers, Phillippe, 28, 190n16

Stein, Gertrude, 41

Stendhal, 30, 32, 180n29; *The Red and the Black*, 30–31

Sterne, Lawrence, 11, 13, 77, 83, 115, 127, 135, 138, 193n15; *Tristram Shandy*, 135, 136, 137, 138, 193n15

Stoppard, Tom, 125

Surrealism, 116

Swift, Jonathan, 159–160, 195n5; "A Modest Proposal," 159–160; *Gulliver's Travels*, 195n5

Thackeray, William Makepeace, 15, 16, 19, 20, 21, 68; *Vanity Fair*, 21

Thornton, Lawrence, 126

Time in the Modernist novel, 111, 163–175

Töppfer, Randolphe, 195n2

Tradition in the Modernist novel, 2, 3, 9, 10, 31, 36, 48, 49, 77, 78, 87, 89, 91, 95, 100, 132, 150, 160

Trollope, Anthony, 7, 20, 21, 22, 35, 36, 52, 56, 189n24; *Barchester Towers*, 21

Trudeau, Gary, 155–156

Truffaut, François, 156

Tzara, Tristan, 190n12

Updike, John, 195n6

Victorian narrative, 10, 15, 20, 21, 22, 27, 32, 33, 34, 35, 39, 48, 49, 52, 62, 63, 64, 68, 74, 77, 84, 93–95, 96–98, 103, 123, 163, 167, 168, 170

Vitrac, Roger, 116; *Free Entry*, 116, *The Mysteries of Love*, 116

Vollmann, William T., 126

Wagner, Richard, 114

Wain, John, 118, 125

Watt, Ian, 10, 18

Wells, H. G., 164

Woolf, Virginia, 5, 7, 8, 28, 30, 47, 69, 79, 91, 92, 95–101, 108, 119, 124, 126, 153, 163, 170–173, 175, 186n3, 187n8, 187n13, 187n14, 188n15, 188n3, 188n4, 189n5; "Anon," 100–101, 187n11, 187n13, 187n14; *Between the Acts*, 172; "Modern Fiction," 119; "Mr. Bennett and Mrs. Brown," 96, 119, 187n7; *Mrs. Dalloway*, 102–103, 106, 115; *To the Lighthouse*, 79, 170–173; "Street Haunting: A London Adventure," 188n3, 189n5; *The Waves*, 79, 95–101, 115, 116, 170, 172, 188n15

Wordsworth, William, 69, 155